D0225419

The Wall Street Primer

The Wall Street Primer

The Players, Deals, and Mechanics of the U.S. Securities Market

Jason A. Pedersen

Westport, Connecticut
London

Library of Congress Cataloging-in-Publication Data

Pedersen, Jason A.
The Wall Street primer : the players, deals, and mechanics of the U.S. securities market / Jason A. Pedersen.
p. cm.
Includes bibliographical references and index.
ISBN: 978–0–313–36515–7 (alk. paper)
1. Securities industry—United States.   2. Wall Street (New York, N.Y.)   3. Stock exchanges—United States.   4. Investments—United States.   5. Stocks—United States.   I. Title.
HG4910.P422   2009
332.64′273—dc22   2008033900

British Library Cataloguing in Publication Data is available.

Library of Congress Catalog Card Number: 2008033900
ISBN: 978–0–313–36515–7

First published in 2009

Praeger Publishers, 88 Post Road West, Westport, CT 06881
An imprint of Greenwood Publishing Group, Inc.
www.praeger.com

Printed in the United States of America

The paper used in this book complies with the Permanent Paper Standard issued by the National Information Standards Organization (Z39.48–1984).

10 9 8 7 6 5 4 3 2 1

To Heather, Alise, Brooke, and Dane

Contents

Preface

Shortly before my departure from a long career in investment banking, I was asked for a favor: Would I present to a group of students at University of California-Berkeley's Boalt Hall School of Law regarding Wall Street or, more to the point, career opportunities across Wall Street for young lawyers seeking non-legal jobs? Recalling my own graduate school questions and career decisions, I gladly accepted.

I had not attended Boalt, but I was a former lawyer who had managed to find such a job and, in fact, several of them. My time on Wall Street had spanned roles in securities law, capital markets, and investment banking. In addition, as an investment banker for the majority of the time, I had worked on corporate finance and merger and acquisition (M&A) transactions across a wide range of industries, including real estate, lodging, gaming, restaurants, retail, consumer products, software, semiconductors, technology hardware, electronics manufacturing, communications equipment, and Internet services. I had dealt with private companies, public companies, venture capitalists, private equity funds, mutual funds, hedge funds, chief executive officers, chief financial officers, business development executives, and a host of entrepreneurs. I felt uniquely qualified to cover the topic requested and the opportunity to help eager young minds at a great educational institution like Boalt to better understand their options appealed to me.

On the day of the presentation, I arrived at the school early to meet with the event's coordinator, Boalt's career counselor. I asked what I should cover and how the discussion would be structured. It would be a free-form event geared primarily to questions and answers and would last 60 to 90 minutes. It was suggested that I begin with a little of my background and follow with an overview of potential career paths in the securities industry for ex-lawyers.

There had been significant interest in the day's topic and, as a result, there would be a good turnout. I was cautioned, however, that I should not confuse interest with knowledge. Boalt had terrific students and brilliant young legal minds, but it appeared that when it came to the real world, they, like their peers elsewhere, were basically clueless. They could analyze case law, recite provisions of federal securities legislation, and construct compelling legal arguments, but, for the most part, they did not have any experience or understanding of the practical application of such matters beyond the four walls of a lecture hall. I reflected on my own transition from student to professional and my own knowledge at the time and concluded that I, too, had been clueless.

I first entered the securities industry as a fresh-out-of-law-school corporate and securities attorney with a leading U.S. law firm. I cannot pinpoint exactly what led me to this career choice. I was not raised around Wall Street. My parents were not stockbrokers, bankers, or buyout specialists, and I had grown up far away from the hustle and bustle of New York City or other financial centers. In fact, I entered law school immediately after my undergraduate studies believing that I would become a specialist in international law, or at least that is what I spelled out in my admissions essays. But during my three-year tenure as an ambitious young law student, my path changed.

I took courses on corporate and securities law. I enjoyed them, and I liked reading Wall Street's many tell-all books even more. It was the late 1980s and there was no shortage of good ones—*Liar's Poker* and *Den of Thieves* come to mind. Doing deals sounded cool and, from what I gathered, the money was not bad either. So I pursued securities work and managed to land a good entry-level position. With my course work, bedtime reading, and a few supplemental classes in business, I felt prepared to get into the action, ready to do deals. I soon learned that I was not.

After taking the California State Bar exam and returning from my post-Bar carefree trip abroad before facing the world of responsible working adults, I began my legal career as a first-year associate. As fresh meat in a busy environment starved for resources, I was quickly assigned as the junior associate on several deal teams. These transactions included an initial public offering (IPO), a venture capital financing, an acquisition, and even a "kitchen sink" shelf registration statement for Intel (an instrument that allowed the company to sell virtually any type of security to investors at a moment's notice and one of the first of its kind).

It was great. I quickly discovered, however, that book learning and the real world have little in common. I had strong analytical skills, a good understanding of securities law, and a passing familiarity with the celebrity financiers of the day, but what I needed was a practical overview of deal process and the parties with whom I was now doing business. I did not know the organizational structures of investment banks, accounting firms, venture capital funds, private equity funds, mutual funds, or even corporate executive teams. Furthermore, I did not understand how these players actually interacted on deals. Their names could be found on working group lists but what they did and how they did it was a mystery to me. The same could be said for aspects of my own job, even some of the simplest things.

I remember attending my first IPO organizational meeting with a team of more senior attorneys from my new employer. It was held in a large conference room of a leading law firm in Orange County, California. The room was packed with executives, board members, bankers, lawyers, and accountants. The meeting lasted all day, and the whole time I kept thinking, "who are all of these people, what are they doing on this deal, and how did they find themselves here?" Most of them I would not see again until the deal's closing dinner. After a few deals, I began to appreciate all of their roles. After many more, I started to understand the roles of a much longer list of market participants who never attend such meetings.

Early in my legal career, I also recall combing through volumes of corporate records as part of the "due diligence" process for a financing. My firm was billing out thousands of dollars for my time in this pursuit. I knew that I was looking for irregularities and issues evidenced by the documents, but as a practical matter I did not know what this meant or how to most efficiently complete the task. I knew how to spend hours in the library researching and writing legal memoranda but nobody ever explained to the green-behind-the-ears associate that due diligence was intended to identify risks and problems in a business and ensure that disclosures were complete and accurate. Of course, it did not take long to learn this but it stands in my mind as a clear example of the gulf between academic and real-world knowledge.

As they say, there is no substitute for experience. Through experience you learn the practical aspects of a career and an industry. You learn how things really work, how things really get done. What I needed when I entered my legal practice, and later when I switched careers to become an investment banker, was experience. Sure, this would come with time, but even a little practical knowledge would have allowed me to interview better, make more informed decisions, avoid mistakes, and be a more effective and productive professional from the get-go. Why take the long road on knowledge accumulation when a shorter road can provide the same foundation and permit quicker growth? I searched high and low for a book that would arm me with this knowledge. Though some touched on useful topics, I found none that provided the full picture. It was in those long-ago days that the seeds for *The Wall Street Primer* were planted.

WHAT THE WALL STREET PRIMER IS NOT

Rather than start by telling you what *The Wall Street Primer* is, I shall first tell you what it is not. Beyond a few historical works, reference manuals, and narrowly focused career guides, almost every book concerning Wall Street falls into one of three categories: (1) the salacious tell-all; (2) the "how to" for picking stocks, getting rich, planning for retirement, et cetera; or (3) the technical finance or legal treatise geared to the academic market. Although these topics can be educational and are often entertaining, *The Wall Street Primer* does not fall within these categories.

This book will not teach you how to value an option, calculate a company's discounted cash flow, or draft a merger agreement. It will not teach you about finance theory, accounting, securities law, or recent regulatory reform. There are several well-respected academic publications that serve these purposes. Similarly, it will not guide you on where to invest your hard-earned money, how to save for retirement, or how to get rich by "beating" the Street. Again, there are many books on these topics. Finally, it is not a salacious tell-all book. Though it does contain a story and a few anecdotes to help illustrate certain points, its purpose is not to give you the sordid details of a takeover battle or the mixed-up private life of some high-profile financier. Once again, there are many other books addressing these topics (and could be many more given the volume of material authors have to work with).

WHAT THE WALL STREET PRIMER IS

The Wall Street Primer is about practical knowledge and providing context for better understanding the dealings of Wall Street. It is, as its name indicates, a primer. It is intended to be a concise narrative for those looking to quickly gain a real-world understanding of Wall Street and, more specifically, who the players are; what they do; how they interact; and how, when, and why deals get done—both corporate finance and M&A transactions. In conveying this information, frequently used terms and phrases from the industry have also been included and are generally denoted by quotation marks.

I am by no means the world's leading authority on the matters covered in this book. What I am is someone who is well versed in how the pieces of the Wall Street puzzle actually fit together. Hopefully, this book will arm students, young professionals, and executives with useful information about the dealings of the U.S. capital markets. It attempts to distill what I wish I had known when I started on Wall Street.

Acknowledgments

I wish to express my deepest gratitude to all of those who helped make this book a reality. In particular, I would like to thank Ian Batey, Janet Chino, Paul Gelburd, Andrew Kimball, David Lamarre, Toshie Neely, John O'Neil, Allan Pedersen, Doug van Dorsten, my agent Larry Jackel, and the team at Praeger, especially Jeff Olson. Your contributions, feedback, guidance, and support have been invaluable. I would also like to convey my appreciation to the many unnamed friends, colleagues, clients, and others who provided enriching experiences, meaningful lessons, and lasting words of wisdom throughout my professional life. And last but not least, I would like to acknowledge my family for their love, encouragement, and patience. Everything has been possible because of you.

CHAPTER 1

The Basics

➤ The primary financial instruments found in the securities market: stocks, bonds, and others.

➤ The principal organizations, professionals, and service providers operating on Wall Street: those commonly known as the sellside, the buyside, and others.

When average people think of Wall Street, they probably think of stockbrokers and day traders. They may even think of some high-flying IPO that minted a new billionaire or the celebrity executives and financiers who routinely grace the covers of *Business Week* and *Forbes* or find themselves in the *Wall Street Journal* or on CNBC. Wall Street, or at least the concept of Wall Street, with its perceived riches and high-profile deals, is well known. Its impact on our culture, economy, and psyche is far reaching. Yet, its day-to-day dealings are not well known or understood.

The securities industry in the United States directly employs a tremendous number of people. In Manhattan alone roughly 280,000 of its 1.7 million inhabitants work on Wall Street and this figure does not include those in closely aligned professions such as securities lawyers, accountants, and regulators. It is a complicated and diverse ecosystem. It is composed of a wide array of institutions and professions who, by and large, share one thing in common—a passion for money and capitalism. Likewise, they do one thing in common—deals. Whether the deal is just trading a stock or involves a complicated leveraged buyout, people on Wall Street do deals. Some plan deals, some execute deals, and some fund deals, but all need and do deals.

Though the ethos of Wall Street (and perhaps American business in general) can probably be summarized as "if you can help me make money, you'll make money and if you can't, you won't," the principal purpose of Wall Street is to provide capital for businesses to fund their operations and growth. Much of the market's daily activities concern trades and transactions between investors long after companies have issued their securities and received this capital. Still, everyone on Wall Street directly or indirectly impacts this primary function (even the great speculators and hedge fund managers who build vast fortunes while never placing a single cent in the coffers of a business). In their dealings, Wall Street's players compete for returns and performance and thereby drive market efficiency. When seeking capital and investors, companies benefit accordingly.

The roles, activities, and incomes of the market's participants differ significantly. To help illustrate what the players do and how they do it, this book's subsequent chapters follow the lifecycle of a fictional company. Beginning with the company's formation and moving through its maturation as a publicly traded corporation, these chapters discuss those who impact the establishment and expansion of a business from Wall Street's perspective. More specifically, they chronicle typical financings and strategic transactions and the Wall Street professionals involved at each stage.

Prior to this discussion, however, we should briefly set the stage and its cast of characters. Each will be discussed in greater detail later in the book.

SECURITIES

Wall Street deals in securities. According to Webster's Dictionary, a security is "any evidence of debt or ownership." To those on the Street, securities mean stocks, bonds, and a growing array of more complicated financial instruments, including hybrids, options, and other derivatives that trade publicly and privately. The sale of securities is governed by the Securities Act of 1933, as well as state and federal laws that outlaw fraud.

Stocks

Stocks represent ownership, or equity, in a business and typically come in two flavors—common and preferred. If you own a share of common stock, you own a portion of a business. The extent of your ownership depends upon the number of shares of common stock the business has issued and outstanding. For instance, if you own 1,000 shares of ABC Corp. common stock and there are 100,000 shares issued and outstanding, then you own 1 percent of ABC Corp. (1,000/100,000 = 1%). It is worth cautioning, however, that your ownership stake may sound better than it actually is. The rights of common stockholders and, correspondingly, the value of their shares are subordinate to other securities and obligations of a company, including outstanding preferred stocks, bonds, and other debts. In Wall Street parlance, common stock "sits lower in the capital structure" than these other instruments.

Preferred stock also represents ownership in a business but it has specific ownership rights that are defined in a company's Articles of Incorporation (also known as a company's "charter"). These rights typically entitle the preferred stockholder to a pre-defined dividend, special priorities in the event the business is sold or dissolved (so-called "liquidation preferences"), and, possibly, special board representation.

For the most part, when one thinks of the public stock market and indexes such as the Dow Jones Industrial Average, S&P 500, and Nasdaq Composite, these are composed of common stocks.

Bonds

Bonds represent debt of a business or governmental entity. If you own a bond, you are owed money by the issuer of that bond. You are owed the face value, or par value, of the bond upon its maturity date. Prior to that time, bondholders typically receive interest on a quarterly basis. Bonds that mature on a single date are called "term" bonds. When principal is required to be repaid across multiple dates, the bond is a "serial" bond.

Bond instruments with maturities under ten years are called notes. Prior to repayment, many bonds trade between investors in a manner similar to publicly traded stocks. They have par values of $1,000 and are quoted relative to 100. For example, a bond trading at 90 reflects that it is being sold and purchased for $900.

Bonds and notes are typically graded according to their credit quality, or level of risk, by one or more of the debt rating agencies—S&P, Moody's, and Fitch Ratings. Those on the upper end of the grading continuum are deemed to be "investment grade." Those on the lower end are known as "high yield" or "junk" bonds. The grade dictates how the bonds are treated by investors and the terms and interest rates required of them when issued. The debt of roughly 70 percent of public corporations in the United States are rated below investment grade.

Convertible Securities

A convertible security is a bond or preferred stock that may be converted into common stock when certain conditions are met. Convertibles have some traits that are similar to equity and some traits that are similar to debt. For this reason, they are sometimes called "hybrids." Most convertibles entitle their holders to interest payments.

Options

Options are financial instruments that provide their holders with acquisition or disposition rights over another security, generally a specified common stock. There are two types of publicly traded options—call options and put options. The owner of a call option has the right to acquire the "optioned" security at a set price. Conversely, the owner of a put option has the right to dispose of the "optioned" security at a set price. Call option holders are typically "bullish" (believe a stock's price will increase) whereas put option holders are generally "bearish" (believe a stock price will decline). These option "contracts" trade in many stocks and give the holder the right to put or call 100 shares of the underlying stock.

In addition to options traded in the open market, options are also often granted by companies to employees as a component of their compensation. Options of this sort are generally provided to senior and mid-level employees and are used extensively by public and private companies in certain fields, such as technology. Options to purchase shares may also be sold by companies to outside investors. These instruments are called warrants.

Derivatives

Derivatives are contracts, the underlying value of which is derived from the movements in other financial instruments such as stocks or bonds. They allow the owners or issuers of certain securities to adjust their rights, obligations, and risks by contracting with a counterparty to assume those rights or obligations in exchange for another set of rights or obligations. A common derivative is the interest rate swap found in the debt market, which enables a company with one interest rate obligation to exchange it for another such obligation (e.g., swapping a fixed-rate for a floating-rate obligation).

Closely related to derivatives are futures. A futures contract entitles an investor to purchase items such as pork bellies or other commodities at a set price at a later date.

ISSUERS

The issuer is the entity that forms and originally sells a security to an investor. It is the party selling its stock or issuing bonds. An issuer may take the form of a corporation, partnership, trust, limited liability company, or governmental entity such as a municipality. *The Wall Street Primer* focuses on the private sector and corporations in particular.

The Securities Exchange Act of 1934 governs the ongoing reporting and disclosure obligations of public corporations as well as certain other matters concerning publicly traded securities.

THE SELLSIDE

The "sellside" refers to the institutions and professionals who work with issuers to sell their securities. The sellside also provides trading, research, and investment ideas for investors in existing publicly traded securities. The sellside receives commissions and fees for these services from issuers and investors. The primary sellside institution on Wall Street is the investment bank.

Investment banks vary in size and scope. The largest banks, referred to as "bulge bracket" firms, have global operations. They underwrite stocks and bonds, provide M&A advisory services to corporate clients, trade an extensive range of securities, provide research on these securities, and may even supply office space and back office services to clients. Typically, they also conduct "buyside" oper-ations (described subsequently). These firms employ legions of bankers, traders, stockbrokers, institutional salespeople (in effect stockbrokers for institutional accounts such as mutual funds and hedge funds), research analysts, and other professionals. Smaller firms, including the "boutiques" and the securities opera-tions of some commercial banks, provide similar services and have similar person-nel but operate more narrowly. For example, they may not have bond operations or may focus only on issuers and investors in certain industries.

THE BUYSIDE

The "buyside" refers to the institutions and professionals who invest in securities—primarily equity and debt—and act as principals rather than agents in this pursuit. The buyside loosely falls into two groups.

Private Investors

Prior to issuing securities to public investors, companies are privately held. Depending on size and financial characteristics, a privately held company can look to several sources for capital, including individuals, venture capital firms, and private equity firms.

Small, young companies typically obtain their funding initially from founders and friends, family, and "angel" investors. An angel investor is usually a well-heeled individual with some expertise and interest in a particular industry. As a company's prospects brighten, "institutional" money, namely from venture capital firms, becomes an option. Venture capitalists oversee and invest funds pooled from wealthy individuals and large institutions such as endowments, pension funds, and foundations. Private equity firms do the same but invest later in a company's development cycle. Beyond issuing securities, private companies also rely on loans from commercial banks and other lenders to satisfy their capital needs.

Public Investors

When a company reaches a certain scale, it has the option to fund its capital needs by issuing securities to public investors. These securities then trade on an exchange (e.g., the New York Stock Exchange or American Stock Exchange) or in the over-the-counter market (e.g., the Nasdaq Stock Market).

Beyond retail investors (people such as you and I, who buy stocks or bonds through a stockbroker, online trading account, or an account managed by a regis-tered investment advisor), public investors include a range of sizable institutions such as mutual funds, hedge funds, endowments, pension funds, sovereign wealth funds, and foundations. The most notable institutional investors in public se-curities are mutual funds and hedge funds. Mutual fund organizations, typically referred to as mutual fund complexes, generally contain several individually man-aged mutual funds with distinct investment objectives (e.g., large capitalization stocks or technology stocks). They may also operate separately managed accounts (SMAs) for larger investors. These contain stock selections that resemble those found in mutual funds.

Today there are several hundred mutual fund complexes, including market leaders like Fidelity, Putnam, and T. Rowe Price. In total, mutual funds manage more than $12 trillion, of which roughly 55% is in stocks and 45% is in bonds. Mutual funds control more than 25% of all U.S. stocks. Investors in mutual funds include individuals (both directly and through retirement accounts such as 401Ks) and institutions, such as endowments and pension funds that have outsourced some or all of their investing activities, generally referred to as "asset management" or "money management" operations.

Hedge funds are closely held, loosely regulated investment vehicles intended for wealthy individuals and institutions. Witnessing significant growth in recent years, there are now more than 8,000 hedge funds with assets totaling roughly $2 trillion. With the use of leverage (that is, the ability to fund their purchases with borrowed money), hedge funds possess significantly more buying power than this amount on Wall Street. Unlike mutual funds, hedge funds can buy stocks in hope that values will increase and can also "short" stocks on the bet that values will decline by selling and then later replacing borrowed securities. Generally speaking, mutual funds are not permitted to short stocks. Hedge funds also deploy a host of investing strategies in derivatives, futures, private investments, and distressed debt that are mostly unavailable to mutual funds. Hedge funds, together with venture capital and private equity, are often called "alternative investments" in reference to their position relative to publicly traded securities and investment vehicles available to the broader public.

Simplistically, the relationship between an issuer, the sellside, and the buyside in the contexts of both newly issued securities and previously issued securities can be depicted graphically as shown in Figure 1.1.

OTHER PROFESSIONALS AND SERVICE PROVIDERS

In addition to those who sell and those who buy securities, there is a related group of service providers who enable securities transactions to occur. Among these are lawyers, accountants, financial printers, investor relations firms, debt rating agencies, and stock registrar and transfer companies. All are vital to the functioning of Wall Street. Their roles are discussed in varying detail later.

THE REGULATORS

Throughout history, the financial markets have been a prime target for fraud and manipulation by those seeking unjust profits. Today is no different. As a result, the activities of Wall Street, including those of issuers, the buyside, and the sellside are monitored by several regulatory bodies charged with enforcing federal

Figure 1.1. Buyside and sellside activity.

Newly Issued Securities

Previously Issued Securities

and state securities laws. At the federal level, the primary regulatory authority is the Securities and Exchange Commission (SEC). At the state level, there are the State Attorney Generals and Secretaries of State or similar agencies. In addition to these governmental bodies, the sellside is governed by the rules of self-regulatory organizations (SROs), namely the Financial Industry Regulatory Authority (FINRA).

Personal Observations on the Wall Street Environment

Following several chapters in this book, I have included a short section distilling my views on a notable topic. While these sections are based upon my observations and experiences as an investment banker and securities lawyer, they contain only my opinions and should be considered accordingly. I have limited each such section to just five primary observations, though a more exhaustive list undoubtedly could have been produced. Here are my five perspectives on the environment of Wall Street and, correspondingly, the temperament of its professionals.

1. *It is a money culture.* The overriding obsession and focus of Wall Street professionals is money. For most, this goes well beyond their professional dealings. They openly talk about it, complain about it, gossip about it, and keep score by it. Money is not a taboo topic, probably because it is the primary product of their daily work. It

is like mechanics talking about cars or writers talking about books. Although this phenomenon affects some Wall Street professions more than others, it touches them all.

2. *It is fiercely competitive.* Wall Street is filled to the brim with Type A personalities—people who like to win and need to win in order to survive. They compete in everything, especially business. Within firms, they vie for the biggest titles and juiciest bonuses. Between firms, they fight for transactions, trades, fees, and returns. Many begin to treat this as just a game, particularly as they advance in seniority. As one grizzled veteran enthusiastically quipped to me many years ago, Wall Street is the closest thing to a contact sport in the business world. I later concluded that he may have been right.

3. *It is political.* Wall Streeters like to act as if the system for compensation and advancement is purely merit-based. They, particularly those at the top of the pyramid, treat success as simply the byproduct of their intellects, talents, and efforts. These ingredients play critical roles but so do politics and cunning. Many successful professionals achieve senior titles and stellar incomes by developing internal alliances and carefully navigating the power structures within their organizations. Upon reaching seniority, they then become the beneficiaries of an institution's reputation, inertia, and largess.

4. *It is mercenary.* Loyalty is increasingly uncommon on Wall Street. This holds true in the relationships between firms and their employees and firms and their clients. Most professionals constantly have their ear to the ground in search of better, or at least more lucrative, career opportunities. When a situation pops up that offers a more senior title and more compensation, they pursue it. In doing so, they may stay at their original firm but only after negotiating a better pay package. Similarly, firms are often in search of professionals who may have better skills and client relationships than their existing teams. When found, they are hired, displacing their predecessors (in my experience, many such "upgrades" look better on paper than they prove to be in practice; nevertheless they are a fact of life). The views of firms and professionals regarding each other also extend to clients. Firms frequently provide services to competitive enterprises rather than remaining committed to just one player in an industry. Likewise, clients swap out longstanding and supportive banking relationships for new ones when it is deemed to be advantageous.

5. *It is self-serving but professional.* The actions of Wall Street and its constituents are almost always colored by self-interest and should be considered accordingly. That being said, most of the players are ethical and very professional. They adhere to the rules and work diligently to achieve the goals specified by their clients.

CHAPTER 2

The Three Principal Ingredients of a Business

➤ Ideas, people, and capital.

There are literally millions of businesses in the United States. They range from mom-and-pops to the *Fortune* 500 and are engaged in everything from yard maintenance, to manufacturing, to software development. Together they make up our $13 trillion economy. Most of these businesses employ fewer than ten people and will never be directly exposed to Wall Street. They are the backbone of our economy but will not issue securities to public investors or seek other forms of institutional capital due to limited needs, goals, or business models. Although indirectly impacted by the affairs of Wall Street, as they are by the affairs of Washington, these businesses are not the focus of *The Wall Street Primer*. This book is focused on Wall Street and those businesses that want and need capital to achieve loftier ambitions.

At their core, successful businesses require three critical ingredients—good ideas, good people, and access to capital. Arguably the two most important of these are the good ideas and good people, because capital is always available to enterprises that can claim both.

When we speak of good ideas, we mean viable business plans to produce and sell products or services that the market needs, desires, and will buy. It is the entrepreneurs who are responsible for ideas. They conjure them up and possess the passion and will to make them realities.

As for people, we mean employees who possess the right combination of talents, both individually and as a team, to successfully execute on a business plan or idea. Although good people are important throughout an organization, arguably the most critical to this undertaking are those at the top, those entrusted with formulating strategy, hiring personnel, building culture, driving growth, and, basically, making all of the key decisions. For a corporation, this means the executives and the board of directors. Executives, including the Chief Executive

Figure 2.1. The three ingredients.

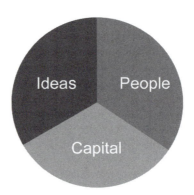

Officer (CEO), Chief Operating Officer (COO), Chief Financial Officer (CFO), and vice presidents charged with functions such as production or sales, are responsible for the day-to-day management and decision making at a corporation. Their activities are overseen by the board of directors (frequently just referred to as the board). Directors are elected by the shareholders and meet several times a year to review corporate operations, strategy, and performance. They also decide upon matters outside of the executive team's authority (e.g., CEO compensation or committing the corporation to a material acquisition). In addition to these roles, directors provide ongoing advice, guidance, and connections in their fields of expertise to executives for the benefit of the corporations they serve.

ENTREPRENEURS AND GOOD IDEAS

Ultimately, every business is started by an entrepreneur—someone who has the vision, commitment, work ethic, and business sense to successfully develop and sell a new good or service while risking personal reputation and resources in a new and unproven venture. There is no prototypical entrepreneur. They come from various backgrounds and assume varying degrees of risk. Some are young, some are old. Some are educated, some are not. Some start businesses with limited formal training whereas others refine their skills and industry knowledge as employees elsewhere before heading down the entrepreneurial path. As a practical matter, I have found that most entrepreneurs who successfully grow their ideas into attractive public companies or acquisition targets fit into one of three categories.

First, there are those who build up a strong base of skills and knowledge working for someone else and decide that they should be running their own show. Perhaps they have a new spin on an idea or just believe they could do it as well, better, or cheaper than their existing employer. They are people like my mechanic Darren. Darren spent ten years working for a local car dealership, gaining valuable technical experience and certifications. One day, Darren decided that he was tired of working for someone else. He figured that he could probably make a pretty good living by charging only half the dealer's hourly rate. He also figured there were probably some car owners who were tired of paying $150 an hour to have their car serviced. He was right. After six months, Darren was so busy he had to hire a second mechanic.

This category of entrepreneur is arguably the largest and most diverse. Virtually every industry in our economy has businesses started by such people. These include traditional employees as well as those employed by consultants and advisors to a particular industry or company. Typically they leave their employers when they are young and have less invested in their careers and less at risk, like needing to feed a family, than their older colleagues.

If they are older or come from higher-level management and decide to take the entrepreneurial plunge, the move is often prompted by a change in corporate circumstance (for instance, their employer is acquired or downsized). A sub-category of this group could be called "serial" entrepreneurs. These are people who build businesses and have seniority but seek exit opportunities once a business reaches a certain scale, typically when it gets sold or handed off to "professional" management.

The second category of entrepreneurs includes those who formulate and incubate their ventures within another organization such as a university research lab or related business. It also includes those who devise new ventures to satisfy class projects in business school. These entrepreneurs differ from the first category insofar as they enjoy the security of an employer or academic pursuit while openly laying the foundation for their other ambitions. Nevertheless, they develop a vision and fully devote their energies to making the vision a reality rather than taking the more predictable path to landing a traditional job (if you could call this more predictable in this day and age).

Some very noteworthy entrepreneurs fall within this category, particularly in the field of technology. Examples from the academic arena include Sergey Brin and Larry Page from Google and Jerry Yang and David Filo from Yahoo. These entrepreneurs developed technologies as part of their studies and then developed enterprises to commercialize them.

Corporate examples are a little different. These typically involve businesses that originally seem like good ideas to senior management but later prove to be distractions or fail to deliver results within an acceptable timeframe. In some cases, they may also be projects promoted by a few executives that never get any funding or institutional traction. The executives who champion these initiatives, particularly as support wanes and the parent company looks to spin them off (or permits them to be spun off instead of just shutting them down), are very much entrepreneurs. One notable such company was Pixar. Prior to its acquisition by Disney, Pixar was a very successful public company. However, it was originally carved out of Lucasfilm in the late 1980s when the computer animation business was young and there was apparently a lack of focus and support for it within the broader Lucasfilm enterprise.

The third category of entrepreneur is those who learn and succeed at a business by simply doing it. These are a rarer breed of entrepreneur. Through luck, pluck, and hard work, they manage to create commercial enterprises of significant and lasting value with little support and no formal training. They generally involve businesses outside of technology, where deep technical skills and expensive lab facilities are not required. They more often involve consumer-oriented businesses. The founder of Papa John's Pizza, John Schnatter, was one such entrepreneur.

There is an interesting viral quality to entrepreneurship as well. It is common for some geographies to possess several similar businesses whereas others possess none. For instance, Wichita, Kansas, a relatively small city, was the birthplace of several successful franchising companies. Some of this may be coincidence but some is definitely fueled by the intellectual capital developed in a region by an academic institution or successful business. People learn about an opportunity and then pursue it on their own. People in these areas seem to be empowered by the can-do perspective that flows from the success of others.

One final observation on entrepreneurs is the frequency with which sizable businesses are cofounded by two partners. Many of the market's most significant companies were started by partners, whether of equal or differing status. These include old-line companies like Procter & Gamble and more recent creations such as Microsoft. These arrangements often involve individuals with complementary skill sets (e.g., a big-picture strategy person and a get-it-done detail person). Other times, the individuals may have very similar skills (e.g., two great technologists). In either event, the productivity and psychological benefits of a collaborative dynamic appear to work well for many startups.

THE PEOPLE

Beyond a narrow group of licensing businesses (those built around royalty streams from patents, trademarks, or celebrity endorsements), most enterprises need more than just the entrepreneur. Successful businesses need good people. They need winning teams.

At the beginning, most businesses are composed of just the founders. These entrepreneurs must nurture an idea to a sufficient scale to either generate sales or attract capital for continued growth. Some entrepreneurs are able to grow with their businesses well beyond the startup stage and learn the new skills necessary to manage and direct expanding operations—notable examples such as Bill Gates and Michael Dell come to mind. More often, entrepreneurs are idea people who have the skills, risk tolerance, and dispositions to run smaller businesses but lack the managerial talents and appetite for detail required to be the CEO of a larger enterprise.

Smart entrepreneurs recognize their limitations and seek outside talent when needed. They hire experienced managers and personnel in all facets of the business, such as marketing, manufacturing, sales, finance, business development, and the like. In doing so, the good ones set aside their egos and accept the opinions of the new hires (albeit with questions and challenges). New additions are usually poached from competitors or found in related fields.

At senior levels, many experienced executives act as modern-day mercenaries. This is particularly true in industries in which venture capitalists and private equity players are active. These "serial" executives have learned to play the game and been rewarded for it. They typically learn the ropes at one company, trade up to more responsibility at one or several others, and develop a network of valuable industry and financial contacts in the process. They then leverage these contacts in their hunt for better opportunities, seeking more seniority, better pay and stock option packages, and ventures with promising futures to best drive the value of their equity stakes and reputations. Their tenure at a particular venture can vary but is generally dictated by the venture's level of success. If the venture begins to look shaky, serial executives often leave when their options vest. They may also be considered part of the problem and be sacked by the board of directors and financial backers. If the venture succeeds and continues to grow, they leave after they become old or fabulously wealthy. Their tenure may also be cut short by a sale. If the business is sold, they may be out of a job or may find themselves uninterested in working for the new owner (a pretty common occurrence when a "hot" young company is bought by a "stodgy" old company).

CAPITAL AND OUTSIDE INVESTORS

The third ingredient for success is access to capital. Virtually every business needs capital. Among other things, capital is needed to hire people, lease space, buy inventory, and fund working capital (the funding gap between when a business must pay its expenses and when it actually receives payment for its products and services). Without it, a great idea and a great team can languish in obscurity while a competitor conquers a market. Capital is especially important for early stage companies and for growth.

Young companies rarely have revenue and profitability levels sufficient to satisfy their capital needs. Take, for instance, a new clothing store; the store may hold great promise but it needs to sign a lease and buy inventory before it even opens its doors. Similarly, more mature businesses may generate sufficient cash flow to fund existing operations but not possess sufficient capital to expand to new markets.

Capital is what Wall Street is all about. It is about money for every stage of a venture and investors looking to turn a profit by providing it. As pointed out earlier, the Wall Street ecosystem ranges from early stage players such as venture capitalists to later stage public investors such as mutual funds. In order to better illustrate the myriad of players and the types of deals they pursue, this book's subsequent chapters follow a fictional company on its journey through the capital markets. This company will provide a framework for our discussion going forward. It is intended to provide a context for better understanding how the pieces of Wall Street fit together. The names of the company, its characters, and the investment banks and other firms it encounters are purely fictional.

OUR FICTIONAL COMPANY

The *Primer* needed a hypothetical that could effectively illustrate capital forma-tion through each stage of a company's development as well as provide some rudimentary insights into how venture-capital-backed companies grow and mature. It had to be a business that could attract capital at an early stage, grow through additional private funding rounds, ultimately go public, pursue more public financings, consider M&A opportunities, and finally face issues associated with maturity and slowing growth.

I pondered options across several industries and settled upon one that fit the bill. It is a technology company, and it seemed appropriate for our times. I recognize the pedagogical limitations of using one business from one industry to illustrate the functionings of Wall Street. The issues, transactions, and players on Wall Street differ in varying degrees from industry to industry. No hypothetical can address every nuance and situation, particularly in a book characterized as a primer. Nevertheless, the experiences of our company and its associated cast of characters, though not all-inclusive, are representative of those found in the real world. In describing the company's progression, transactions, and dealings with the financial community, I have tried to avoid using terms such as typically, generally, usually, and often. Please be aware that almost every sentence in this book could be qualified with them. Wall Street has common practices but is also riddled with exceptions. With those caveats in mind, here is the company and its story:

Envision two graduate students, Larry and Jerry. While completing their dissertations in physics and mechanical engineering at a prestigious Western university, the two began collaborating. At first, they simply discussed their ideas to gain further insights for their own work. But over time, they blended their efforts into one cause and, with the support of their respective departments, worked day and night grinding away in the lab to test their theories. Slowly but surely their efforts began to pay off. Their research was yielding some very promising results, and these began to attract the attention of senior faculty members. It appeared that Larry and Jerry were on the verge of a monumental discovery.

With energy prices escalating and oil becoming a never-ending source of international tensions, Larry and Jerry had set out to crack the code on perpetual energy. In doing so, they engineered a device that appeared to safely and cleanly produce perpetual energy on a small scale using commonly found elements. They named their device the perpetual energy machine or PEM for short.

Encouraged by their early findings and the recent successes of other ex-graduate students who had taken and commercialized their discoveries, Larry and Jerry decided to leave their studies and start a company. They named it The Perpetual Energy Machine Corporation and began referring to it as just PEMCO. Peers and academic advisors were supportive and hopeful. The university was as well. After all, Larry and Jerry's university had rights to the intellectual property of their discoveries and wanted to see it commercialized. Larry and Jerry, like other faculty members and students whose work produced marketable discoveries, were given the exclusive right to commercialize the PEM in exchange for royalties (a policy common to most universities).

CHAPTER 3

Seed Capital and Related Matters for Startups

➤ The initial funding options for companies at the startup stage: personal savings, friends and family, angel investors, and others.

➤ The primary structural considerations in private financings.

➤ The role and activities of securities lawyers in the marketplace.

The first thing on Larry and Jerry's agenda was to officially form PEMCO and then raise some "seed" capital for the venture.

Figure 3.1. Funding progression—Seed financing.

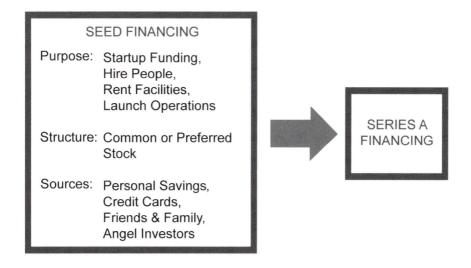

Private companies can take several organizational forms. Most small businesses are sole proprietorships. They are owned by one person and are basically the business alter ego of that person. Companies owned by more than one person can be structured as partnerships, limited liability companies, or corporations. There are a host of considerations used in selecting the best structure. The most important considerations involve taxes, governance, and liability. With few exceptions, private companies with institutional outside investors are structured as corporations ("C corporations" to be more specific in reference to the Federal Tax Code). This structure shields outside shareholders from any personal liability associated with the actions of the company. It also permits a company's capital structure to be greatly customized to meet the demands of investors. Upon the advice of counsel, Larry and Jerry chose the C corporation structure for PEMCO.

When Larry and Jerry left their graduate studies to form PEMCO, they knew they needed capital to get things going. Beyond hiring a lawyer to incorporate the company and finalize the royalty agreement with the university, they needed space and people to continue their research and development efforts.

The amount of seed capital a new venture requires can vary significantly. Though it rarely exceeds six figures, the amount is very case specific and depends heavily upon the industry involved. Usually, the money goes to funding the venture itself but on occasion it may be used to fund a subsidiary project that possesses different ownership than the primary venture. This is common in real estate ventures and some multi-unit restaurant and hotel operations.

Larry and Jerry decided to seek $100,000. Though more than many startups, this was a modest amount given the expenses that they were likely to incur in the near term. They needed lab space and experienced technical personnel. Fortunately, Larry and Jerry had a jump on things. They had already performed much of the work typical of a seed-stage venture while pursuing their graduate studies. They just needed a little money to carry them to their Series A financing and a better valuation for the company.

Most new ventures are initially funded with money from the founder's own pockets or credit cards. But Larry and Jerry were just poor graduate students; thus they had to look elsewhere for their seed capital. They drafted a cursory business plan outlining their discovery and plans to commercialize it. They then turned to the second main source of capital for startups—friends and family. These supporters provided some money, but not enough, so Larry and Jerry were forced to look to the third main source of startup capital—"angel" investors, wealthy individuals who operate individually or collectively to fund early stage investments in areas where they possess unique interest and expertise. Larry and Jerry turned to their former colleagues and professors for thoughts and with a few introductions were able to secure the needed capital from a wealthy alumnus.

Founders usually receive common stock for their contributions. Oftentimes, seed investors do as well. Since Larry and Jerry had agreeable investors, they were able to issue common stock in the seed round. As common shareholders, the new investors would have the same rights and preferences as Larry and Jerry. Just like Larry and Jerry, they would have the right to vote their shares to elect members of the board of directors and to approve material corporate events such as a sale of the business. Of course, their weight in these matters would be limited to their ownership percentage of the company. The only key term of the investment that they had to agree upon was valuation. They all agreed that the $100,000 total investment would represent 10% of the company, thereby placing a $1 million post-money, or $900,000 pre-money, valuation on the company. As 50/50 owners of the venture before the financing, Larry and Jerry were now each worth $450,000 on paper.

When a company raises equity capital, the company's owners and new investors must agree upon the terms of the investment. These include:

1. **Type of security** to be received.
2. **Valuation**, or what percentage of the company new investors will receive for their money.
3. **Governance**, or what involvement and authority new investors will have in the company through board representation and voting power.
4. **Participation rights** in future financings to allow the investors to maintain their ownership percentage in the company.
5. **Antidilution protection** to guard against the negative impact future financings completed at lower valuations could have on their ownership positions. Such occurrences are commonly known as "down rounds." Investors also use this provision to protect against the dilutive impact of excessive equity compensation to employees.
6. **Liquidation preferences** delineating how new investors will be treated relative to other investor classes upon a change of ownership or other liquidation of the company. New investors almost always require that they be returned some or all of their investment before funds are dispersed to other classes. Note, however, that an initial public offering (IPO) is a liquidity event that generally does not trigger the protections contained within this provision. Rather, an IPO, assuming it fits certain predefined parameters, generally prompts the mandatory conversion of all outstanding preferred stock into common stock.

These and other provisions are distilled into a "term sheet," then a stock purchase agreement and, finally, a company's articles of incorporation. Shareholder voting agreements and certain other documents also may be involved.

Private companies, particularly those envisioning future investment rounds, typically issue preferred stock to outside investors following the seed round. This is necessary to satisfy the demands of new investors regarding shareholder rights and protections. For tax and accounting purposes, it can also justify price disparities between an outside investment and the prices paid by founders and employees for their common shares. The preferred stock is issued in different series (also known as "tranches," borrowing from the French word for "slices"). Ventures following a traditional multistage financing path refer to each stage in an alphabetical sequence—Series A Preferred, Series B Preferred, and so on. The terms of each series reflect those agreed upon at the time of the financing round. These are then detailed in the articles of incorporation and filed with the secretary of state in the company's state of incorporation.

A Briefing on Securities Lawyers

Law is big business in this country. Fees paid to law firms exceed $200 billion annually, and this figure does not include the salaries of tens of thousands of lawyers employed directly by companies. By this measure, law is one of America's largest industries and readily surpasses all other "professional, scientific, and technical services" industries as defined by the federal government.

The practice of law is very diverse. It includes sole practitioners and firms of all sizes. There are local firms, regional firms, national firms, and international firms. Some specialize, some do not. Even by service industry standards, law is a highly fragmented business. There are more than 1.1 million lawyers in the United States and the top 100 law firms based on revenues employ fewer than 10% of these.

Law firms are staffed with professionals—partners, associates, paralegals—and support staff such as typists and secretaries. Each of these plays a role in legal work for the client and each professional carefully tracks the time devoted to the client. The client is then billed for these hours and minutes (some firms bill in six-minute increments) at different hourly rates. Clients also pay for related expenses such as travel and document production. Billable rates for partners and associates increase with seniority.

The career track from associate to partner is usually eight or more years. During this time, an associate is classified by years of experience (e.g., a "second-year associate" or a "fifth-year associate"). On their progression to partner, associates are expected to bill at least 1,800 hours a year, if not significantly more. In the past, law firms had a pyramidal organizational structure. Generally there were several associates for every partner. This permitted partners to work fewer hours and focus more attention on business development efforts (such as the afternoon golf game at the club). Partners demonstrating the greatest ability to gather clients, fees, and business are called "rainmakers."

Today, law firms have much flatter organizational structures. Associate-to-partner ratios now approach one-to-one at many firms. Though rainmakers still bill less, rank-and-file partners now bill as many hours as associates (or more). Business considerations have driven this shift in the practice of law. In the new world of 24/7 connectivity, clients want partner-level attention at all times and competition requires that firms provide it. Partners cannot offload as much work to junior colleagues. The positive corollary to this situation is higher revenues or "billables" to law firms since partners charge much more per hour than their junior colleagues.

For the most part, attorneys at large law firms are paid on a lockstep basis during their tenure as associates. There is little variability among peers and the majority of their incomes is paid in salary rather than year-end bonuses (unlike many other Wall Street professions). Upon reaching partner, an attorney's income becomes more closely tied to productivity and business development abilities. Partners usually own a certain percentage of their firms and are entitled to that percentage of the profits. Ownership is adjusted annually and incomes sometimes are augmented with discretionary bonuses for unique contributions.

Early stage ventures rarely require heavy-hitting legal expertise. Services for companies at this stage are typically limited to preparing company formation documents, reviewing a few material contracts, and perhaps advising on some employment matters. As a result, most early stage companies are adequately supported by smaller local firms, or possibly even sole practitioners, which charge much less than larger law firms. These are usually found by word of mouth or by interviewing a couple of firms found through online research.

Some larger law firms seek to be retained by early stage ventures, particularly in regions like Silicon Valley, in hopes that the ventures will succeed and their legal budgets will grow. When hired in these situations, larger law firms often staff less senior resources on a client's projects. This is done to lower fees for the client and to help the firm train less experienced lawyers. In my experience, the success of this arrangement largely depends on the expectations of the client. Some firms also gamble on the potential success of startup clients by accepting stock as payment for their services.

Whether working with a small firm or a large firm in forming a business, companies at the outset should adhere to common, time-tested organizational and ownership structures. Overly customized and unusual charters, bylaws, and securities can create significant issues for companies later in life.

As a business matures, its legal issues and attendant risks become more complicated. A business may also require unique expertise such as that involving the protection of intellectual property. When businesses face these topics and transitions, they look to more sophisticated and experienced legal counsel that can justify higher hourly rates. This is particularly true when companies look to raise institutional money.

At this stage, a company may interview a handful of firms, or conduct a small "bake-off," as it is known, to find new counsel. Key considerations in the selection process include reputation, securities law/transaction experience, current market knowledge, and financing and industry contacts. A partner generally takes point for the firm in these discussions. It is this person who will nurture the relationship and coordinate legal teams to work on matters for the client. Of course, the best legal relationships extend beyond pure legal advice. They involve trust, chemistry, and helpful introductions and input on broader matters.

Most securities transactions also require legal representation for the investors, agents, or underwriters. Beyond working with companies, law firms actively court investment banks, venture capitalists, and private equity firms for their business. Marketing efforts include referring opportunities, presenting on continuing education matters, and cosponsoring conferences and similar events. In today's competitive world, these efforts and developing strong personal ties are necessary complements to providing top-notch legal representation in winning business.

CHAPTER 4

Early Stage Institutional Capital

➤ What is meant by institutional capital in privately held companies.

➤ The funding progression of institutional capital in early stage private companies: Series A and beyond.

➤ The process of raising institutional funding in early stage companies.

➤ The role and characteristics of venture capitalists.

SERIES A

The first financing following a seed round is referred to as the Series A round. The amount of progress between the seed and Series A rounds varies widely, especially across industries. Some business models never require additional funding

Figure 4.1. Funding progression—Series A financing.

or only need it for growth initiatives after a business has matured significantly. Others have voracious appetites for capital and may do several financings before turning a dollar of revenue. As such, it is important to note that all Series A rounds, like other rounds, are not created equal. Based on company characteristics, they can vary dramatically with respect to size, valuation, and other material terms.

With those caveats in mind, there are some rules of thumb for venture-backed enterprises. Series A in technology and health sciences is considered early stage for venture capitalists (VCs). Those who focus in this area rarely invest in something that could be considered a "real" business. Instead, they are presented with concepts and entrepreneurs hoping to exploit existing or emerging market opportunities. Basically, they invest in business plans and people. Rarely is there a product much less customer traction. For this reason, Series A is treated as the "proof-of-concept" round. In the consumer sector, on the other hand, the Series A round tends to be later and after a concept has demonstrated its appeal with customers. An early stage consumer company may be a retailing or restaurant business with one or two successful locations that needs capital to roll out more units. In these situations, consumer VCs look for concepts and formulas with demonstrated appeal that can be readily expanded to new sites.

In light of their circumstances, Larry and Jerry chose to pursue a Series A financing shortly after the seed round was completed. They had not done much more than hire a few people and rent lab space but the seed round had allowed them to get established and now it was time to more aggressively expand their research and development (R&D) efforts. Larry and Jerry revised their business plan, noting new developments with the company and technology, and set out to raise more money. They were hopeful that their progress would warrant a higher valuation in this round, the Series A round, than they had experienced in the seed round. Like most founders, they wanted to avoid being diluted (i.e., having their ownership percentages notably reduced by new investors).

With business plan in hand, they discussed the proposed financing with their outside counsel. In forming the company, they had interviewed several lawyers and firms. They had created a list of candidates based on references, reviewing SEC filings for recent IPOs, and the clients noted on firm Web sites. Ultimately, they selected a partner at Love, Law & Howe (LL&H) because of his and his firm's experience and reputation in working with technology startups. He had worked on many financings and was well versed in completing the legal work. As importantly, he knew what terms other companies were getting in Series A rounds and had valuable contacts in the VC world. Larry and Jerry's business plan was converted into a Private Placement Memorandum (PPM) with a few modifications. This document would serve to describe the company and investment opportunity to prospective investors. Their new counsel then made some introductions. Their angel investor from the seed round did the same.

Larry and Jerry sent out the PPM to about twenty VCs. This included the introductions and some firms they had identified independently that had similar but noncompeting investments. They were hoping that whoever invested could

Figure 4.2. Venture funding process.

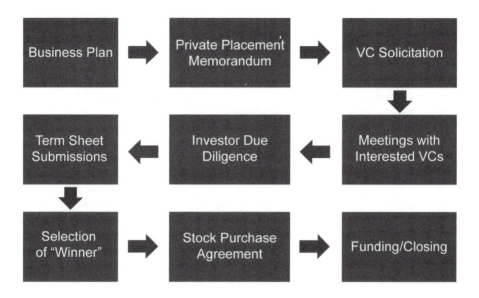

bring more than money to the table, namely industry insights, experience, and contacts. However, they did not want an investor with a competing agenda. From the twenty targets, they met with several and ultimately obtained a few term sheets (proposals outlining the terms of a potential investment). These were received after the interested firms had completed due diligence on Larry and Jerry, their technology, and the market opportunity. The terms were negotiated and a "winner" was selected, Alpha Ventures.

Alpha Ventures had a long history of backing successful technology companies. The firm also had unique expertise in the alternative energy sector, having financed the market's leading hydrogen fuel cell company and a top developer of next-generation batteries for the mobile device market. Alpha proposed that they, together with another VC who had voiced interest as a co-investor in the round (POC Ventures), would invest $3 million for a 30% stake in the company, thereby valuing the company at $7 million pre-money and $10 million post-money. Although this was big step up from the recently completed seed round, Alpha was encouraged by the state of PEMCO's technology and excited by the size of the market opportunity.

The investment would be made in a Series A preferred stock and would fund in one closing rather than being left open to allow more investors to participate subsequently—such extended closings can sometimes last several months. Holders of the Series A stock would be entitled to elect one director on PEMCO's board of directors. They would also have the right to participate in future financing rounds and the right upon a sale or liquidation of PEMCO to receive their $3 million back before other investors received any proceeds (in other words, Alpha

Table 4.1 Series A Financing

	Pre-Round Ownership	New Capital Commitment	Post-Round Ownership	
			%	$ (millions)
Larry	45.0%	$0.00	31.5%	$3.15
Jerry	45.0%	$0.00	31.5%	$3.15
Seed Investors	10.0%	$0.00	7.0%	$0.70
Alpha & POC	0.0%	$3.00	30.0%	$3.00

and POC would get more than 30% of the company if it was valued at less than $10 million).

With the Series A completed, the ownership stakes of the prior investors, including Larry and Jerry, had increased in value but had been diluted to a lower percentage of the overall company. The investment allocations and ownership percentages and values for the round were as shown in Table 4.1.

SERIES B

Over a year passed following the close of PEMCO's Series A and things were going well at the company. Larry and Jerry had used the funds wisely and avoided many of the missteps common in the dot-com era, namely operating with a high "burn rate" by prematurely spending on space and people. With the help of the money, some of Alpha's industry contacts, and attractively priced employee stock option grants (as customary, the Series A agreements reserved a pool of options for employees—in this case an amount equal to 10% of the company), PEMCO had hired a small but top-tier team of engineering talent and now had a fully operational prototype of a small perpetual energy machine. It was time to take the company to the next level.

Figure 4.3. Funding progression—Series B financing.

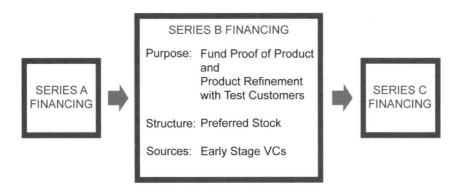

PEMCO needed to convert its working prototype into a commercial product. Technology for the device was sound but could not yet be scaled down to meet the size requirements of the consumer battery market or scaled up to address the power requirements of larger items such as homes or cars. It was decided that certain power-hungry devices and appliances would work well for the perpetual energy machine's current specifications. Management and the board (Larry, Jerry, and representative from the Series A round, a Partner from Alpha Ventures named Richard Veesy) considered a number of paths to commercialization and settled on an OEM strategy to address the markets for these applications.

"OEM" is the acronym for original equipment manufacturer. OEMs are responsible for designing and producing everything from computers to toasters. Some use their own brands for marketing products and some produce the products to be sold under brands owned by other companies—a phenomenon very common in the consumer electronics world. An OEM strategy refers to selling a product to an OEM that, in turn, will use it as a component in one or more of its own products. The concept is appealing to cash-strapped companies. Rather than spending dollars on distribution, sales, and marketing to reach end users, the approach allows a company to sell to one or a few customers who, in turn, will sell thousands or millions of units via distribution of their primary products.

The OEM model also is common in technology. Intel is a shining example. Its processors are sold almost exclusively through the computing and networking products of other vendors (albeit with some independent branding—"Intel Inside").

Although the OEM strategy sounds simple, it is complex and expensive in practice. It typically involves a long, grueling sales cycle to a handful of potential customers. These customers run the product through a series of tests and trials to ensure that it is well suited to the primary product and market. In the process, OEM vendors, as they are known, are required to adjust and modify their components to meet the OEM's requirements and demands. This requires resources and money. These expenses are referred to as nonrecurring engineering expenses or NRE. Despite these drawbacks, PEMCO's product seemed well suited to the OEM market.

PEMCO needed to hire sales people and additional engineers to support the OEM development efforts. With capital from the prior round depleted, Larry, Jerry, and the board decided a Series B financing was warranted. Series B is sometimes referred to as the "beta" round or the "proof-of-product" round. In technology, the goal is typically to develop a "beta" stage product, meaning a product that is placed with a few customers for testing and preliminary use.

With or without an OEM strategy, the task of producing a beta product involves identifying a group of "beta" customers and convincing a subset of them to expend resources to test and provide feedback on the product. To find willing participants, the product's value proposition must be compelling (some in the VC community like to say 10X faster or 10X cheaper). Likewise, the supplier must be viewed as stable and sufficiently capitalized. Potential beta customers often ask for cash and balance sheet information prior to proceeding with trials to assure that they are not sinking money and time into a lost cause.

The fundraising process for a Series B is virtually identical to a Series A. It involves producing an updated PPM, identifying investors, and targeting them with mailings and meetings in hope of securing several attractive term sheets. The primary difference in the Series B is the role played by the Series A investors. The Series A board member will work actively behind the scenes to market the opportunity to potential investors. VC board members contribute in this capacity during each fundraising for a company. In doing so, they pursue other VCs with whom they have had good experiences in past dealings. They also leverage their networks for other introductions.

Another difference between prior rounds and subsequent rounds lies in the interest level from VCs that may have passed on previous deals or submitted term sheets that were insufficient to win. These VCs will maintain an ongoing dialogue with a company if it operates in an area of interest. They do this for several reasons. Sometimes they want to position themselves to lead the next round and, in fact, may encourage a company to do another round of fundraising to satisfy this objective. Other times, they may be trolling for information. It is common for a handful of companies with very similar business models to crop up at the same time. VCs who miss one frequently invest in another. These VCs like to keep in touch with the competitive set. Executives need to be aware of these agendas. They should maintain a dialogue but take care not to reveal too much about strategy, positioning, customers, and product launch dates.

With the aid of outside counsel and the board member from Alpha Ventures, PEMCO was able to complete its Series B financing in less than two months from start to finish, faster than many Series Bs. Larry and Jerry were pleased with the terms offered by Beta Ventures and selected the firm to lead the round. Beta was an early stage VC with a lot of experience with OEM vendors. Many of Beta's portfolio companies had pursued this strategy and been successful. Beta had developed many relationships with consumer and industrial product conglomerates and was well versed in how to effectively target these potential partners.

Beta Ventures, along with Alpha Ventures and POC Ventures, which exercised their participation rights from the Series A round, would invest $7.5 million in PEMCO for a 25% stake, valuing the company at $22.5 million pre-money and $30 million post money. The investment would be made in the form of Series B preferred stock. Its holders would have preferential rights similar to those of the Series A shareholders. In particular, they would be entitled to one director on PEMCO's board of directors. They would also have participation rights in future rounds and a liquidation preference on their $7.5 million, giving them the right to receive this capital, or "be made whole," as they say, before any payout to the common stock and Series A shareholders.

The investment allocations and ownership percentages and values for the round were as follow (excluding the impact of employee stock options):

Table 4.2 Series B Financing

	Pre-Round Ownership	New Capital Commitment	Post-Round Ownership %	Post-Round Ownership $ (millions)
Larry	31.5%	$0.00	23.6%	$7.09
Jerry	31.5%	$0.00	23.6%	$7.09
Seed Investors	7.0%	$0.00	5.3%	$1.58
Alpha & POC	30.0%	$2.25	30.0%	$9.00
Beta*	0.0%	$5.25	17.5%	$5.25

* Beta was only able to invest 70% of the round due to the Series A participation rights.

A Briefing on Venture Capitalists

In today's market, the exact definition of a VC can be difficult to pin down. The role of the VC has expanded over the last several decades. Historically, VCs did not invest in going concerns—at least not when making an initial investment in a company. VCs were those who backed good people with good ideas who wanted to build new commercial enterprises. They invested in ventures, not businesses. By and large, this remains true today. There are, however, VC firms that devote all or a portion of their capital to later-stage private companies with proven products and business models. In some cases, they even invest in pubic companies.

There are hundreds of VC firms in the United States. In total, they manage more than $250 billion. They have varying sizes and areas of expertise. Some focus on industry sectors (e.g., biotech or software), others target geographic regions (e.g., the Southeast or Rocky Mountain states), and a few invest according to ideological themes such as promoting green technologies to help the environment. The U.S. government even sponsors a fund, In-Q-Tel, the mission of which is to fund and help develop better security technologies. VC investment portfolios range in size from several million to several billion dollars. Except for the venture investing arms of corporations (a limited pool given the losses suffered in the dot-com meltdown) almost all VC firms raise capital and invest via funds that are structured as limited partnerships. They refer to these limited partnerships by a fund number such as Fund I or Fund II (note the use of roman numerals).

The limited partnerships have two classes of partners, general partners (GPs) and limited partners (LPs). The GPs are responsible for directing the partnership's activities. Technically, VC firms serve as the GPs of the funds. As a practical matter, however, the senior members of the VC firms are considered to be the GPs and carry this title since they serve as GPs of the venture firms themselves, which are also structured as partnerships, albeit typically composed of just the firm's investment professionals.

Outside investors in the funds are the LPs (or "Limiteds" as they are also known). Limiteds include pension funds, foundations, university endowments, sovereign wealth funds, and wealthy individuals. To avoid issues with the U.S. securities laws, all need to be "qualified institutional buyers" or "accredited investors"—essentially, well-funded institutions and wealthy individuals. At the time a fund is raised, the Limiteds commit a certain amount of capital. This amount is not funded immediately. It is "drawn down" as needed for investments over the life of the fund. VCs hold annual meetings for their Limiteds to discuss their portfolios and showcase a handful of investments (typically the most promising ones).

VCs raise their funds based largely upon reputation and experience. The fundraising process for a fund, particularly a new one, can last several months. Sponsors for a proposed fund first identify a group of potential investors. Several of these are contacted about the fundraising for input and preliminary interest. Firms with existing funds rely heavily on past investors for this. An offering memorandum is then prepared, taking into account feedback from these discussions. The memorandum contains the investment records and backgrounds of the sponsors and other investment professionals as well as a preliminary term sheet. This document is then sent to an even broader group of investors and meetings are arranged with interested parties. This set of meetings is known as the "road show."

The road show and ultimate decision making for several classes of institutional investors include both staffers from these institutions as well as outside advisors. Larger pension funds, endowments, sovereign wealth funds, and foundations rely upon internal investment teams for due diligence and recommendations. They also look to opinions from outside advisors. Trustees and investment committees may, in fact, be required to use advisors to assure objective decision making.

Although specifics may vary, partnership agreements for VC funds generally contain the following key provisions:

1. **Fund size and duration.** Funds limit their period of active investing from seven to ten years.
2. **Sponsor co-invest.** Sponsors are required to invest their own capital in the fund. The amount of the co-investment may vary. This gesture helps ensure prudent investment decisions on the theory that people are more thoughtful with their own money than other people's money (OPM).
3. **Management fee.** Fees of 2% of committed capital are paid out annually to cover salaries and operating expenses of the VC firm (e.g., the annual management fee would be $2 million on a $100 million fund). This fee is sometimes lower, particularly on much larger funds.
4. **Profit participation.** This is more commonly known as the "carried interest" or the "carry." VCs receive 20% of a fund's profits (e.g.,

they would receive $4 million on a $100 million fund that produced a 20% or $20 million profit). This amount is generally paid after investors recoup the previously paid management fees. The management fee and carry constitute the "2 and 20" compensation structure commonly referenced in the press and elsewhere for VCs, private equity funds, and hedge funds.

5. **Key personnel protection.** Investors in a VC fund are betting on the people. Investors want the option to terminate their funding obligations if key sponsors depart a fund.

Once a fund is raised, the investing process begins. To get a jump on things, investment commitments are sometimes made prior to closing a fund.

Beyond the GPs and their slightly less-senior peers—partners—VC firms are staffed with investment professionals who generally have four titles—analyst, associate, vice president, and principal. Firms may also have "venture partners," who work on specific ventures, and entrepreneurs-in-residence (EIRs), former executives who incubate new ventures in-house. Firm heads are known as managing GPs.

VCs generally possess one of three backgrounds. Many are hired directly out of elite graduate business school programs with previous industry experience helpful to a firm (e.g., a former software engineer hired by a technology-focused firm). These people start out as associates and work their way to more seniority. Others make lateral career moves out of financial fields such as investment banking—at the junior ranks, many analysts fit this description. And finally, some VCs are former executives with valuable connections and industry expertise. These VCs normally start at more senior levels. Good VCs contribute more than capital to a company; they bring experience and contacts to help build a business and facilitate liquidity options.

Many VC firms maintain relatively small professional teams even when their funds grow significantly. In many instances, this limits senior-level openings at established firms. Other than truly exceptional talent, few GP-level promotions occur without corresponding departures. As such, VCs

Figure 4.4. Venture capital organizational structure.

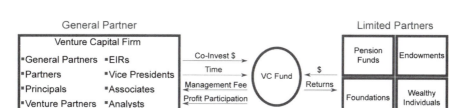

approaching partner-level tenure frequently defect for attractive opportunities elsewhere or to start new firms. Sometimes, departure threats are used to force out less-productive older partners.

GPs usually have responsibility for specific industry sectors and work with teams of more-junior personnel to identify, perform due diligence, and craft term sheets for potential investments. VCs source deals through their relationships with executives, industry gurus, bankers, and other VCs. They also receive a significant volume of unsolicited business plans from entrepreneurs seeking capital. If successful in closing an investment, members of the investment team stay involved with the investment and monitor its developments. They also are compensated based on the investment's success by receiving a percentage of the carry associated with it.

Prior to committing capital to a company, the opportunity is reviewed by an "investment committee" from the VC firm. This committee is composed of senior members of the firm. The review process includes presentations from the investment team concerning the merits of the proposal. It may also include meeting with company management. These discussions are often done on Mondays, the day most VCs reserve for internal meetings to review existing investments, debate new opportunities, and discuss industry trends and other noteworthy matters. Because VCs have a finite pool of capital to deploy, and thus carry to generate, some have suggested that the investment committee process can be political, with scrutiny varying according to the investment sponsor. Rightly or wrongly, up-and-coming professionals have argued that their deals must meet higher standards than those of their senior colleagues.

A VC firm may serve as the lead investor or a co-investor in a financing. As a lead investor, the VC takes a board seat (usually occupied by the sponsoring GP) and plays an active role with the company. Co-investors are more passive and do not take board seats. They rely upon the lead investor to finalize the terms of the investment and to actively oversee it. Given the role trust plays in this arrangement, certain firms often develop a pattern of working with each other on several deals and switching off roles.

Whether as a lead investor or a co-investor, overseeing investments is a time-intensive process. For this reason, most VCs seek to make larger investments to reduce the number of companies in their portfolio and to assure that all their investments can impact the fund (doubling a $1 million dollar investment in a $1 billion fund cannot do this). Minimum investment sizes vary by fund but are generally $5 million for smaller funds and $20 million for larger funds. This amount may take into account future financing commitments to a company. Private companies generally do multiple financings before experiencing a liquidity event. VCs in early rounds will reserve one or two times as much capital for future financing rounds as they invest initially. So, a $2 million commitment on the first financing may ultimately result in $4 to $6 million being invested over the life of the investment.

Venture capital funds have limited life spans set by the terms of their formation documents. Within these timeframes, VCs seek to produce returns by selling their portfolio companies, taking them public, and sometimes selling their stakes to "secondary investors" in the private market (in effect other VCs and private equity funds that buy stakes in private companies from earlier investors).

CHAPTER 5

Mid-stage Private Capital

➤ The common definition of a mid-stage private company.

➤ Institutional funding options for mid-stage private companies.

➤ The characteristics and process of a typical mid-stage institutional financing round.

➤ The role and activities of accounting firms in the securities market.

After the ink dried on PEMCO's Series B, work began on implementing the first phase of the OEM strategy. Management and the board had chosen the military submarket as their initial target. The size, cost, and power characteristics of the PEM were well suited to applications and devices in this arena and Uncle Sam was a steady customer. Sales and support teams were hired for the initiative and, with the help of Beta Ventures and some of its other portfolio companies, contacts were established at several OEMs that supplied the Department of Defense.

The subsequent twelve months were difficult but fruitful. The strains on Larry and Jerry were particularly high. As the chief technologists and Co-CEOs, they were forced to do two jobs during this time—take lead on refining the PEM and work hand-in-hand with sales to court potential OEM partners. Day after day, Larry and Jerry felt as if all they saw was the inside of a lab, conference room, or airplane, but PEMCO emerged with several product wins. These were scheduled to go into production in the coming months. Additional capital would be needed to fulfill anticipated production volumes.

SERIES C

PEMCO's board, now composed of Larry, Jerry, Richard Veesy from Alpha, and a representative from Beta Ventures, knew a Series C round was needed. They also

Figure 5.1. Funding progression—Series C financing.

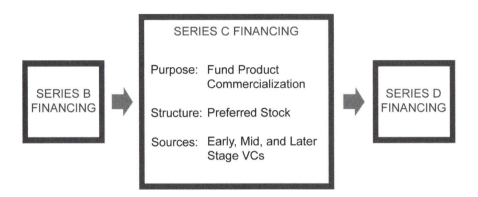

knew that certain structural matters at PEMCO needed to be addressed before proceeding with a new financing. For most technology companies, a Series C financing is pursued at the early commercialization stage. The round is done when a product has successfully completed beta testing and is proceeding to "general availability" or GA. GA means commercial release and thus more customers and real sales.

PEMCO was now approaching revenues and needed to upgrade its financial infrastructure. To date, the company's accounting had been relatively simple. With nothing but expenses to worry about and no revenue or revenue recognition policies to consider, the job of maintaining the company's books had been given to a staffer at Alpha Ventures who played a similar role at several other companies. Likewise, PEMCO had used a small accounting firm for its annual audits. These things needed to change. PEMCO now needed an experienced in-house accounting staff. It also needed a larger, more reputable accounting firm. Although other hires would also be necessary to scale up the company, these items took top priority and the board wanted them resolved before the next funding.

Through its expanding network of relationships, PEMCO quickly found several highly qualified candidates to lead its accounting department. It was unclear whether any of them possessed the skills necessary to become the CFO of a larger enterprise, but this could be addressed in time. For now, Larry and Jerry interviewed the candidates and selected one who had previously worked as an accountant with one of the "Big Four" accounting firms. He had left prior to making partner to join a hot but now defunct startup and was eager for a new opportunity. He seemed knowledgeable, smart, and ambitious.

The board then took on the task of hiring a new accounting firm. Although the last firm had been responsive and competent, PEMCO now needed one that had a national reputation and resources well versed in more complicated accounting matters. They considered their options and, like most companies, chose to work with a Big Four firm. After a small bake-off, they selected their new hire's former employer to be PEMCO's new outside accounting firm—his former mentor was the point partner for the account.

With an appropriate accounting and finance team now in place to support PEMCO through its next stage of development, the board green lighted the Series C and targeted a $20 million raise. The fundraising process was almost identical to Series B. Larry and Jerry drafted a new PPM with the help of outside counsel (this time with more detailed financial projections), identified and contacted potential investors, and so on. The main difference was the targeted pool of investors. Although PEMCO had no revenues to speak of, it did have customers that believed in its products, and potentially lucrative design wins. These factors appeal to later-stage VCs.

Successful early stage VCs excel at identifying and nurturing teams, technologies, and concepts with large market opportunities. This approach takes patience and is fraught with risks. Early stage VCs structure term sheets and valuations to compensate for these factors. Later-stage VCs on the other hand, structure their term sheets to compensate for commercialization risks, their primary focus. They typically seek opportunities where the team, technology, and concept have proven themselves and continued success now depends on execution. Although not all Series C rounds are conducted at this stage, PEMCO was there, and later-stage VCs would be interested with better terms and higher valuations.

Like PEMCO's former round, the Series C was well received. A buzz had developed within the VC community and PEMCO was becoming known as a "hot" company given the early customer wins and the PEM's promising future. Even Alpha and Beta had contemplated keeping the round all to themselves but they wanted and needed a new, outside lead to set the terms. Like most VCs, their policies and fund agreements discouraged "internal rounds" in order to thwart any temptation to overinflate the value and prospects of existing investments. Besides, they knew Larry and Jerry were smart and would see that a broader marketing effort would almost certainly result in better terms than Alpha and Beta would be willing to propose.

Several term sheets were put forth by top-tier VCs. Some were straightforward later-stage VCs with great track records. Others were VCs with larger funds that had been successful at both early and late-stage investing—each of which are now needed to effectively deploy billion-dollar funds in a timely fashion. One was a fund affiliated with Alpha. Together with a few other successful early stage VCs, Alpha had helped form and now served on the investment committee of a separate firm with a later-stage fund. The fund compensated Alpha out of its fees and Alpha helped guide the fund to promising investments. All of the interested VCs had strong reputations and would be great choices to lead the round.

Larry, Jerry, and the board ultimately settled on Carto Ventures, the affiliate of Alpha, to lead the round. Carto had offered a strong valuation and a "clean" term sheet, referring to one without onerous or unusual provisions regarding governance, liquidity preferences, or valuation resets for failing to meet certain goals and objectives (increasingly common in late-stage rounds). Carto's term sheet called for a $100 million pre-money valuation ($120 million post-money)

Table 5.1 Series C Financing

	Pre-Round Ownership	New Capital Commitment	Post-Round Ownership	
			%	$ (millions)
Larry	23.6%	$0.00	18.9%	$23.63
Jerry	23.6%	$0.00	18.9%	$23.63
Seed Investors	5.3%	$0.00	4.2%	$5.25
Alpha & POC	30.0%	$7.50	30.0%	$37.50
Beta	17.5%	$4.38	17.5%	$21.88
Carto*	0.0%	$10.50	8.4%	$10.50
Strategics*	0.0%	$2.63	2.1%	$2.63

*New investors were only able to invest 52.5% of the round due to existing participation right.

along with other customary provisions, including a board seat for the Series C investors.

During the fundraising process, PEMCO had also been approached by two of its OEM partners about participating in the round. Unlike many companies, which ceased making such investments after the dot-com crash, both customers still had internal funds dedicated to strategic investments. Both wanted to serve as co-investors behind a credible lead investor. Believing that these strategic investors would be helpful to PEMCO's future initiatives, the board discussed upsizing the Series C to include them. This proposal was put forth to Carto, and Carto agreed. The round would be $25 million, resulting in a $125 million post-money valuation. Carto Ventures and the strategic investors would take 80% and 20% of the round, respectively, after accounting for the Series A and Series B participation rights.

The investment allocations and ownership percentages and values for the round were as shown in Table 5.1 (excluding the impact of employee stock options).

VENTURE DEBT

A financing alternative to traditional venture capital for private growth companies is venture debt. Young companies without established businesses, much less revenues and profits, have very limited borrowing options from conventional lenders. For the most part, banks will not lend to such organizations except on a full recourse basis to the founders. Venture debt providers are different. They assess a young enterprise on the basis of its prospects much as do VCs, and lend funds for infrastructure and working capital. This debt is secured by a blanket lien over all of the assets of the business, including intangibles such as patents and other intellectual property. Beyond interest, venture debt lenders participate in the equity upside of their borrowers via warrants. Although PEMCO, like most other traditional venture-backed companies, chose not to explore this alternative, it can be an attractive option for some companies.

A Briefing on Accounting Firms

Accounting services in the United States, excluding payroll services, amount to more than $70 billion annually. As with the practice of law, the business of accounting is highly fragmented at the local level. There are thousands and thousands of accounting firms throughout the country. These firms and independent certified public accounts (CPAs) provide a range of services to their clients, who include individuals, companies, and nonprofit organizations. The largest service offered by them is tax preparation work.

At the national and international levels, the business of accounting is concentrated. Following several mergers and the collapse of Arthur Andersen after the 2001 Enron scandal, there now remain only four large accounting firms that are responsible for the bulk of work completed for public companies and larger institutions. These are referred to as the "Big Four" and each employs more than 100,000 employees and generates over $10 billion in annual revenues. The Big Four are Deloitte Touche Tohmatsu, PricewaterhouseCoopers, Ernst & Young, and KPMG.

Larger organizations gravitate to the Big Four for their services because of the depth of their resources and the familiarity and comfort level public investors have with them. Among other things, these firms audit and prepare financial statements filed with the SEC, audit and review internal bookkeeping systems and procedures, and conduct forensic and analytical work for strategic initiatives such as acquisitions. Aside from the Big Four, there are a handful of national firms with the resources and reputations to also garner assignments from larger companies. These include BDO Seidman, Grant Thornton, McGladrey & Pullen and Moss Adams. Some of these employ tens of thousands of people.

The process of selecting an accountant is similar to selecting a law firm. Companies typically interview a couple of firms after identifying which have experience in the company's industry. This sort of experience is extremely important. Accountants must interpret and apply the rules, policies, bulletins, pronouncements, and standards of certain governing authorities, namely Generally Accepted Accounting Principles (GAAP). Among other things, GAAP and Financial Accounting Standards Board (FASB) strictures address the appropriate methods for recognizing revenues and expenses. How this is done varies by industry. Accountants must be conversant in these and stay abreast of new developments that may impact accounting within an industry. Outside accountants for public companies often interface with SEC staffers regarding the contents of certain public filings. Having an existing rapport with the SEC staffers, who are generally assigned to industries, can also be valuable.

The career progression within the Big Four and the national firms is pretty consistent. The entry-level job is as a staff accountant or associate. One is then promoted and gains more responsibility through the sequence of senior accountant, manager, senior manager, and partner. Each of these steps lasts a couple of years. As in the law, clients are billed at different hourly rates based on seniority. Partners are responsible for overseeing and maintaining client relationships.

With respect to public company accounting, the profession has changed over the past decade. Given the threat of liability and fear of becoming another Arthur Andersen, accountants have become much more guarded with their clients. In some cases, the accountant/client relationship has turned contentious and adversarial. Accounting engagements are largely protected in these situations. Unlike the situation with other service providers, a client cannot simply fire and replace an accounting firm over a disagreement. Changing accountants requires significant expense and added public disclosures. Fearing the worst, it also spooks investors. This environment, coupled with the added demands of new regulatory schemes such as the Sarbanes-Oxley Act, which emerged after recent accounting scandals to protect investors, have put a greater strain on accountants and forced longer working hours. Whereas this has been a financial boon to the firms, it has caused many junior and mid-level accountants to seek new employment opportunities.

CHAPTER 6

Later-stage Financing and Investment Bankers

➤ Institutional funding options for later-stage private companies.

➤ The nature of investors who typically invest in later-stage private companies.

➤ The role, activities, and motivations of investment bankers when calling on private and public companies.

PEMCO shifted into high gear following the completion of its Series C financing. As the company moved into volume production, all other operations ramped up their hiring and activity levels to fulfill internal demands and enable continued growth. The R&D department worked feverishly to improve the PEM and broaden its capabilities and applications. The sales department expanded its calling efforts to OEMs in several new markets, including consumer appliances and other products where the PEM could replace larger batteries or conventional power sources (the PEM's specifications had progressed but could still not meet the size and output requirements needed for bigger applications). PEMCO also moved to larger headquarters and deepened its administrative functions in order to support its increasing girth. This entailed hiring a human resources department, additional accounting professionals, and a general counsel (a senior associate from PEMCO's outside counsel who, like several of his past colleagues, had opted out of firm life and the "partner track" for an in-house position with a client). PEMCO's growth was controlled but just barely.

The products constituting PEMCO's first design wins were more successful than originally anticipated. Demand had outstripped supply and, as a result, the OEMs were constantly pressuring PEMCO and other component suppliers for more parts. Although this was better than the reverse scenario, it put an added strain on the system and ultimately forced PEMCO to outsource virtually all of its PEM production to an electronics manufacturing services company. Fortunately,

PEMCO had already been in manufacturing trials with the market leader and was confident that the organization had the supply arrangements and manufacturing expertise to meet the increased demand.

It had now been four years since Larry and Jerry left their studies to found PEMCO and over a year since the Series C closed. The company had raised $35.6 million, deployed it judiciously, and made tremendous progress. The company now had products, customers, sales, and even a catchy tagline recently devised by its marketing team—"PEMCO: More Power to Ya." It also had new markets to pursue, a large infrastructure, and a depleted cash balance. The company had high gross margins (PEMs sold for three times as much as the cost to make them) but was not yet profitable given the overhead for sales, R&D, administrative support, and facilities. The time was right for another fundraising.

PEMCO's board had several financing options to consider. The company was at a unique point. It was no longer a startup but still lacked significant revenues and a meaningful financial profile. Investment bankers from several prominent firms had begun visiting with PEMCO's management and board members to learn more about the company and to provide their feedback. Some had done so by invitation while others did so unsolicited, by making cold calls after hearing continued buzz about the company. They offered a range of advice on how best to proceed and finance continued growth.

A few bankers indicated that the public market would be receptive to PEMCO's story in light of the alternative energy angle, strong customer wins, and promise for the future. They encouraged the company to consider an IPO as the next step. Most bankers, however, indicated that PEMCO should secure one more round of private capital before proceeding to an IPO or other liquidity event (PEMCO was also starting to draw attention from potential acquirers). A private round would enable PEMCO to gain further scale and customer traction, develop a longer history of revenue growth, and get closer to profitability. These elements would increase interest from the buyside and significantly improve the value of the company, whether it was sold, taken public, or remained private.

The bankers proposing a private financing for PEMCO suggested several options. Financings at the company's stage of development are commonly referred to as "mezzanine financings"—implying their status "in between" venture and public capital. "Mezz" rounds, as they are also known, can take several forms. Most involve Series D (or later) preferred stock issued at attractive valuations and with relatively "clean" terms. They may also take the form of debt or equity with terms structured to be advantageous to the issuer if everything goes well and advantageous to the investor if it does not. An example of this would be equity issued at a very high valuation to minimize the dilution to existing investors, but which is structured to reset to a much lower valuation with much greater dilution if an IPO or sale of the company does not occur within a specified timeframe.

Debt issued in a mezz round (not to be confused with mezzanine debt involved in financing buyouts referenced later in this book) typically includes warrants and interest payments that are due monthly, quarterly, semi-annually, annually, or upon maturity or another triggering event such as an IPO. The interest, or "coupon," may be in the form of cash or the issuance of more debt as payment-in-kind (PIK).

In the end analysis, the decision as to what type of financing to pursue rests upon a cost-of-capital analysis (i.e., what is the least expensive and least dilutive capital) and one's comfort level with a business's prospects, markets, and the future impact of unique and potentially onerous financing provisions. After weighing these considerations and dismissing a possible sale of the company as premature, PEMCO's board elected to pursue a traditional Series D financing. It now needed to determine the best approach for pursuing the round.

A Briefing on Investment Bankers—Part I

Calling Efforts

The topic of investment bankers is broad and is therefore covered in two sections in this book. At this point, it is worth having a brief discussion regarding how and why investment bankers become involved with private companies.

As noted in Chapter 1, investment bankers work with companies to raise capital through the sale of securities and also work with companies to buy and sell businesses. Their stock and trade are capital, information, and relationships. In their pursuits, they call upon public companies, private companies, and investors such as VCs and private equity firms. Contrary to what the title suggests, investment bankers constitute only one group of professionals employed by investment banks—others include stockbrokers, institutional salespeople, research analysts, and traders.

At most investment banks, bankers fall into one of two categories: They are either industry specialists or product specialists. Industry bankers are tasked with the responsibility for calling on and having expertise in a specific industry. Product bankers specialize in a certain "product" (e.g., private placements, leveraged finance, or M&A) and work with industry bankers to pitch and execute assignments where their product expertise is required. Product bankers also act as internal gatekeepers overseeing access to the bank's resources in the product area. Some firms also have bankers responsible for covering important investors. Financial sponsor coverage bankers, as they are known, call upon private equity and VC firms, learn about portfolio companies and banking opportunities, and marshal the resources of the investment bank to win and execute assignments for them.

It should be noted that investment banks may also use geographic coverage models for building and maintaining client dialogues. Geographic coverage officers are common for operations in foreign countries where regional business ties and relationships are critical to winning mandates. Like their financial sponsor counterparts, geographic coverage bankers leverage colleagues with industry and product expertise to support their calling efforts.

An industry banker typically begins the process of calling on a private company (venture backed or otherwise) and its board members when the company has reached revenue stage or has generated some notable attention for its products or technology. Bankers hear about interesting prospects through the media, competitors, investors, trade shows, and other word of mouth—one great resource is *VentureWire*, an online information source for new financings owned by Dow Jones.

The banker will arrange an introductory meeting with company management, generally the CEO and CFO, and begin an ongoing dialogue regarding progress and new developments. The banker will also keep the company abreast of noteworthy activity in the markets such as related IPOs and M&A transactions. The banker will place particular emphasis on deals involving his or her firm, given the marketing impact of such activity. Clients want bankers who do the important deals and are in the flow.

The banker's ultimate goal in pursing these dialogues is to earn fees. Fees are earned by winning and successfully executing assignments. For a private company, an assignment could include being selected as: (1) an agent for a private placement, (2) an advisor for a sale of the company, or (3) an underwriter for an IPO.

During the first several meetings with a banker, managements tend to be very noncommittal and vague about what type of banking opportunity might exist over the foreseeable future. When asked about a possible sale, private placement, or IPO, a common refrain is "for now we are just interested in building a good business and we'll wait to see what makes sense for us in the future." Board members with a financial stake, such as VC or private equity representatives, tend to be more forthcoming with bankers about their objectives and longer-term outlook for a company. Because of their focus on achieving returns, their views may differ from the hopes and aspirations of management—particularly when the end result may involve a sale and management becoming jobless.

Dialogues with private companies also produce market intelligence that can be used to win other assignments. Industry bankers call upon public companies and larger industry players as part of their routine. These companies, and their business development departments, which oversee M&A activity, always like to hear about interesting private companies, potential competition, and acquisition ideas. In these discussions, most bankers are cautious not to cross the line and release information gained in confidence from other companies.

Many private companies like to get their stories out and speak openly with bankers in the hopes of doing so. They do this for a handful of reasons but mainly to generate interest on the part of potential suitors. If they want to be sold, it is good to get the word out that they have real customer traction and are doing well—whether this is truly the case or not (exaggerated claims are not uncommon).

Public companies reward bankers for these "strategic dialogues." If a banker brings a unique idea and the company acts upon it, most public companies have an unwritten policy that the assignment, referred to as a buyside engagement, will go to that banker. Some companies, however, have longstanding institutional relationships with only one or two investment banks and maintain a heavy bias to working only with them irrespective of the source of an idea. Bankers look to understand these dynamics when budgeting their time and expending energy on a company. Buyside engagements generate advisory fees and fees for rendering fairness opinions. A banker with a long history of supplying helpful knowledge and thoughtful insights may also be rewarded for the effort with an unrelated assignment. This might include a buyside engagement on another project or an underwriting role in a financing.

CHAPTER 7

Late-stage Financings and Private Placements

➤ The characteristics and process of a typical institutional funding for a later stage private company.

➤ The role and potential benefits of private placement agents.

➤ The structure and purpose of investment banking engagement letters.

➤ Important considerations for private companies to take into account when pursuing institutional funding.

Figure 7.1. Funding progression—Series D financing.

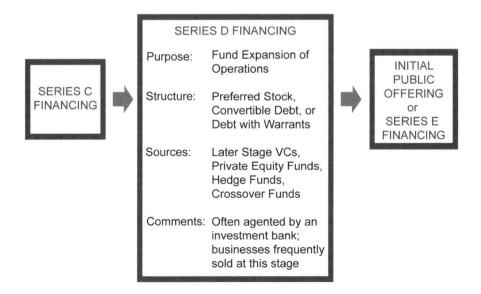

Most investment banks, large and small, have private placement departments that raise money for later-stage private companies. Together with industry bankers, these departments pitch for private placement mandates and, if selected, orchestrate the process of preparing the PPM, identifying and contacting potential investors, scheduling the road show to meet with interested parties, coordinating investor due diligence, and negotiating term sheets. Throughout these steps, the private placement team will work closely with the industry bankers, management, and the company's outside counsel. Counsel for the investment bank might also be hired. The bankers will also keep the board apprised of the deal's progress through regularly scheduled updates. From start (the organizational meeting) to finish (the closing), the fundraising process lasts about three months and often longer, but rarely shorter.

Companies engage private placement "agents" for several reasons. First and most importantly, they do so in hopes of accessing more investors and generating better terms for the round. Mezzanine financings with their more mature companies appeal to private equity funds, hedge funds, crossover funds, and selected mutual funds. Early and late-stage VCs have fewer relationships within these groups, whereas investment banks have many such relationships given the breadth of their activities. Agents are also used for their familiarity with current markets and investor appetites. Companies want insights on how far to push potential investors on terms and what the market will bear. Last, agents help reduce the time commitment and distraction to management during the fundraising process. This can be valuable when a company is experiencing tremendous growth, is at a critical inflection point, and needs management's full attention.

PEMCO's board considered the merits of using an agent for the Series D and concluded it would be the best approach. They assessed the input and feedback of the investment banks that had visited the company and selected a few to pitch for the business. Bankers from the firms were notified and provided with more detailed information on the company and its financial outlook. The bankers were also given a date and a ninety-minute time slot to present their thoughts and qualifications. All of the meetings would occur back-to-back on a single day to accommodate the schedules of management and the board.

Three investment banks pitched for the private placement. In attendance from the company was the entire board. This included the two cofounders and representatives from the lead investors from the Series A, Series B, and Series C financings. The company's previous accounting hire, who had been elevated to vice president of finance and acting CFO, also attended. The general framework of each banker presentation was very similar although the details varied.

Each investment bank brought a banking team and a set of materials known as a "pitch book." The banking teams consisted of the senior industry banker, one or two junior industry bankers, the senior private placement banker, one or two junior private placement bankers, and a representative from senior management (e.g., the head of technology investment banking). Each of these parties was responsible for discussing a section of the pitch book. Information in these sections included the bank's views and opinions concerning: (1) its private placement qualifications and experience, (2) market conditions for the round, (3) how to best position the company to investors, (4) the anticipated company valuation and transaction terms, (5) investors targeted for the deal, (6) process calendar and timeline, and (7) fees and terms of engagement.

Following pitch day, the acting CFO contacted several references for each bank, including previous private placement clients and investors, to discuss their experiences. He reported his finding to the board. After considering all factors, PEMCO selected I.L. Bankit & Co. (ILB) to agent the round. ILB was a growth- and technology-focused firm with a solid track record in private placements, a good reputation with investors and issuers, a strong presence in alternative energy, and a platform that could scale to meet PEMCO's future needs if they chose to pursue an IPO or sale of the company (this is helpful as busy directors and executives have only so much time to educate bankers and develop banking relationships). The board had briefly considered selecting another bank to "co-agent" the round but dismissed the notion. A co-agent was not customary and would unnecessarily complicate the deal. After notifying ILB, PEMCO proceeded to execute an engagement letter with the firm regarding the assignment.

A Briefing on Engagement Letters

Investment banks sign engagement letters with clients when they are mandated on M&A and fundraising projects. The exception to this rule is for public offerings, for which, instead, an underwriting agreement is executed by the parties. Investment banks each have "form" engagement letters that are tailored to different assignments. When being negotiated, the appropriate form letter is customized and provided to the client for comment. Principal terms for an engagement letter include:

1. **Fee.** For most assignments, the fee equates to a percentage of transaction value, generally 5% or 6% for private placements and much lower for M&A deals (usually less than 1.5%). An agent may also receive warrants to purchase stock for services it renders in a private placement. Except in situations in which other services are also provided (e.g., a "fairness opinion" delivered in the context of an M&A transaction) or a small retainer is paid upon signing the engagement letter, bankers are only paid when a transaction closes. Some engagements stipulate that compensation will only be paid for deals consummated with parties specifically identified in the engagement letter.

2. **Term.** The term refers to the duration of the engagement. Most engagements range from six to eighteen months with either party having the right to terminate upon earlier notice. Clients like short terms and bankers like long terms. In fact, the form letters at many

Wall Street firms are "evergreen"; they have no set termination period.

3. **Tail.** Closely linked to the term is the tail, which refers to the period of time a client must pay a banker's fee after an engagement is terminated. Tails exist to cover situations in which work is done on a transaction and the transaction, for whatever reason, closes after the engagement period.

4. **Rights of first refusal.** Some transactions end up differently than originally contemplated—for instance, a private placement that morphs into a sale of the company after the fundraising process generates interest from potential buyers. Bankers want to be protected in these circumstances. The right of first refusal gives them the opportunity to work on the new transaction. It may also cover an unrelated future transaction such as an IPO after a private placement is completed.

5. **Expense reimbursement.** In executing assignments, bankers incur out-of-pocket expenses for items such as legal fees, travel, document production, and shipping. Engagement letters provide for reimbursement and typically require client permission for expenses that exceed some predetermined aggregate amount or "cap."

6. **Indemnification.** Investment banks insist on being contractually protected, or "indemnified," by clients against claims that may arise from engagements.

Engagement letters are always negotiated, sometimes heatedly, and at times a client may negotiate several of them simultaneously with different banks to secure the best terms before making the final banker selection.

ILB's engagement letter called for a 5% fee on the money raised in the Series D. It also gave ILB the right of first refusal to serve as the company's advisor if it were sold during the engagement period (although this was not being contemplated). PEMCO's board agreed to these provisions but reduced the term and tail of the letter to six months and six months, respectively. They also refused to give ILB the right to act as the company's lead underwriter if it chose to pursue an IPO in the next two years.

With the engagement letter signed, PEMCO and ILB set out to raise $50 million with hopes of a $300 million pre-money valuation. The fundraising process was similar to the prior rounds but involved more structure and organization. It also involved preparing a more comprehensive PPM. Although not necessary for all Series Ds, ILB advised PEMCO to prepare a PPM that had the look and feel of an IPO prospectus in order to appeal to a broader group of investors.

The process began with an organizational meeting—also called an "org" or "all hands" meeting—for the bankers, executives, lawyers, and accountants. The purpose of the meeting was to: (1) discuss proposed terms for the transaction and a detailed schedule, (2) conduct due diligence and gather information on the company for the private placement memorandum, and (3) begin drafting the PPM. At the meeting, ILB circulated an "org book" containing a meeting agenda, due diligence request list, transaction calendar, working group list, and a rough draft of a PPM based on revisions to the Series C PPM. The meeting was chaired by the senior and mid-level ILB bankers.

After the organizational meeting, there were a series of drafting sessions to revise and improve the PPM. These sessions were conducted by a subset of the overall team and were held one or two times a week for three to four consecutive weeks. The result was a strong marketing document—one that accurately reflected the business to comply with the securities laws but also conveyed PEMCO's promise for the future.

The PPM was sent to a broad group of investors. Although wealthy individuals can be targeted for deals of this sort, ILB and PEMCO limited distribution only to institutions and those that could help the story going forward, either by their actions or their reputations. The distribution list included many institutions with charters to invest in both pubic and private companies as well as a few that only invest in private companies. As before, it excluded funds with competitive investments in the alternative energy sector.

The goal of the fundraising process was to secure one new investor that could lead the round. The remainder of the Series D would be taken by the existing VCs and strategic investors. As typical, the early stage VCs (Alpha, POC, and Beta) would invest but not to the fullest extent of their participation rights given the likely terms of the financing—the terms would be considered too "rich" for their charters. Carto and the strategics, on the other hand were committed to taking as much of the round as they could get. They would exercise their full participation rights and take any amounts not spoken for by Alpha, POC, and Beta.

Following a four-week period used to distribute the PPM, solicit preliminary interest, conduct a road show, arrange follow-up due diligence, solicit term sheets, and negotiate term sheets, ILB's process left PEMCO with several offers from potential leads. Two of these were much stronger than the rest.

One strong offer was from Smart Capital, a large hedge fund that had invested in several late-stage "pre-IPO" financings and had been rewarded handsomely for it. Most of its deals had gone public at valuations much higher than the private rounds. This, in turn, had helped the fund's overall performance and enabled it to generate "alpha," a term referring to a better return than the fund's market benchmarks. Smart had been good at picking winners and believed PEMCO would add to the list.

The second strong offer was from Crossover Technology Partners. CTP was dedicated to investing in technology companies that were either late-stage privates or were public with market capitalizations below $1 billion. It had a long and successful history of doing nothing else. CTP had just raised a new fund, its fifth. The fund was $1.5 billion and CTP's partners were anxious to put it to work.

Smart's and CTP's term sheets differed on two material points—valuation and board representation. CTP valued the company at $375 million post-money and

Table 7.1 Smart and CTP Valuation Methodologies

Assumptions	Smart	CTP
Time to IPO in months	18	18
NTM[1] Earnings at IPO	$20.0	$19.0
NTM[1] P/E of Comparables[2]	35×	32.5×
Calculations		
Value at IPO	$700	$618
Size of IPO	$100	$100
Pre-Money Value at IPO	$600	$518
Targeted Rate of Return	30%	25%
Post-Money Value	$405	$370
Rounded Post-Money Value	$400	$375

Note that dollars are in millions.
[1] NTM refers to Next Twelve Months.
[2] Valuation of comparables based on current NTM trading levels.

required no board seat, only the right to attend and observe board meetings. Smart valued the company higher, at $400 million post-money, but required a board seat.

Though different, Smart and CTP had arrived at their valuation levels by applying similar methodologies. Using PEMCO's projections (with some adjustments and customization) and the trading characteristics of their own sets of "comparable" public companies according to their price-to-earnings ratios, both had made an assessment of the likely timing and valuation for an IPO of the company. They had then discounted the IPO back to a present value based on their internal risk-adjusted targeted rates of return. In simple terms their analyses are shown in Table 7.1.

Smart and CTP also valued PEMCO assuming scenarios in which: (1) the company was sold outright at multiples and values paid in similar transactions and (2) it remained private longer. Subject to the assumptions, these values produced results similar to the IPO calculations.

PEMCO's board debated the merits of the two proposals. Directors were inclined to proceed with Smart given the higher valuation and the role they believed the hedge fund could play after PEMCO became public. Contrary to the "quick flip" practices of some hedge funds, Smart had a solid reputation as a long-term holder that added to its public positions whenever there were signs of weakness in a stock. This type of "aftermarket support" could be helpful. However, the board was not looking for another director who was an investor or insider. The board already contained three VCs and two founders. The company now wanted to bring in a couple of highly credentialed outside directors in anticipation of an IPO. ILB conveyed the board's position to Smart.

Knowing that it would ultimately seek to vacate any board seat prior to the IPO in order to allow greater flexibility in buying and selling PEMCO's stock once it was public, Smart agreed to forego a director's seat in exchange for observation rights on the board and an increase in the size of the round to $60 million. Smart also asked for an informal say in the selection of the new directors. The board granted these requests and the round closed three weeks later, after allowing for confirmatory due diligence and the completion of documentation.

PEMCO's Series D was $60 million at a $400 million post-money valuation. Net of ILB's fee, the company received $57 million. Unlike many agented rounds, the deal exceeded the company's expectations and its banker's earlier representations. It closed at a higher valuation and in a shorter timeframe than originally set forth in the ILB pitch book, a rare occurrence given competitive pressures and the inclination of bankers to make exaggerated statements in order to win business. Experienced VCs are aware of this phenomenon and urge bankers to give them honest opinions. Unfortunately, these same VCs often award assignments to bankers with the most aggressive views on matters such as valuation on the basis that it shows enthusiasm for a deal. An aggressive approach also finds a receptive audience with management, who invariably like to be told how pretty their baby is. It is necessary to point out that VCs have also been known to stretch the truth when it comes to driving an agenda, promoting a portfolio company, or otherwise looking after their own interests.

When the dust settled, the investment allocations, ownership percentages, and values for the Series D were as shown in Table 7.2 (excluding the impact of employee stock options).

In total, PEMCO had now raised $95.6 million with total invested capital of $15.8 million for Alpha and POC, $15.6 million for Beta, $31.1 million for Carto, $7.8 million for the strategics and $25.2 million for Smart. On paper, the investors, particularly the early stage VCs, had already shown an attractive, albeit

Table 7.2 Series D Financing

	Pre-Round Ownership	New Capital Commitment	Post-Round Ownership	
			%	$ (millions)
Larry	18.9%	$0.00	16.1%	$64.26
Jerry	18.9%	$0.00	16.1%	$64.26
Seed Investors	4.2%	$0.00	3.6%	$14.28
Alpha & POC	30.0%	$3.00	26.3%	$105.00
Beta	17.5%	$6.00	16.4%	$65.50
Carto	8.4%	$20.64	12.3%	$49.20
Strategics	2.1%	$5.16	3.1%	$12.30
Smart*	0.0%	$25.20	6.3%	$25.20

* Smart was only able to invest 42% of the round due to participation rights from earlier rounds.

unrealized, return on their investments. With more than $60 million in cash, PEMCO was well positioned for further success.

OTHER OBSERVATIONS ON PRIVATE FINANCINGS

PEMCO's experience of proceeding smoothly from one institutional funding to the next is atypical. More often, companies stumble over unforeseen challenges to their growth. Technologies take longer to develop, products take longer to produce, customers take longer to surface, and markets take longer to emerge. All of these factors, and others, conspire to consume more capital and produce weaker results than originally contemplated. Companies are forced to complete additional financings and make downward revisions to their projections. Of the hundreds of private companies that I have visited over the years, these are the rule. In fact, I would be hard pressed to count on one hand the number of companies that came close to, much less exceeded, their early financial projections. For this reason, experienced executives at early stage companies almost never discuss detailed financial information with outsiders (even with nondisclosure agreements in place). They are vague on the topic and contain their commentary with bankers to higher-level matters such as notable customer wins, industry awards, and product accolades.

Failing to produce projected results can be costly to existing shareholders as well as employees with stock options. This is especially true following large later-stage rounds completed at high valuations. When a company has raised a lot of money, liquidation preferences can add up to an amount beyond the pre-money value offered for a company in a new round. Take for instance PEMCO: It has now raised $95.6 million. Of this, $95.5 million is entitled to liquidation preferences—every dollar raised except money from the seed round. While this preference works when the company is worth $400 million, it would be problem if the company needed more capital and was only valued at, say, $75 million. Without some form of adjustment to the capital structure, the company would not be able to attract new capital or retain employees who have compensation tied to the value of common stock. The common stock would be worth-less because its value is subordinate to liquidation preferences of the preferred stock.

The problem just noted became acute to many private companies following the 2000 technology collapse. The result was a series of recapitalizations in which the capital structure of companies was reconstituted and preferences were restructured to keep employees and enable new financings. Dubbed "cram-down" rounds, most of these converted preferred stock investors into small common shareholders and allowed employee stock options to be reset to lower valuations.

One variation on the cram-down round is the "pay-to-play" round. In a pay-to-play, existing investors from each class of preferred stock are rewarded for continuing to invest in a company. The reward comes in the form of preferences that are preserved on previously invested capital. For example, terms of a recapitalization round may provide that existing investors will maintain their previous preferences for funds committed to the new financing on a dollar-for-dollar basis (i.e., for each new dollar invested, the preference associated with one previously invested dollar will be maintained). The pay-to-play structure was required in many recapitalizations in order to gather sufficient support among each class of investors to vote in favor of new fundraisings. Suffice it to say, there is a lot of boardroom brinksmanship at the time of these discussions.

One other consideration closely linked to liquidation preferences is knowing when a private company should be sold rather than raise additional capital. A new fundraising may allow a company to continue to grow but the amount of growth many not be sufficient to offset new preferences and reward employees and common shareholders for the effort. As a simple example, consider a small private company with preferred stockholders who currently have $10 million in liquidation preferences and who currently own 50% of the company if they converted their shares to common stock. The company receives an offer to be purchased for $20 million. At this level, the common shareholders and option holders have $10 million in value ($20 million less the $10 million in liquidation preferences). If the company chose to raise a $10 million round at a $30 million post-money valuation instead of proceeding with the sale, the company would also be valued on paper at $20 million with $10 million for the common shareholders and options holders. However, management and the employees would have to work hard to make the company worth $30 million and would only be entitled to one third of every dollar in value created above that amount. Subject to the opportunity, this may not be a good trade off.

Personal Observations on Private Institutional Capital

1. *Many businesses are not well suited to private institutional capital.* Although a large pool of private capital may sound appealing to an entrepreneur, some business models are not well suited to it. Only businesses that require the capital and can generate substantial growth and value from it should consider it an attractive option. Otherwise, VCs and private capital can be unnecessarily dilutive to a founder's ownership stake or, worse, can result in a business being shut down or sold prematurely to repay investors. Those considering their financing needs should be realistic about their plans and consider all of their options.

2. *Many entrepreneurs are not well suited to private institutional capital.* Even if a business fits the description of one that should consider private institutional capital, an entrepreneur should carefully consider whether it fits his or her style and personality. Many entrepreneurs are hardheaded and accustomed to calling all of the shots. They find it very difficult to listen to, much less to follow, outside opinions. Being accountable to outside investors is a fact

of life an entrepreneur must accept when a company takes outside capital.

3. *Some VCs and private equity firms have the ability to create tremendous value for their companies and investors.* Some private financiers have the Midas touch. They provide invaluable experience, insights, connections, and credibility to their companies and generate huge returns for their investors. Assuming a company accepts and follows their guidance, these individuals and firms are worth far more than the capital they bring to the table. Entrepreneurs should do their homework to find these players and aggressively pursue them—even if it means accepting inferior terms in a financing round to get them.

4. *Some VCs and private equity firms offer nothing more than money and headaches to their companies.* There are many private financiers that unfortunately fit a description opposite to that in #3. These players talk a good game but lack substance and follow-through. Instead, their oversight and input only amount to substantial burdens for their companies. Obviously, these firms and individuals should be avoided at all costs. Entrepreneurs should look to track record and reference checks for direction on a financial partner rather than be lured by attractive financing terms and silver-tongued salesmanship.

5. *The paramount agenda of private institutional capital is to make money.* Companies accepting private capital should never lose sight of this fact. Although VCs and private equity firms may have good rapport with an entrepreneur and a company's executives, their mission is to make money. Ultimately they will take whatever steps are necessary to achieve this goal. They will fire founders, restructure management teams, overhaul operations, force a sale, or do whatever else they can to serve their own investors and generate or preserve returns. After they have been sacked or demoted, I have seen many entrepreneurs shocked and in disbelief that their VCs would take such steps, particularly since they had grown to consider their VCs as friends and confidants.

CHAPTER 8

Paths to Liquidity for Private Companies

➤ The primary options for providing liquidity to private company shareholders: recapitalizations, private company sales, and IPOs.

➤ The necessary ingredients for an initial public offering.

Over a year passed since the Series D financing and PEMCO continued to make tremendous progress. It had a booming business supplying PEMs for military applications, and the consumer appliance market had proven to be a winner. Early sales of PEM-powered refrigerators, dishwashers, and ovens had been brisk. When remodeling a kitchen or building a new house, it appeared that the public liked the notion of paying a little more up front to lower their power bills and conserve resources. With improvements to the device, PEMCO was now exploring opportunities in the automotive and small generator markets. Preliminary discussions looked promising.

PEMCO now employed almost 300 people and had sales and development offices in the United States, Europe, and Asia. Throughout the past twelve-plus months, the company had continued to focus attention on infrastructure and assuring that the necessary systems and personnel were in place to support the growing enterprise. This included comprehensive and expensive rollouts of enterprise resource management (ERM) and customer relationship management (CRM) software packages from leading vendors in these areas. It also included audits and input on PEMCO's financial controls and systems from the company's outside accountants. These would be needed if the company chose to go public or to sell itself (financial and strategic buyers demand better bookkeeping and accounting practices in larger acquisitions).

As foretold in the last financing, the board had been expanded to include two highly qualified and well-connected outside directors. One had a deep background in the consumer electronics industry covering operations and marketing. The other was the former CFO of a *Fortune* 500 company. This person would serve as head of the board's audit committee, a necessary but difficult-to-fill position following the accounting scandals of recent years.

With Larry and Jerry's support, some notable changes occurred in the executive ranks as well. Recognizing the cumbersome nature the arrangement and his own interest in developing technology rather than managing people, Jerry stepped down from his roles as co-CEO and co-chairman to become the company's chief technologist. Knowing the market's general dislike for co-CEOs and co-chairs, the board encouraged this move. Jerry would still have a seat on the board. Larry became sole CEO and retained the chairman title even though combining these roles often rankles investors who prefer nonexecutive board chairs. Shortly following the move, Larry joined the local chapter of the Young Presidents Organization (YPO). While not much of a joiner, Larry was encouraged by a few board members to seriously consider the opportunity. Offered by invitation only, the YPO is a national networking and support organization for CEOs who are under 50 years old.

In addition to these moves, the board had retained an executive search firm to find a chief operating officer (COO) qualified to better manage the company's expanding operations. The firm, Head & Hunter, was well suited to the task. It had extensive relationships throughout the electronic components and technology hardware industries. The new COO would be critical to the company's continued success and ideally would serve as an informal mentor to the smart but unseasoned Larry. Head & Hunter found the right candidate, a *Fortune* 500 executive with a wealth of experience in global operations at some of the world's largest companies. The new COO was lured to PEMCO with a pay cut but options on 1% of the company (exercisable at the Series D valuation). Given the difficulty of valuing the options, Head & Hunter was paid a flat finder's fee for the COO rather than the conventional 25 percent to 33 percent of a hire's first-year income.

Beyond building the business, the board had been spending time considering PEMCO's future as well as liquidity options for the investors. Alpha and POC had been invested in the company for five years. Although the typical holding period for their investments was roughly five to seven years, they and the other VCs knew that some liquidity paths take longer to achieve than others. They also knew that planning and preparation for a certain-to-be-needed liquidity event was wise. The board did not want to create distractions to management at this critical juncture but agreed that it would be prudent to begin exploring its exit options more seriously.

Private companies basically have three options when it comes to providing liquidity to shareholders. Besides distributing profits, they can: (1) recapitalize the company with debt and pay out proceeds of the debt to shareholders as a special dividend, (2) sell all or a portion of the company, or (3) take the company public. Options #2 and #3 were available to PEMCO. Option #1, at least with conventional debt, was not.

RECAPITALIZATIONS

Recapitalizations replace or modify a company's existing capital structure. They can involve the issuance of new debt or equity to replace existing debt or equity. Those involving new debt, whether or not proceeds are distributed to shareholders, typically involve mature businesses. Banks and other lenders, including bond investors, like businesses with strong historical financial performance. They want to be repaid and make lending decisions based on whether projected and historical cash flow characteristics make repayment likely.

Typically, companies borrow on terms referenced according to a multiple of annual cash flow. Cash flow is generally defined as earnings before interest, depreciation, and amortization expenses (EBITDA). Lenders want to ensure that a company's cash flow is sufficiently high to cover interest payments and other debt servicing obligations. For example, a $20 million loan at 5 percent interest to a business with $5 million of trailing annual EBITDA would be characterized as one with 4X EBITDA coverage ($20 million/$5 million) and 5X interest coverage ($5 million/$1 million)—both would be acceptable to a bank. PEMCO was growing rapidly and was continuing to invest in that growth. This produced negative EBITDA each year since its inception. Although last quarter it reached cash flow breakeven, with EBITDA moving out of negative territory, it was not a viable recapitalization candidate.

Over the preceding five years, PEMCO had the financial profile shown in Table 8.1.

SELLING A COMPANY

A sale was a very real opportunity for PEMCO and could involve the entire company or simply a portion of it. With respect to providing some shareholder liquidity via the latter, a sale could take two forms. PEMCO could sell an ownership stake through a new financing and then use the proceeds to repurchase some of the outstanding stock from existing investors. Alternatively, interested shareholders could sell their positions directly to one or more buyers (assuming the sales complied with securities laws and were not otherwise limited by contractual obligations). In either event, PEMCO would need to be involved. Buyers

Table 8.1 PEMCO Summary Financial Profile

	Year 1	Year 2	Year 3	Year 4	Year 5
Round(s)	Seed & Series A	Series B	Series C	Series D	
Revenues	$0.0	$0.0	$2.0	$20.0	$75.0
Gross Profit	$0.0	$0.0	$1.3	$13.3	$50.0
EBITDA	($1.3)	($4.0)	($8.7)	($18.7)	($5.0)
Net Income	($1.4)	($4.4)	($9.6)	($20.4)	($9.4)
Ending Cash	$0.9	$2.6	$14.6	$47.8	$34.0

would look to the company for information, financial and otherwise, to arrive at a valuation and assess the merits of the purchase.

The company continued to be approached by potential suitors in response to its successes and increasing notoriety. Some of these approaches were made directly by business-development executives from larger companies. Others were made indirectly by investment bankers who had attempted to play matchmaker by arranging introductory meetings between PEMCO's management and executives from potential buyers. These meetings were often characterized by the bankers as opportunities to "open dialogues" and see whether there were ways that the companies could work together.

PEMCO's board could not rule out selling all or a portion of the company, but it was not prepared to proceed exclusively down this path. The board considered several factors in reaching this decision. First and foremost, it believed that PEMCO was poised for further growth and would continue to increase in value. It was not a one-product company with limited potential for expansion, nor was it a company facing competition from new or existing players with me-too products. Similarly, it was not created to be sold, as is the case with many VC-backed companies that target specific product or service holes of larger companies. PEMCO's VCs had seen such scenarios and chosen sellside paths for them in order to lock in gains and avoid seeing a valuable, hot company turn into a not-so-valuable, has-been company. In PEMCO's case, it was decided that selling today would be leaving money on the table.

The second primary consideration was the founders and employees. Behind closed doors, the VC directors debated how the team would react to a potential sale. Despite the financial rewards involved, they concluded not well, given the company's culture and management's emotional connection to the business. The topic of a sale was never discussed extensively with Larry and Jerry to avoid creating any ill will or board-level schisms.

GOING PUBLIC

A company's ability to pursue an IPO is impacted by several factors, most of which are related to the company and some, related to the market. To be a viable IPO candidate, a company must possess the right mix of scale, growth, profitability, and opportunity to appeal to public investors. This mix varies from industry to industry. It can also vary from company to company within an industry.

1. **Scale.** Scale is an absolute and relative concept but is basically synonymous with size—size in terms of revenues and operations and size vis-à-vis competitors. A company must be large enough to be relevant to an industry and preferably be an industry leader (or at least a noteworthy challenger). It must also be large enough to sustain itself as a viable long-term commercial concern. In light of the added costs and burdens of being public caused by new regulatory concerns, public companies require more scale today than in the past.

2. **Growth.** Investors purchase stocks they believe will increase in value. Stock prices are driven by perceived value and are the product of two variables—earnings and valuations multiples (price-to-earnings or otherwise). An increase in either of these will drive a stock price higher, and growth fuels both. It improves earnings and strengthens investor sentiment and thus trading multiples. Companies are valued at their IPO on the basis of projected future earnings discounted for risk (execution or otherwise). Projected growth supported by historical performance is a key consideration for investors.

3. **Profitability.** Profitability, as used here, has a double meaning. It refers to (1) the level of a company's actual historical earnings and projected earnings and' (2) the ability of a company's business model to produce earnings from incremental sales (i.e., does revenue growth produce earnings growth and to what extent—this is called "operating leverage"). Both forms of profitability are important to investors and thus an IPO. There is no bright-line rule on sufficient profitability. Many venture-backed, high-growth companies have completed IPOs with very little or no historical profitability (perhaps only a quarter or two) but with business models possessing high operating leverage and strong outlooks for future profitability.

4. **Opportunity.** By opportunity, we mean market opportunity. A company must have an attractive market opportunity to appeal to investors. This can be a large, existing market or an emerging market that has demonstrated growth and holds significant promise.

Generally speaking, less of one ingredient can be offset by more of another and vice versa. Investors have demonstrated a willingness to buy IPOs with modest scale and limited historical profitability so long as they had compelling growth and opportunity characteristics. In fact, many of the market's best-performing deals fall into this category. Conversely, investors also purchase slower growth stories with significant scale and profitability.

Market factors also affect the viability of an IPO. Investment bankers refer to the IPO market as having "windows" when it is "open" or "closed" to new deals. To go public, there must be investors willing to put capital at risk in the untested stock of a newly minted public company. How investors view the market overall, the market for new issues, and the market for comparable stocks (those in and around the company's industry) all influence investor appetites. If the market has been choppy, if recent IPOs have performed poorly, or if there have been issues with comparable companies (fundamental, trading, or otherwise), potential buyers will be reluctant to venture into an IPO even if it has appealing investment characteristics. The market window will be closed or, at a minimum, the negative market sentiment will reduce receptivity and drive lower valuations.

It is worth noting that the market window is generally open to some deals and closed to others at any given point in time. The buyside has trillions of dollars to invest in public stocks and is constantly looking for new opportunities that can generate favorable returns. IPOs provide such opportunities. Industries and companies within them, however, move in and out of favor with investors based on their operating characteristics and outlooks. IPOs rarely occur in out-of-favor sectors. Investors do not want them and are not willing to pay enough for them to prompt an issuer to take the leap into the public sphere.

PEMCO possessed all the ingredients for a successful IPO. It had scale, spectacular growth, and a huge market opportunity. It also had a business model with attractive gross margins and operating leverage that could produce strong earnings via incremental sales. The only element it did not yet have was absolute profitability. Historically it had lost and not earned money, but this was about to change. The company projected that it would earn more than $20 million next year, its sixth year of operations.

Investors seemed eager to put money to work in alternative energy plays. Stocks in the sector had performed well and recent industry deals had been very successful. Each had "priced" at or above "the high end of the range" (the price per share range noted on the cover of the marketing prospectus) and traded up in the "aftermarket" (the days following the offering, or "pricing"). The overall market was also strong. While things could change, it appeared that a PEMCO IPO would have a receptive audience and the board decided to proceed accordingly.

CHAPTER 9

Considerations for Selling a Private Company

➤ The two general categories of buyers for private and public companies: strategic buyers and financial buyers.

➤ The differences and similarities between strategic and financial buyers regarding their acquisition initiatives.

➤ The role, activities, and structure of private equity firms.

Although PEMCO's board had decided not to pursue a sale of the company, it is worth discussing what the sale process for a private company involves, as this path to liquidity is far more common than an IPO. Most private companies simply do not possess the requisite traits to become public, and with increasing frequency, those that do choose to pursue a sale over an IPO given the burdens associated with being public. Once a company is public, additional expenditures and infrastructure are required and executives face greater scrutiny and personal liability. Moreover, liquidity for inside shareholders remains limited due to securities laws and underwriter "lock ups" (to be explained later).

Whether it is a local restaurant, a mid-sized regional business, or a $300 million-a-year venture-backed enterprise, most private companies consider and often actively pursue a sale at some point in their history in order to provide liquidity to their owners. The smallest of these businesses are advertised online or through local print media (if marketed at all) and sold directly by the owners to employees, family members, or other budding entrepreneurs. Slightly larger businesses are typically sold by local and regional business brokers engaged by the owners. These brokers maintain several listings and market them to entrepreneurs, investor groups, and others with whom they have relationships within the business community. Beyond these two categories are the enterprises that possess sufficient scale or other unique elements to attract the interest of larger buyers. This chapter addresses sales involving these companies.

THE BUYERS

Purchasers of public and larger private companies fall into two categories: strategic buyers and financial buyers. Strategic buyers are companies with complementary products and services that look to acquisitions, both large and small, to expand their offerings for either offensive or defensive purposes. Offensive purposes include growing a market or expanding into a new market. Defensive purposes mean fending off a new or existing competitive threat. Virtually all public companies explore strategic acquisition opportunities from time to time, and many maintain an active program of making such acquisitions. These come complete with well-staffed business-development departments that are tasked with finding and analyzing opportunities. Some purchases are rational and some are merely poorly contemplated reactions to market pressures or fears. Some of the market's leading acquirers include household names such as Microsoft and Proctor & Gamble.

Financial buyers acquire businesses and then create value for themselves by growing operations, improving financial performance, applying financial leverage, divesting assets, selling to higher bidders, or some combination of the above. For larger businesses, financial buyers include private equity funds and, to an increasing extent, hedge funds. They also include a handful of publicly traded conglomerates and specialized financial entities such as special-purpose acquisition companies.

There are some rules of thumb regarding strategic and financial buyers:

1. **Strategic buyers typically pay more.** Unlike financial buyers, strategic buyers have infrastructure that can be leveraged to increase the sales and/or reduce the operating expenses of companies they acquire (assuming they are of real strategic value). Referred to as revenue and cost synergies, these positively impact the financial profile of an acquisition, thus enabling a better price to be paid. When a company is sold, the seller attempts to quantify the synergies and extract value for them from strategic buyers. The other factor impacting strategic buyers is fear. They often pay more to eliminate competitive threats. It is worth noting that this who-pays-more rule has been challenged recently given the quantity of capital in the hands of financial buyers, the availability of low-cost debt, and the creative hedging and financing structures now deployed by financial buyers.

2. **Sometimes financial buyers are strategic buyers.** The exception to rule #1 is when a financial buyer owns a business that would be a strategic buyer. Many private equity funds invest in companies that can serve as platforms for future acquisitions. They make these platform investments in order to reduce the number of companies in their portfolios, thus freeing up investment professionals to dedicate more time and energy to their existing investments. Private equity firms also generate incremental advisory fees from their platform investments when they work with them to make such "add-on" acquisitions. These deals are strategic in nature.

3. **Strategic buyers do not like minority investments.** Strategic buyers often have more than just financial returns in mind when making acquisitions. They buy businesses to achieve broader goals and objectives that cannot be satisfied without possessing control over the agenda of the target companies. Minority stakes typically fail to offer this level of input. Some financial buyers also steer clear of minority investments. That being said, strategic buyers sometimes do make minority investments to gain toe holds in companies that may possess strategic value in the future as either acquisitions or business partners.

4. **Financial buyers like larger, more mature businesses.** As noted previously, financial buyers attain attractive returns from acquisitions by deploying several techniques. Almost all of these, including the use of financial leverage (i.e., debt) and improving operations after an acquisition (i.e., reducing expenses), require a business to be of scale. The business must have cash flow to borrow against and cost centers, such as head count and facilities, to reduce.

5. **Financial buyers pay cash.** Financial buyers use cash almost exclusively to fund acquisitions, although they may reserve some stock to retain management and employees. Except for smaller deals, strategic buyers often use some combination of cash and stock when making acquisitions. Sellers always prefer cash.

6. **Financial buyers move faster.** Strategic buyers require certain board and shareholder approvals for material acquisitions. These take time. They also have internal politics and agendas to address in order to gain support for most acquisitions. Financial players are not encumbered by the same formalities and issues and therefore can move faster in deciding upon and closing acquisitions. There may also be fewer antitrust issues to address, as compared with an acquisition by a direct competitor. Sellers appreciate speed and certainty although they can also be harmed by them. In transactions with limited competition, financial buyers sometimes revise their offers with take-it-or-leave-it "down bids" after values have already been agreed.

A Briefing on Private Equity Firms

As with VCs, there are hundreds of private equity firms in the United States. Sometimes referred to as buyout shops, these firms vary by size and focus but possess a common objective: to generate investment returns by acquiring established businesses, or at least significant stakes in them. Private equity firms manage more than $750 billion in equity capital. With leverage, this provides them with several times this amount in buying power for acquisitions.

The organizational and funding structure of private equity firms is virtually identical to that of VCs (see discussion in Chapter 4). Most firms are operated as partnerships that, in turn, oversee funds of pooled capital from institutional investors (pension funds, foundations, university endowments, sovereign wealth funds, etc.) and wealthy individuals. Unlike VCs, many private equity funds rely upon placement agents to spearhead fundraising efforts. These agents, of which only a few are notable, have longstanding relationships with fund investors and their advisors. Agents receive a fee upon the closing of a fund as well as an ongoing percentage of management fees and carry.

Typical fee arrangements for private equity funds differ slightly from those of VCs. Like VCs, the firms receive a management fee (usually 1.5% to 2%) based on capital committed to a fund and a carried interest on the profits of a fund (usually 20% on amounts above some set rate of return such as the federal funds rate). Unlike VCs, private equity firms also receive separate fees from their portfolio companies. They receive fees for the time and energy they dedicate to the companies as well as advisory fees for working on projects such as M&A transactions. Private equity firms may also receive commitment fees when they deploy capital for new investments.

Private equity firms are staffed along the same lines as VCs. Investment professionals have titles progressing from analyst, to associate, to vice president, to principal, to partner. The background of these individuals leans heavily toward finance and banking. Many analysts are hired from investment banking analyst programs, associates from top-tier graduate business school programs, and more senior lateral hires from investment banks, other private equity funds, or the ranks of successful management teams. The two core competencies for senior private equity professionals are investment acumen and the ability to open doors. For this reason, private equity is home to the well-connected, including many ex-politicians, ex-military brass, and ex-government officials.

On average, private equity firms and their funds are larger than those found in the VC community. In fact, the trend lines for the two groups have been going in opposite directions over the past several years. Many VCs have scaled back their operations and fund sizes to better mirror the capital needs of early stage opportunities or have expanded the scope of their investing activities to encompass later-stage opportunities and small buyouts. Gone are the days of the $50 million Series A round, even though collectively VCs now manage several times as much capital as they did in the late 1990s.

Private equity firms, on the other hand, have experienced a boom in transaction volumes as waning capital markets and a challenging regulatory environment for public companies have notably increased the number of corporate divestitures, going-private transactions, and large private-company sales. Many of the latter come from other private equity funds. In these transactions, buyers try not to overpay for an asset or get "stuffed" by the competition as it is often referred to by the players.

Private equity firms have responded by staffing up and raising more money to make investments. In 2007, for instance, buyout shops raised more than $300 billion for new funds and acquired businesses valued at more than $700 billion. Some critics have charged that increased funding and the emergence of multibillion-dollar "mega" funds have shifted the focus of many private equity professionals from generating above-average returns to simply maintaining performance levels that allow them to retain assets and gather larger and larger management fees. The same has been said of developments in the hedge fund community. There is probably some truth to this assertion. Actions and incentives often differ when one is building versus preserving an organization and economic base.

As controlling shareholders, private equity firms tend to also dedicate more resources to portfolio companies than their VC brethren. Though they may, in some instances, acquire a minority stake or pool resources with other firms to make a large, complicated, or hotly contested acquisition, private equity firms generally hold the majority of board seats and have ultimate decision-making authority over companies in their portfolios. Their investment professionals maintain daily dialogue with company executives and often spend several days a week at a company's headquarters analyzing operations, initiatives, and opportunities.

Firms within the private equity universe are distinguished from each other by several factors. First and foremost among these is a firm's predominant investment style. Fundamentally, there are two investing approaches for private equity firms—leveraged investing and growth investing.

Leveraged Investing. Almost all private equity firms use debt and financial leverage to help fund their acquisitions and produce returns. Some firms rely extensively on this approach. They possess deep expertise in leveraged finance and generate returns primarily by creatively using debt and then divesting assets, reducing expenses, and improving cash flows. While they also benefit from revenue growth at their portfolio companies, driving notable growth at the top line is a secondary focus. The acronym LBO, short for leveraged buyout, was coined to describe this investment approach. Subject to the credit markets and the availability of debt for a particular deal, acquisitions are usually funded with roughly 25 percent to 35 percent equity and 65 percent to 75 percent debt. Structured in tranches bearing different levels of risk such as senior debt, subordinated debt, secured debt, and unsecured debt, debt for these transactions is supplied by commercial banks, large investment banks, bond investors, and mezzanine debt funds.

Growth Investing. Rather than relying upon financial engineering and the use of other people's money, some private equity firms focus on producing returns by growing the businesses they acquire. This approach may involve some debt but much less than that found in true leveraged investing. Cash flows are used by these firms to expand a company's operations rather than to repay debt, make interest payments, and fund special dividends. Firms targeting this approach may also acquire distressed businesses that cannot support heavy debt loads with the idea of improving their operations and returning them to good health.

In many respects, the investing styles just described dictate many of the other differences between private equity firms. These differences tend to surround four variables—organization size, investment size, industry focus, and geographic focus.

1. **Organization size.** Some private equity firms dedicate their energies to one fund and limit their advisory work to smaller projects and acquisitions for portfolio companies. Others manage several funds simultaneously through separate investment teams (each with a different objective) and have large advisory practices that work with portfolio companies as well as unaffiliated entities. Larger organizations such as these often focus on leveraged investing and may use more than one fund to make an acquisition (e.g., an equity fund plus a mezzanine debt fund).

2. **Investment size.** Private equity firms scale their investments to correspond to their staffing levels, resources, and capital under management. Smaller firms do smaller deals and larger firms do larger deals. What constitutes larger or smaller depends on investing style. Given the higher equity levels required for growth investing, a large deal for a growth investor may be considered a small deal for a leverage investor. Those considered large on an absolute basis, say over $1 billion, almost always involve leverage investors (note that they may only need $250 million in equity for such a deal). Most firms have limits on what they can commit to a single investment without special approval from their limited partners (typically 10% to 20% of a fund's capital).

3. **Industry focus.** The private equity business historically has been more about numbers than industry expertise. In many respects, it still is for leverage investors. These firms focus primarily on traditional industries with large cash flows that can be leveraged and improved. Understanding the value of knowledge and familiarity, they may gravitate to sectors where they have experience and often rely upon input and advice from advisory board members who are retired executives from specific industries. Growth-focused firms, on the other hand, tend to be very industry focused. They rely heavily upon their history and expertise within particular areas. For instance, several firms focus on retailing and restaurant companies.

Historically, technology has been a less active area for private equity firms. A few growth-investing firms have been successful in technology but almost no leverage investing has occurred in the sector because many lenders and rating agencies have long viewed technology companies, even established market leaders, as too risky for sizable debt loads. This has started to change. In recent years, a few leverage-focused firms have started paying greater attention to the segment.

4. **Geographic focus.** Private equity is a national business. Most firms have investments spread throughout the country and do not limit their activities by geography. Nevertheless, many firms end up with some geographic concentration given their industry focus, physical location, and ability to source deals in communities where they have had past success. Except for much larger firms, most domestic firms limit their investment activities to North America.

Besides managing their investments intelligently, arguably the most critical task for private equity firms is finding and closing attractive acquisitions. This is particularly true today given the availability of capital and heavy competition for deals. Firms rely upon their reputations and contacts to source transactions. Many also promote a pro-management image to solicit deals. Executives pursuing a management-led buyout generally need equity capital and want management-friendly partners.

One key source for deals is investment bankers. As previously discussed, bankers spend a substantial amount of time visiting with companies (public and private) and learning about their operations, strategies, and goals. They then traffic in this information. Private equity firms want acquisition ideas generated from these discussions and are willing to pay for them.

Private equity firms produce substantial fees for Wall Street. When they buy companies, they pay bankers for M&A advisory services and for structuring and arranging debt financing. When they own companies, they pay bankers for M&A advisory services and for structuring and arranging refinancings and recapitalizations. And when they seek liquidity for companies, they pay bankers for M&A advisory services and for underwriting IPOs.

Among other things, private equity firms reward investment banks with mandates and fees for bringing them good ideas. They are especially interested in proprietary ideas—those that are not shared with other firms or "shopped" via a formal auction process. In most cases, a private equity firm will pay a banker an advisory fee for an idea that results in an acquisition (note that this requires more than just an idea, it requires introductions and helping put a deal together). They will also involve the banker in future underwriting and M&A activity for the company. On leveraged deals, upfront fees usually also include those paid for structuring and arranging debt financing. In light of the potentially lucrative stream of fees for good ideas, most large investment banks have dedicated financial sponsor groups who routinely call on and provide proprietary ideas to large private equity firms. Recognizing their lower position in the pecking order, many smaller private equity firms maintain an active program of reaching out to investment banks to cultivate idea-generating relationships.

CHAPTER 10

The Process for Selling a Company

➤ The two general approaches to selling a company: targeted discussions and auctions.

➤ The step-by-step process undertaken with each approach.

➤ The function and potential benefits of a sellside advisor.

➤ Important considerations for companies when contemplating a sale.

➤ The principal differences between selling a private company and a public company.

After a company has decided to sell, it can take several paths to pursue a transaction. Sellside processes basically fall into two categories: targeted discussions and auctions. Which path is best depends largely upon the pool of potential buyers, the company's characteristics, and the circumstances that prompted the decision to sell.

Targeted discussions. Here, a company contains the scope of its process to discussions with only one or a few buyers. Invariably these discussions involve strategic buyers. They are conducted "quietly" without the knowledge of employees or others so as to not disrupt business, upset customers, or create negotiating issues with potential buyers.

One version of a targeted discussion involves negotiations with only a single buyer. This approach is rare and is typically limited to circumstances in which there is only one logical suitor for a company and that suitor has approached the company with an attractive offer. Generally, these discussions occur when a buyer and a target have a pre-existing relationship such as an OEM agreement, distribution agreement, or joint venture.

A more common version of a targeted discussion extends the process to encompass a handful of potential suitors. This path is typical when a company has been approached by a serious buyer and there is at least one other logical buyer. Other buyers are approached discreetly when negotiations are underway with the original interested party. Some boards use an indication of interest from one possible suitor, even if it is relatively weak, as a catalyst to shop a company to a handful of other possible buyers.

Auctions. When a company has a large pool of potential suitors—usually both strategic and financial—and is less sensitive to information about a possible sale becoming public knowledge, the company will use an auction process to sell itself. In a typical auction, a set of materials describing the company and its financial profile is prepared and sent to a targeted group of buyers. If the group is large, say greater than 20, it is referred to as a broad auction. If the group is smaller, it is called a narrow auction. Auctions may be conducted whether or not a company has previously been approached by potential suitors (though this is often the case).

Except for the occasional situation involving a single-buyer negotiation, most private companies valued over $20 million or so will engage an investment banker to spearhead the sellside process. Companies engage bankers for their knowledge of the market and relationships with potential buyers. Bankers orchestrate the sellside process and bear the day-to-day burden for marketing the sale. They also play "bad cop" in difficult negotiations, an important service to prevent hurt feelings and ill will between a buyer and a seller who need to work together after a transaction closes.

Companies sometimes make the mistake of looking to hire a banker only after they have unsuccessfully shopped the company themselves. This can be a disastrous strategy. The buyer universe for most companies is limited. It is very important to approach potential suitors with a carefully scripted message and thoughtfully constructed process. Buyers have long memories and limited time. Many refuse to devote energy to opportunities that they believe they have already explored and rejected—even if they misunderstood a deal's merits.

As in selecting private placement agents, boards generally conduct small bake-offs before hiring an investment banker to serve as a company's sellside advisor. A board will invite a handful of banks to present their views and qualifications for the assignment. Banks are usually invited based on their past dealings with the company, reputation in the industry, sellside experience, and prior transaction history with board members (even when they do not control the board, representatives from financial firms such as VCs hold significant sway over these selections, given their perceived expertise). Boards also narrow the field of potential advisors based on anticipated transaction size. Boutique investment banks and M&A advisory firms that generally do smaller deals are invited to pitch smaller deals and vice versa for larger firms and larger deals. Clients want expertise and focus, and they know that some firms are not equipped to handle larger, more complicated deals and others will not take, much less focus on, smaller deals.

In the sellside bake-off, potential advisors are invited to make a presentation to the company—typically all or a subset of the board plus senior members of management. The hopeful participants bring a banking team and pitch materials to the meeting. Bankers at the meeting generally include the senior industry banker, one or two junior industry bankers, a senior M&A banker, and one or two junior M&A bankers. As with the previously discussed private-placement bake-off, a representative from senior management, such as the head of investment banking for a particular sector, may also be present. Each of these individuals, at least the senior ones, is responsible for a portion of the presentation. The pitch includes the bank's perspectives regarding: (1) how to best position the company with potential suitors; (2) who the potential suitors are and why (included in this is a discussion of strategic rationale, past acquisition history, and ability to fund a deal); (3) the likely valuation for the company; (4) the best process for the transaction, including a timeline; (5) the firm's M&A qualifications and experience, especially with respect to the industry, similar transactions, and the potential suitors; and (6) the proposed fees and terms of engagement (these often are excluded from the pitch book and reserved for verbal discussion). When appropriate, the pitch may also include a discussion of the bank's ability or willingness to provide financing for potential buyers to fund the deal. This is referred to as a "stapled" financing.

Bake-off presentations may be formal or more relaxed and interactive, but they always have time reserved for questions and answers, which could more appropriately be called banker interrogation. Competitive pressures and the drive to win business sometimes lead bankers to make inflated claims in a pitch. To test their knowledge and the veracity of their statements, company representatives quiz bankers on all aspects of their presentations. They direct particular attention to valuation assumptions and the list of potential suitors. They drill into the bank's transaction experience and buyer relationships. Having positive past dealings and an ongoing relationship with potential suitors, especially the strategics, can be critical to a successful sellside process.

Once a bank is selected to serve as a company's advisor, an engagement letter is entered into by the parties. Sellside letters typically have at least a one-year term with a six-month tail. The banker's fee is usually a percentage of the ultimate transaction size subject to some minimum. Many letters contain a "fee schedule" that adjusts the fee percentage down based on increasing deal values to allow the fee to increase with an improving sale price but stay within an acceptable band. Some letters reverse this structure at certain breakpoints to create an added incentive to get a higher price. A sellside letter may also contain a list of buyers who must be involved in the acquisition in order for the banker to receive a fee.

Bankers generally receive a retainer from the seller upon signing an engagement letter. Though modest in most cases, bankers request retainers to cover up-front costs and, more importantly, to assure that the seller is serious and not just using the banker to test the market for interest.

Though less common in a private-company sellside, the engagement letter may also provide that the bank render a "fairness opinion" to the seller's board prior to the company signing a definitive acquisition agreement with the buyer. The fairness opinion helps the board justify its decision to proceed (or not) and thus deflect liability for any claim that it failed to exercise reasonable judgment and fulfill its fiduciary obligations in connection with the transaction. If included, the bank receives a separate fee for the fairness opinion at the time that it is delivered. The fee is a pre-set amount defined in the letter. Retainers and fairness opinion fees are generally credited against the overall fee to be paid when a transaction closes.

Buyers routinely attempt to renegotiate sellside banker fees after they make an acquisition, particularly when the fees are considered to be above the market. Technically, these fees are the concern of the seller. Buyers, however, generally pay the seller's fees when a transaction closes out of the purchase price for the deal. Accordingly, any savings on the fee results in a savings to the buyer, not the seller. Discussions along these lines can be contentious, with buyers sometimes resorting to subtle threats about a bank's reputation and opportunities for future mandates.

Once the engagement letter is negotiated and signed, work begins on selling the company. The specific steps taken by the banker and the seller depend upon the process agreed to by the parties.

TARGETED DISCUSSION PROCESS

If the circumstances warrant targeted discussions, it is likely that the company has been approached by and has already started discussions with a potential buyer. At this point, the decision is generally made to extend the process to other possible suitors without the knowledge of the original interested party. Sometimes, the banker assumes the lead role in discussions with the original buyer; other times, this is left to the company to avoid disrupting the dialogue. In either event, the seller attempts to slow down talks to allow time for contacting and receiving preliminary feedback from other possible suitors. In targeted discussions, timing is critical. The company must be shopped quickly and quietly to avoid turning off the lead contender.

The marketing effort is spearheaded by the banker. With careful coordination and scripting, members of management or the board of directors may also be involved if they have relationships that can be useful. In a targeted discussion process, the pursuit of other buyers usually involves the following sequence of events:

1. **Preparing a teaser.** The banker quickly prepares a brief descriptive memorandum on the company called a "teaser." Often, it will not refer to the company by name. Aliases are used for confidentiality.

2. **Contacting the potential buyers.** The banker and the company agree upon the best person at each buyer to contact regarding the opportunity (e.g., the CEO, CFO, or head of business development in the case of a strategic buyer). A member of the banking team calls each contact to describe the opportunity and follow up with the teaser if the contact is interested in learning more.

3. **Signing nondisclosures.** If the contact would like to pursue further discussions after reviewing the teaser, the potential buyer is asked to sign a nondisclosure agreement (NDA) concerning the opportunity and information to be obtained in any discussions. This brief document is typically negotiated and may take several days to execute.

4. **Meeting with management.** A meeting between the seller and the potential buyer is arranged to discuss the company in greater detail. The meeting includes key executives and bankers from both sides (if the buyer chooses to hire a banker). The parties also explore the strategic rationale for a possible deal. After the meeting, the buyer may request additional information to aid in its review of the opportunity. The scope of this information may be limited by the seller until the party submits a term sheet and is selected as the leading suitor.

The steps just outlined are somewhat fluid and generally take a few weeks to complete. The pool of potential suitors is then narrowed to those that have indicated a serious interest in the seller. This group, along with the original potential buyer, is asked to submit term sheets. In the process, the banker hints at the seller's expectations and the interest others may have in acquiring the company. For targeted discussions, the number of term sheets is small. It may be as few as two but this is sufficient to create competition and drive better terms. The term sheets are discussed with the board and a "winner" is selected. Leading up to this point, the board will have already received frequent updates from the banker on the process and the status with interested buyers. The winning term sheet, usually with modifications, then is signed by the two parties (this document may also be called a letter of intent or LOI). Sometimes, however, a public strategic buyer resists signing a term sheet on the basis that it might require early disclosure of the possible deal under the buyer's securities-law disclosure obligations. This concern is mitigated when a deal is relatively small and not "material" to the buyer.

Term sheets contain the material terms of the offer and, most importantly, price and consideration. A term sheet also provides for an exclusivity period for the buyer and seller to agree upon a definitive acquisition agreement (depending on the company and the deal's structure, this agreement may also be called a purchase-and-sale agreement or a merger agreement). Referred to as a no-shop provision, this period of time also allows the buyer to complete its due diligence review of the seller, often with the assistance of outside counsel and accountants. The exclusivity period is normally thirty days. Definitive acquisition agreements are long, complicated documents requiring extensive negotiation and input from the bankers, the company, and company counsel. Once a definitive agreement is reached by the parties, there is a subsequent period of time reserved for closing the transaction. This period of time is left open for obtaining necessary shareholder and regulatory approvals, such as the Hart-Scott-Rodino (HSR) antitrust filing, which must be made with federal officials for many acquisitions. Major shareholders, such as the VCs represented on the board, will be asked to sign an agreement to vote their shares in favor of the acquisition at the time the definitive acquisition agreement is signed.

AUCTION PROCESS

An auction follows a series of steps similar to those found in targeted discussions, but is more structured, less discreet, and less subject to day-to-day adjustments. It also involves preparing a more comprehensive informational memorandum on the seller, simply called a "book" by bankers and buyers. An auction usually tracks the following sequence of events:

1. **Preparing a teaser and a book.** Along with a teaser, the banker and the seller prepare a "book" on the company. Akin to an offering memorandum for a later-stage private placement, this document includes detailed historical financials and projections as well as a description of the company, its operations, and its strategy. The teaser rarely includes the seller's actual name.
2. **Contacting potential buyers.** Here the list is much longer than in targeted discussions and almost always involves financial buyers. Potential buyers are provided with the teaser. If interested in the opportunity, they generally are asked to sign an NDA before being given the book.
3. **Signing NDAs.** Some broad auctions do not use NDAs. Though they are typically required, some financial buyers, even those that are a good fit for an opportunity, refuse to sign them.
4. **Sending out the book.** In many auctions, the book is the only source of information that potential buyers have on the company prior to submitting a first-round term sheet. Suitors are not even given the opportunity to meet with company management until they make it to the next stage of the process.
5. **First-round term sheets.** With some coaching and guidance from the seller's banker, interested buyers are asked to submit a preliminary, or first-round, term sheet. These are commonly referred to as first-round bids. This document is more cursory than a full term sheet. It is often just a brief letter outlining timing, price, proposed consideration, and contingencies. The valuation may be a range rather than a specific price for the company.

6. **Narrowing the field.** The banker collects the first-round bids and follows up with the submitters to clarify any open issues or questions. These then are discussed with the board and a subset of the bidders are invited to the next stage of the process.

7. **Management meetings.** Buyers who make it to the next stage, or the second round as it is called, are given the opportunity to meet with management for a comprehensive presentation on the company and a question-and-answer session. These meetings generally last the better part of a day and take place at the seller's headquarters.

8. **Access to the data room.** Along with management meetings, second round bidders are given access to a company "data room" to complete their due diligence. This room, now often provided online with special access and tracking software, is organized and monitored by the seller's banker and contains all material documentation on the seller (e.g., contracts, leases, and financial records).

9. **Second-round term sheets.** With some further banker coaching and guidance, second-round bidders are asked to submit detailed second-round term sheets. Sellers often request that this term sheet be accompanied by a "mark-up" of a definitive purchase agreement supplied by the seller. Sellers want to move quickly to signing the agreement after selecting the winning bid and thus want any material issues in the agreement hammered out beforehand. Given the extent of due diligence completed to this point, buyers are generally in a position to accommodate this request, albeit sometimes begrudgingly.

10. **Picking a winner and going exclusive.** The banker discusses and clarifies each second-round term sheet with the submitting bidder. The term sheets and marked-up purchase agreements then are discussed with the board, which selects the winning bidder, with whom the company will negotiate on an exclusive basis.

11. **Signing a definitive agreement.** As noted earlier, the process is structured to permit a quick signing. The agreement is often signed within a week of selecting the winning bid.

12. **Closing.** As with the targeted discussion sellside process, a period of time is reserved between signing the purchase agreement and closing the acquisition to allow for any required shareholder and regulatory approvals.

The amount of time to complete an auction can vary, but is generally tied, more or less, to a predefined timeline. Most are targeted to be three to four months with four-plus weeks to prepare materials and receive first round term sheets, another four weeks to receive second round term sheets, two weeks to sign a definitive agreement, and four weeks to close.

Figure 10.1. M&A Sellside Auction Process.

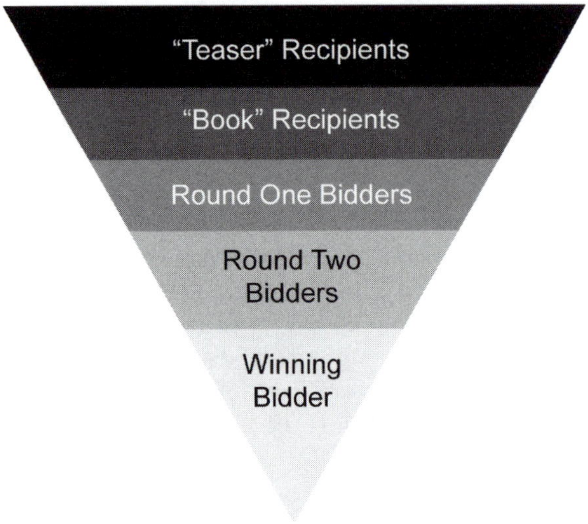

OTHER OBSERVATIONS ON PRIVATE COMPANY SALES

Economics are the principal motivating factor behind selling a company. Whether to generate a handsome return or to prevent a bad investment from becoming worse, shareholder considerations ultimately drive the decision to sell. That being said, other factors and other constituents also play a role. The ongoing success of most companies is highly dependent upon employees, management, and, often, founders. As such, their support throughout a sellside process and their willingness to stay involved after an acquisition are critical to both seller and buyer. Their opinions and interests carry significant weight. For this reason, critical executives without large ownership positions are often paid retention bonuses while a company is being shopped. Likewise, strategic fit and plans for a company's operations, people, and products can be the deciding factors in choosing to sell to a particular buyer. Best price and consideration may not be the paramount concerns behind a deal.

Why bidders pursue an acquisition depends on many factors but the process by which they reach a price typically fits into one of the following molds. Strategic buyers consider the revenue and expense benefits of a combination and then modify projections supplied by the seller to account for such synergies. For many, these pro forma projections are applied to formulas containing internal return thresholds to determine an appropriate valuation—for example, using a discounted cash flow analysis or other return-on-investment calculation. After integrating an acquisition (where the real work happens), strategic buyers who use sophisticated analytical models like these generally track a deal's performance relative to expectations for several years in order to assess and improve upon future acquisition efforts.

Other strategic buyers take a more simplistic approach and determine value based primarily upon what they can afford to pay. They look at their return on cash, earnings per share, and trading multiples and arrive at a price according to what would be accretive or dilutive to their stock price. For example, they may be willing to pay up to 30X forward earnings for a company if they are using stock to make the acquisition that is trading for more than 30X forward earnings. Likewise, a cash-rich company may be willing to pay 20X earnings for a company in cash if its cash is generating less than a 5% after-tax yield. Sometimes known as spread investing, many conglomerates and industry consolidators have deployed these strategies to become market leaders over the years.

Financial buyers tend to use discounted cash flow (DCF) and internal rate of return (IRR) analyses to assess appropriate valuation levels. Like strategic buyers, they modify company-supplied projections to create pro formas that encapsulate their views and opinions of products, markets, and operations. These pro formas are plugged into DCF and IRR calculations containing additional assumptions for use of debt, future capital requirements, and exit values. Exit values are typically based on some multiple of cash flow that the buyer believes the company could obtain in a sale or IPO five to ten years into the future. Interestingly, valuation ranges for financial buyers in a sellside process are usually pretty predictable despite their extensive modeling efforts. Though influenced by the debt market, less stable or lower growth companies generally sell for 6X to 8X EBITDA and more stable or faster growth companies fetch 8X to 10X EBITDA (sometimes much more).

The flipside of the buyer's analysis is the seller's assessment of what constitutes an acceptable price. This, too, depends on many, many factors, including the owner's state of hope or state of desperation. That being said, seller expectations usually tie to: (1) prices and multiples paid in recent comparable transactions, (2) multiples of comparable public companies, and (3) valuations produced by discounted cash flow analyses. Buyers also use numbers 1 and 2 to cross-check their DCF- and IRR-generated valuations.

Multiples, in this context, typically mean enterprise value (equity plus debt minus cash) to EBITDA (trailing twelve month). Subject to the industry, it can also refer to enterprise value to revenues (future or past) or another standard comparison metric. The terms of many acquisitions are not publicly disclosed and thus much of the information on multiples for precedent transactions is difficult to obtain. Much of this information comes through word of mouth and is diligently tracked by bankers. Despite the challenges of obtaining this information, sellers always manage to know about the highest multiple deals and, not surprisingly, often think they deserve at least as much, if not more, for their own companies.

Another key consideration relevant to private company sales is structure and, more specifically, whether a deal should involve the purchase of a company's stock or its assets. With a stock transaction, the buyer acquires the prior owner's stock, leaving the company and its legal framework intact. It simply steps into the shoes of the prior owners. Sellers generally prefer the clean and simple nature of stock deals. Buyers sometimes, however, prefer asset deals, whereby they acquire the assets that comprise a business's operations. This enables a buyer to acquire a business without any of the liabilities or issues that might be attached to the legal entity of the seller (e.g., debts owed by the selling corporation). This may also help the buyer's tax position. Payment for the assets is made to the selling company, which, in turn, remains intact. The business is then dissolved (typically) and the proceeds of the sale are distributed to the owners.

DIFFERENCES WITH PUBLIC COMPANY TRANSACTIONS

Sellsides for public companies are very similar to those of private companies. They can follow a targeted discussion route or an auction route. The differences with public company deals stem from their disclosure obligations and liability concerns. For the most part, the differences can be summed up as follow:

1. **No use of names before an NDA.** A banker will discuss a seller conceptually with prospective buyers and may even provide a no-name teaser but will not release the company's name until NDAs are signed. The fact that a company is being shopped is material nonpublic information, thus requiring this level of secrecy.
2. **Use of a press release.** In situations in which a broad marketing effort is contemplated, companies put out a press release indicating that they have hired an investment bank to help explore "strategic alternatives" for unleashing shareholder value. This is code for a sellside process or at least a significant corporate restructuring. The release preempts unintended leaks and also serves to attract buyers who might otherwise not have been contacted about the opportunity. Public announcements regarding acquisition discussions are also made when the deal being contemplated involves company insiders, such as in the case of a management buyout (MBO). The announcement helps deflect shareholder lawsuits by helping assure fairness and no self dealing in the process to find the best buyer.
3. **Heavy reliance on publicly filed documents.** New marketing materials, aside from those used in management presentations, are rarely created for public sellsides. Instead, buyers and sellers rely upon public filings for information on the company and its operations. By definition, these filings should contain all material information on the seller. In due diligence, buyers still seek undisclosed documentation as well as company budgets and projections.
4. **Fairness opinion.** Before voting upon and accepting the terms of an acquisition, the seller's board requires a fairness opinion on the proposed transaction. This is generally delivered by the investment bank advising on the acquisition, though it may be provided by a separate bank. The

fairness opinion analyzes the financial merits of the transaction and opines on its fairness to shareholders. It is rendered before the deal is signed, announced, and submitted to a shareholder vote.

5. **Careful record of events.** Sellers are required to maintain a careful record of the events leading up to a definitive acquisition agreement. This record is placed in the proxy statement that is submitted to shareholders for their vote on the transaction. The record contains a detailed history of each step in the company's sellside process, including the number of buyers contacted, the number of buyers interested, and material information used in the discussions, such as projections. The disclosure is intended to provide shareholders with data necessary to make an informed decision about whether or not to support a transaction.

6. **Proxy statement and shareholder vote.** Selling a public or private company requires a shareholder vote in favor of the transaction. The process for obtaining this vote is dictated by a company's charter and bylaws. In the case of public companies, it is also dictated by federal securities laws that outline required information and specific steps for submitting a proxy statement to shareholders regarding a proposed transaction. Generally, the SEC reviews proxy statements for adequate disclosure before they are mailed to shareholders. The law usually requires that a public company's shareholder vote be no sooner than 20 business days after the final proxy is mailed. Companies involved in transactions requiring shareholder approval frequently retain the services of proxy solicitors and public relations firms to help secure shareholder votes.

In addition to the factors just noted, the role of management and "corner office" considerations are often different in public-company deals. Executives at public companies generally earn more and own less stock than their counterparts in private companies. They may also enjoy the power and prestige of leading a public company. As such, a company sale may not be management's preferred path, especially in strategic deals. In fact, management and their agendas are frequently obstacles to consummating otherwise intelligent transactions. It is worth remembering that shareholder interests may not be paramount to executives in their decisions for a company. Just look at *The Wall Street Journal*: Battles between entrenched management (and boards for that matter) and activist shareholders looking to unlock value show up over and over again. Of course, the opposite can also be true. Executives may be overeager to do a deal when they stand to receive a large windfall due to change-of-control provisions found in their employment contracts.

As fiduciaries, directors of public companies are required to act in the best interest of their shareholder constituents. In doing so, they must exercise "reasonable business judgment" and accordingly must assess strategic alternatives when presented with legitimate opportunities. However, they are under no obligation to sell a company just because someone has offered a price that exceeds the value of the publicly traded stock. They may consider more than price in determining what would best serve the longer-term interests of shareholders. Continuing to go it alone or taking a lower-priced deal involving stock consideration from a company with a great strategic fit may be an acceptable outcome. However, it is worth pointing out that once a company proceeds down a path where it has demonstrated a willingness to take a cash offer, it may be deemed to be "in play" and thus obligated to consider and pursue the highest-priced offer.

Additional issues and considerations pertaining to public-company sellside transactions are discussed in Chapters 17 and 21.

Personal Observations on Private Company Sales

1. *There are always buyers for a "real" business, though price may be an issue.* There is ongoing demand for profitable businesses with material revenues. Financial buyers want them and so do strategic buyers, assuming there are opportunities for synergies and revenue growth. Price can be an issue, however. A financial track record generates interest but it also provides guideposts around which value can be ascertained and measured. Except in rare circumstances with a strategic buyer, this means that "real" businesses do not achieve the loftiest valuations. These are reserved for earlier-stage businesses that can sell hope instead of reality.

2. *It is very difficult, if not impossible, to find buyers for early and mid-stage private companies, even those with real customers and products, without inbound interest from a strategic suitor.* Without a track record of sales and profits, earlier-stage companies appeal to a much narrower set of buyers. These are limited to strategic players who may have an interest in a concept, technology, or product. Strategic players are almost always public companies, and therefore are very sensitive to buying businesses that can negatively impact near-term financial performance. They prefer to sit on the sidelines and watch a business and its products mature before pursing an acquisition—even if this results in having to pay more. With that being said, strategic buyers do, sometimes, make preemptive moves to buy young businesses when they are deemed to be sufficiently important. This interest can prompt competitors to become interested. Without this catalyst, there is no urgency to act, so prospective buyers usually take a wait-and-see approach.

3. *Many VCs carefully time the sales of private companies to transfer execution risks to new owners.* They may also shamelessly hype the merits of a company, its team, and its products to generate acquisition interest. Sometimes this is sincere, sometimes it is disingenuous. They seek to take profits and hit the optimal balance between risk and reward when hopes are high and risks are discounted

by the buyer community. In technology, this point is shortly after commercialization of a product has started, when sales begin growing swiftly (usually before challenges emerge from competitors). While many such businesses fail to live up to expectations after being acquired, it is worth noting that many failures can be attributed to the post-acquisition decisions of the strategic buyers rather than just the shortcomings of the acquired businesses. Furthermore, strategic buyers continue to look to these types of acquisitions, even if they fall short, to fill product holes. Overpaying for a few businesses can be less risky and more economical than funding large internal research and development projects.

4. *Investment bankers can add real value in a private-company sale.* A carefully orchestrated sellside process from a well-connected investment banker always results in more value for a seller when there is more than one logical buyer. I have never seen nor heard of a situation in which a credible and experienced advisor did not produce returns that exceeded its fee, if not multiples of its fee. Gaining access to the decision makers, understanding their hot buttons, deploying carefully honed negotiating skills, and creating a sense of competition produce this outcome. There is a reason that the market's leading VCs and private equity firms habitually use advisors on their deals. Investment bankers are not miracle workers, however. Even if an advisor can produce the best outcome, it does not mean that it can produce an acceptable outcome for the seller. For a multitude of reasons, some companies are simply not interesting to buyers, at least not at the right price, no matter how carefully and diligently they are sold. Founders and executives are fond of blaming their bankers in these situations. Of course, this is frequently justified (at least somewhat), given claims bankers might make to win a mandate.

5. *The decision to sell or go public is one of economics.* In recent years, much has been discussed about the impact the new U.S. regulatory environment has had on companies considering an IPO. Many have suggested that it has driven companies to sell rather than go public due to the added costs and liabilities of being public. This, without a doubt, has had some influence, but economics are still the overriding driver. All things being equal, it boils down to who is willing to pay more for a business—an acquirer or public investors. When the market's appetite for new issues is subdued, private owners (i.e., VCs, private equity funds, and founders) sell their businesses. When a sector is hot and public investors are hungry for new deals, these owners take their companies public.

CHAPTER 11

Initial Public Offerings: Selecting Underwriters

➤ How underwriters are selected and compensated in an initial public offering.

➤ What investment bankers consider when choosing to accept an underwriting role.

➤ The hierarchy and politics among investment banks.

➤ The departmental organization, roles, and career progression of investment bankers.

Getting back to our story, PEMCO's board had considered its liquidity options and concluded that an IPO would be the appropriate next step for the company. According to bankers, the market was strong and PEMCO possessed all the

Figure 11.1. Funding progression—Initial public offering.

right ingredients for a successful deal. With this in mind, the company set out to put together its IPO banking team. Also known as putting together a cover (in reference to the investment banks listed on the cover page of a prospectus), companies considering an IPO must select a group of "managing" underwriters to work with on the deal. The size of this group depends upon the size of the transaction being contemplated.

Ultimately, the number of managing underwriters on an IPO or other public financing boils down to a question of economics. Investment banks charge 7 percent of the money raised to underwrite IPOs. Exceptions to this rule only exist in very large transactions. This fee, referred to as the "gross spread," is divided between the managers based on their roles as lead managers or co-managers. Typically, there is one lead or two co-leads (possibly more on very large deals). The leads are responsible for directing all of the logistics of the transaction, from drafting the prospectus, to coordinating the road show, to allocating the stock to investors when the deal concludes. If there are co-leads, generally one is designated as the "bookrunner." When more than one is the bookrunner, they are referred to as "joint bookrunners." During the marketing phase of a transaction, the bookrunning lead manager directs the road show and aggregates "indications of interest" from investors. Also known as orders, these indications denote their level of interest in terms of both price and number of shares. The bookrunner manages the order "book" and has final say over investor allocations. When there is a single lead manager, this investment bank generally takes 50 percent of the gross spread. Co-leads usually take 60 percent to 70 percent combined. The phenomenon of co-leads became widespread during the dot-com boom, when busy bankers would only accept lead managed business and routinely turned down co-manager roles. Although the market subsequently witnessed tremendous declines in underwriting volumes, the co-lead structure has endured.

Co-managers participate in all aspects of an IPO but have no real authority over the process. They help draft the prospectus, prepare the road show presentation, and market the company to investors. Among other things, co-managers are hired for their industry knowledge, ability to generate investor interest, and willingness to provide trading support and research after the IPO prices (i.e., the time at which it is sold to investors). Co-managers are often divided into senior and junior classifications. Senior co-managers usually receive 10 percent to 20 percent of the gross spread each. Juniors get 5 percent to 10 percent each. Given their resource commitment to a company during and after an IPO, most investment banks will not accept a co-manager role unless it can generate at least a $1 million fee. Less-established firms and boutiques may be more flexible with fees but rarely agree to less than $500,000.

Despite the sound of it, the economic proposition for co-managers is much less attractive today than ever before. The emergence of the co-lead structure reduced the economics available to co-managers as a group from what was routinely 50 percent of the fees on a deal to what now may be as low as 25 percent to 30 percent. As importantly, this percentage is now often divided among more banks. Issuers have made a habit out of hiring more co-managers and putting together fuller covers. Before 2000, it was common to have only three underwriters on a deal—one lead and two co-managers. Today, it is common to have four or five underwriters on a similarly sized transaction.

Most bankers recommend that an IPO be at least $50 million in order to generate sufficient interest out of institutional investors, namely mutual funds and hedge funds. These institutions account for the majority of demand for deals and fuel the IPO market. They require that IPOs be large enough to allow them to acquire meaningful positions—something that can impact funds measuring hundreds of millions of dollars in size. Investors also want aftermarket liquidity and therefore a sufficient number of shares in public hands to produce sizable daily trading volumes. Large "public floats," as these shares are known, enable investors to buy or sell positions without significantly affecting stock prices. Beyond deal size, most institutions limit their IPO investments to companies with market capitalizations greater than $250 million. A $50 million IPO will generally support three reputable underwriters—one lead with 50 percent to 60 percent of the "economics" and two co-managers with 20 percent to 25 percent each.

Based on preliminary input from the banking community and the company's capital needs, PEMCO was contemplating a $125 million transaction. This amount would be large enough to attract investors. It also fit within another normal IPO parameter. At this size, the deal would represent roughly 15 percent of the company's proposed market capitalization (i.e., the total value of the common stock to be outstanding after the transaction). IPOs typically fall between 10 percent and 30 percent. The board agreed that a $125 million transaction warranted five underwriters—two co-leads, two senior co-managers, and one junior co-manager. They had a group of banks in mind for each of these roles. Before making a final selection, however, they recognized that a bake-off would be in order.

Since PEMCO's Series C round, management and members of the board had been visited by many investment banks. Some, including ILB from the Series D, were well versed in the market and the alternative energy sectors and had proven helpful to PEMCO in making introductions and providing updates on notable financings and M&A transactions. Others had been useless. Of the helpful ones, there were a few from each category of investment bank found in the market, namely: (1) bulge bracket firms with comprehensive product offerings and operations, such as Goldman Sachs, Morgan Stanley, and Merrill Lynch; (2) universal banks with large, global commercial and investment banking operations, such as Citibank, JPMorgan Chase, and UBS; (3) middle-market firms with regional or less extensive commercial and investment banking operations, such as Wachovia and RBC; (4) boutique firms with focused offerings, such as Thomas Weisel Partners, Cowen & Co., and Piper Jaffray; and (5) small boutiques with even narrower offerings, such as those that focus on some niche of the M&A market. The company had gotten to know these firms well and had even attended some of their investment conferences to make informational presentations to institutional investors on the PEMCO story.

As with the private placement bake-off, the company contacted bankers from each of the firms being considered. These firms were assigned a one-hour time slot to present their views and qualifications to the board. They were also given an RFP (request for proposal) detailing each of the topics that the board would like covered in the presentation. These included company positioning, appropriate public comparables, proposed IPO valuation, transaction size, targeted investors, transaction timeline, references, lead-manager experience, trading history in previous IPOs, and other relevant qualifications. It also requested an opinion on what shares, if any, existing shareholders could sell in the deal.

Ten banks were invited to the two-day bakeoff—a longer roster than in the private placement, but this was not a winner-take-all situation. There would be underwriting roles for half of them. Unlike some of its peers, PEMCO had been judicious and not opened the bake-off to an even larger number of less-qualified banks. It had also chosen not to bifurcate the bake-off between one for prospective lead managers and one for prospective co-managers. Leading up to the presentations, bankers were given the opportunity to meet with management for an update on company developments and the story. They were also provided with the latest historical financials and projections.

At this point, the research departments of the investment banks also became involved in the process. As part of their ongoing efforts to stay abreast of interesting new technologies, products, and enterprises that could impact companies within their coverage, research analysts from most of the firms had already visited with PEMCO, some several times. Contrary to practice before the passage of new rules governing sellside research, these meetings had taken place without any coordination or involvement from their investment banking colleagues.

PEMCO would expect the research analysts from its underwriters to "initiate coverage" on the company after the IPO. This was fair. Legally the underwriters could commit to providing research. They could not, however, commit to a "buy" rating or in any way prescribe what research on the company would say. PEMCO wanted to meet with the analysts again to update them and to get a better sense for their knowledge and perspectives on the industry and the company. These get-togethers were arranged before the bake-off.

The research meetings were also helpful to the prospective underwriters. Most firms will not pitch an IPO, much less agree to be an underwriter, without knowing the view of their research analysts regarding the opportunity. The analyst needs to be interested in covering the company. An investment bank's other clients—investors who put money to work in IPOs and other securities offerings—expect coverage after an underwritten IPO and will look to the research analyst for guidance and input. Whereas research analysts cannot be involved in marketing an IPO, they can take inbound calls from investors regarding deals and are generally asked for their views and opinions.

The bake-off went as planned. For two days, banking teams made presentations to the board regarding the contemplated IPO. Most of these meetings exceeded their 60-minute time limit but fully covered the matters requested by the board through the discussions and pitch books. Before and after the bake-off, executives and senior bankers from the prospective underwriters barraged board members with calls voicing their commitment to PEMCO and interest in the IPO. This is how the game is played, and some were effective at winning support.

The board reconvened a week after the bake-off. This gave each of the directors time to reflect on the presentations and review the pitch books in greater detail. It also gave the CFO the opportunity to check references. In addition, the CFO gathered input from the investor-relations (IR) firm PEMCO had recently hired.

IR firms help public companies raise their visibility with institutional investors and sellside research analysts. They coordinate informational road shows, arrange introductory meetings with research analysts and investment bankers, obtain invitations to investor conferences, and help draft press releases and earnings announcements. Most are smaller organizations staffed by former employees of investment banks or the buyside. IR firms are generally paid a monthly or quarterly retainer. They are often hired before a company conducts an IPO to help with the process and to provide input on underwriters. PEMCO's executive team thought these services could be useful.

Going into the bake-off, most of the board, or at least the VCs, had their favorites for the underwriting lineup—firms with which they had strong ties that had done good work for them in the past. Most also had biases about the type of firm that should fit into each underwriting role. The pitches had changed some of these views. A couple of the front-runners had flopped. Their comments demonstrated a lack of understanding for PEMCO and its position relative to competitors and public comparables, and their materials revealed a lack of focus and effort. Simply put, their knowledge and work product were weak. Conversely, other firms had impressed the board with their perspectives, analysis, and qualifications—much more so than expected.

The board convened and discussed and debated the underwriting team for the better part of a morning. Like other smart issuers, PEMCO wanted investment banks that possessed the following traits:

1. **Strong company and industry knowledge.** Understanding both are critical to positioning a company with investors and preparing the prospectus and road show presentation. They are also helpful to ongoing feedback, market intelligence, and M&A ideas.
2. **Experienced and focused banking team.** IPOs are time-consuming and complicated. The team responsible for shepherding a company through the IPO process needs to have bandwidth and experience.
3. **Good reputation and relationships with targeted investors.** IPOs are sold primarily to institutional investors. Mutual funds and hedge funds drive terms and generally buy over 70 percent of a deal. But not all institutional investors buy IPOs, and only a subset of those that do will consider any given deal in light of size and industry characteristics. Selecting underwriters with strong, well-regarded relationships with portfolio managers and investment staffs at the appropriate institutions is very important.
4. **Long and successful track record with IPOs.** Underwriters, particularly lead managers, need to be well-versed organizationally in IPO logistics to assure smooth deal execution. Likewise, investors pay attention to

new "merchandise" from good underwriters. Successful past deals, as defined by aftermarket performance, help capture investor mindshare and generate demand for new issues.

5. **History of trading support for client stocks.** Investors seek and will pay a premium for stocks where they can buy or sell large positions without impacting prices. Trading desks at investment banks provide this form of liquidity to investors, particularly in smaller-capitalization stocks with smaller public floats and lighter daily trading volumes. Trading requires focus, expertise, and capital commitment. IPO investors, and thus issuers, want underwriters that have demonstrated all three through their past leadership in trading client stocks. A top trading position is also indicative of the mindshare an investment bank has with investors in a market sector.

6. **Well respected research in the sector.** While research departments are not legally permitted to be involved in marketing an IPO (or any other transaction, for that matter), good research helps a company's visibility with investors and drives potential interest. Being covered by a well-known and respected research analyst who understands a company and its industry is very valuable to a public company.

In the end, the board agreed upon five firms they believed had these characteristics and should take PEMCO public. The deal would be lead managed by ILB and Burnham Peabody, one of Wall Street's most prestigious bulge bracket firms. Burnham would be the sole bookrunner on the deal and, as such, would be "to the left of" ILB on the cover of the offering prospectus. As senior co-managers, the board selected Deutsche Credit (a universal bank) and Feeman Brothers (another bulge bracket firm). RSF Securities (a focused boutique) was offered the junior co-manager slot.

The board made its choices based on what they believed each firm could contribute to the IPO and to the company once it was public. Throughout the pitch process, they heard negative campaigning regarding each type of firm. Big firms claimed smaller firms lacked heft and broad enough investor rapport to get deals done successfully, particularly if the market turned sour during marketing. Small firms claimed bigger firms lacked focus and commitment—they would assign junior resources to the deal, place stock in the wrong hands at pricing, and fail to provide quality trading and banking support after the fee was paid. In the end analysis, the board chose a diversified cover rather than selecting only one type of firm to underwrite the deal (or only bulge bracket firms to lead it). They wanted their bases covered in the event there was any truth to the warnings.

Now the difficult part began. The company needed to strike the right division of economics, or economic splits, among the underwriters. Discussions over economics are often contentious. Although happy to win an underwriting mandate, bankers always want a better fee and aggressively voice frustration and disappointment in an attempt to get one. Before making a proposal, PEMCO's CEO and CFO needed data on what was customary.

Larry informed the co-leads of their selection and asked them to do a "fee run" on recent IPOs of similar size with similar underwriting teams. The run showed a 7 percent gross spread in every deal, with splits averaging 30/25/20/20/5 for bookrunner/co-lead/senior co/senior co/junior co. Larry agreed to the 7 percent and Burnham and ILB agreed to their 30/25 splits. Larry then went to the co-managers. Although RSF Securities was particularly upset with 5 percent, all accepted the economics. Deutsche Credit and Feeman, however, had significant reservations about being junior and "to the right of" ILB. This matter would need to be discussed with their internal "commitment committees." Each of the banks would need approval from their commitment committees before proceeding with the deal.

The positioning of underwriter names on a prospectus cover is very important to bankers. The line up runs left to right based upon seniority of role and economics. Firms of equal status flow alphabetically. Separate tiers are generally on different lines, top to bottom, or all of the co-managers are cascaded below the lead managers alphabetically with those of differing status being listed out of alphabetical order (i.e., "B" would come before "A" if B was a more senior co-manager). For prestige, branding, and market perception, bankers always want to be on the highest row and to the left of the other underwriters.

When it comes to cover position and economics, firms are very sensitive regarding establishing precedents that can be used against them in future transactions. Accordingly, firms will pass on deals, even for great companies offering high fees, in which they are "junior" to lower-tiered firms. In fact, several bulge bracket and universal banking firms will not serve as co-managers on deals lead managed by smaller firms. PEMCO's board had taken a risk by selecting ILB (a boutique) to co-lead its deal. As a result, its chosen senior co-managers might not agree to do the deal. Assuming all the underwriters did sign on, the bottom of the prospectus cover for PEMCO's IPO would show:

> Burnham Peabody & Co. I.L. Bankit & Co.
> Deutsche Credit
>   Feeman Brothers
>   RSF Securities

Commitment committee procedures vary by investment bank. Most require bankers to have separate committee approvals prior to: (1) attending a deal's organizational meeting; (2) filing a deal's registration statement, known as a Form S-1, with the SEC; and (3) printing a deal's preliminary prospectus, or "red herring," for distribution to investors. Composed of very senior representatives from investment banking, equity capital markets, institutional sales, trading, and the legal department, commitment committees meet as needed to review and opine on underwriting mandates. A similar procedure with different players is generally in place to review and approve other assignments, such as private placements and M&A engagements. Prior to a CCM (the often-used acronym for commitment committee meeting), the banking team prepares and distributes to committee members a memorandum describing the issuer and detailing the proposed transaction, including the firm's role and economics. At the meeting, the senior deal banker presents the opportunity and recaps highlights from the memorandum. Committee members question and push the banker on matters of concern. Without the bankers present, they will also speak to the appropriate research analyst about the issuer. CCMs can go smoothly or they can be a nightmare. With their volatile mix of powerful personalities and competing agendas, CCMs lean toward the scary side of this spectrum even when a deal is certain to get approval.

The pre–organizational-meeting CCMs at Burnham and ILB went well. Burnham was pleased to be the sole bookrunner for the IPO and, though disappointed at not "getting the books," ILB was pleased to be given a lead role ahead of two larger and more established competitors. It would be a good precedent for the firm to set. Both Burnham and ILB would receive credit as lead managers for the deal in the industry "league tables" that track such matters (a valuable measure for underwriters). Things were rockier at Deutsche Credit and Feeman, but after much teeth gnashing, both firms agreed to sign on as senior co-managers. PEMCO was a high-profile deal that every bank wanted irrespective of ILB's role. Besides, the economics of 20 percent each were a little better than some other deals, and they figured that they could explain away the precedent given ILB's unique history with the company (recall, ILB had been a longtime advisor that had acted as agent in the Series D financing). RSF approved the deal without hesitation. The firm was building its reputation and needed every good "print" it could get.

With the cover set, PEMCO's CFO informed the losing banks of the board's decision. Management and the board were relieved to have this behind them. They were also relieved that the winners had accepted their split proposal without too much strife. The advice they received to determine a fair arrangement and stick with it irrespective of banker pressure proved to be correct.

A Briefing on Investment Bankers—Part II

Staffing and Career Paths

Investment banking departments are divided into separate industry groups such as the Consumer Group, the Technology Group, and the Real Estate Group. Each group employs professionals with titles ranging from analyst to managing director. For the most part, the organizational structure of industry groups resembles a pyramid. Industry groups may also contain product specialists such as M&A bankers. Alternatively, these specialists may comprise separate groups. Projects are generally staffed by deal teams that contain one senior banker, one mid-level banker, and one or two junior bankers.

Bankers at all levels are paid salaries and annual bonuses. The bonus constitutes the vast majority of a banker's income and is typically paid shortly after year end. For junior bankers, incomes are in the form of all cash. For more senior bankers, compensation is paid in a combination of cash and restricted stock that vests over several years. The stock and vesting are used as retention tools to deter the mercenary-like firm hopping common to many in the profession. Banker compensation escalates significantly with each year of seniority and can vary dramatically among peers based on productivity levels.

Junior-level bankers include analysts and associates. Analysts are hired out of college and are expected to commit two years to a firm before heading to graduate school or moving on to another job—often with a VC, buyout shop, or corporate business-development department. Obtaining an analyst position is very difficult. Most hail from the Ivy League or other top-tier colleges and possess very strong quantitative and computing skills. Analysts are expected to forego a personal life and frequently work hundred-hour weeks. They are directed by associates and senior bankers and are responsible for the grunt work on projects, such as preparing financial models ("spreading the numbers" in banker parlance), PowerPoint presentations, pitch books, database runs, and other analyses and analytics. They spend most of their time in their office cubicles, many of which are clustered with other analysts in areas known as bull pens. Analysts attend some client meetings, such as due diligence and drafting sessions, and sometimes they travel. In exchange for their blood, sweat, and tears, they are paid well and receive a tremendous amount of highly marketable experience in a very short period of time.

Associates are typically hired out of tier-one graduate business schools (i.e., MBA programs). Most are former analysts. A few are lateral transfers from related industries such as law or consulting. In rare instances, they are promoted directly out of the analyst pool. Associates have primary responsibility for the physical work product of the investment banking department. With guidance and direction, they take point on preparing pitch books, financial models, and other written materials. In doing so, they oversee and rely heavily upon analysts who serve as their laborers to accomplish these tasks. Associates are also delegated specific roles on transactions. For instance, they may be given responsibility for coordinating due diligence or directing other logistical matters. As with analysts, associates are on call 24/7 and are required to work extremely long hours. They are expected to do whatever is necessary to get a job done and done right. Their time is divided between the office (again cubicles) and client meetings, including pitches. Tenure as an associate is generally three years before being considered for promotion. The next step is vice president.

Vice presidents are mid-level bankers. They coordinate the efforts of junior bankers and are the primary go-to people for senior bankers. They review and direct the preparation of pitch books and other materials. More importantly, they are responsible for driving the day-to-day execution of transactions and spend much of their time working with clients in this capacity. VPs are on the road as much as they are in the office. The lines sometimes blur between the role of VPs and the roles of senior associates and junior principals (the next title). VPs are expected to work tirelessly but begin to have greater control over their schedules than their junior colleagues. Assuming they are capable, VPs are promoted to principal after three years. Bankers with aspirations outside of the industry typically leave for new careers when they are associates or VPs, the point at which they have valuable skills but are not too entrenched in their profession.

An investment banker's mission begins to shift upon reaching the title of principal (note that in some firms this level is titled director or senior vice president). They spend less time executing business and more time trying to generate it. At this stage, they are expected to have very strong trans-action and industry knowledge. Their employers now want to see whether they can produce business and are managing director (MD) material. Pri-mary calling responsibility for some existing clients is transferred to them, and they work on cultivating these relationships for new business. This en-tails frequent telephone calls, e-mails, and visits to discuss developments in the market and transaction ideas suited to each client's circumstances and objectives. Principals also work on identifying and pursuing new prospects. Most non-introductory meetings and conversations require unique presenta-tion materials and analyses. Like MDs, principals spend most of their time out of the office and usually reach "platinum" status or its equivalent on several airlines each year. Principals and MDs are considered senior bankers.

After two-plus years, successful principals are promoted to MD. Although well versed in the technical aspects of banking, their chief role is sales. They are expected to identify, pursue, and win fee-generating business—in most cases over $10 million worth every year. They spend all of their time develop-ing ideas and nurturing clients with calls, e-mails, meetings, lunches, dinners, and other activities. The best become trusted advisors who are relied upon extensively for their insights and opinions. MDs must also be capable of effec-tively marshalling the resources of their organizations to serve their clients when executing transactions and providing ongoing support. In their busi-ness development pursuits, it is common for MDs within a firm to clash with one another over coverage responsibility for companies. They also look to tie their names to mandated transactions, even if they were only tangentially involved in winning or executing the business, so as to receive "credit" for the revenues.

As they progress in seniority, MDs take a more active role in firm admin-istration, serving on internal committees, spearheading new initiatives, and becoming group heads. The title "vice chairman" may be given to older MDs who are winding down their careers. Vice chairmen have no sector or com-pany calling responsibilities but remain involved in helping colleagues win business by attending pitches and leveraging relationships.

Bankers with client-facing responsibilities, typically defined as associates and above, are required to be licensed securities representatives known as registered representatives or RRs. As with stockbrokers, they must pass the Series 7 and Series 63 examinations administered by the Financial Industry

Regulatory Authority (FINRA). Principals and MDs must also become licensed "securities principals" and take the Series 24, which pertains to securities professionals with managerial responsibilities. Once licensed, bankers are required to obtain a certain amount of continuing education each year.

Along with the banking team, professionals from the Equity Capital Markets Department (ECM) are integral to pitching and executing equity transactions, including IPOs, follow-ons, private placements, and offerings of convertible securities. (Its mirror-image counterpart, Debt Capital Markets, works on debt and leveraged finance transactions.) Bearing the same series of titles as their banking colleagues, professionals from ECM are the bridge between the banking department and the sales and trading operations of an investment bank.

Typically, ECM is divided into two functions—origination and execution. Those in origination work closely with bankers to identify financing candidates and structure transaction proposals (e.g., optimal deal size, type of security, timing, investors, and underwriting team). They also attend pitches and often maintain an independent dialogue with clients regarding capital market activities in their industries and their stocks (e.g., bringing their attention to unusual trading volumes or noteworthy new financings).

ECM execution, a portion of which is called "syndicate," works on engaged transactions. Some ECM departments staff professionals who attend drafting sessions and are actively involved in the pre-announcement documentation phase of a transaction. More commonly, ECM execution professionals provide input leading up to a deal's announcement regarding terms and structure and then assume the leading role for the bank during the deal's marketing phase. Syndicate determines the road-show schedule, works with sales to arrange investor meetings, gathers orders from investors, keeps everyone apprised of the deal's progress, sets the terms for the deal at pricing, and ultimately allocates to investors the shares offered. The extent of ECMs' involvement in each of these matters, however, is dependent upon whether the firm serves as a lead or co-manager in a transaction.

CHAPTER 12

Initial Public Offerings: Transaction Process and Structural Considerations

➤ The step-by-step details of how IPOs are executed.

➤ The roles and activities of the principal IPO "deal team" members.

➤ The key topics that must be addressed when conducting an IPO, including pre-IPO structural changes to a business.

➤ The role of stock exchanges and how they operate.

➤ The careers and activities of sellside research analysts.

It was late January. The organizational meeting for PEMCO's IPO was scheduled for February 1. Unlike the Series D, there was no need to sign an engagement letter with the underwriters before moving forward. Their contractual arrangement would be covered by an underwriting agreement that would not be signed until just before the deal priced (i.e., the point at the end of the marketing phase, when the share price is determined for the offering and the shares are allocated to investors). This document would contain the fee structure already agreed to by the parties and other customary provisions, the details of which would be negotiated by company counsel and underwriters' counsel. Prior to signing the underwriting agreement, the company is at liberty to fire any of the underwriters and any of the underwriters are free to walk away from the deal.

Technically, there are two forms of underwriting: best efforts and firm commitment. The former provides that a firm will use its best efforts to find investors for the securities being offered without actually assuming any direct financial risk. The latter places the underwriter on the hook to buy the securities that it cannot sell. Most IPOs are firm-commitment transactions but, as a practical matter, are conducted as best-efforts underwritings. The underwriting agreement for most public financings, including IPOs, is not signed until after the marketing phase of the deal is completed, buyers have been found, and shares have been allocated. Only if a buyer subsequently refuses its allocation does the underwriter become the proud new owner of the securities. This occurs only in the rarest of circumstances.

The lead underwriters had to accomplish several things before PEMCO's organizational meeting. They needed to: (1) hire underwriters' counsel, (2) gather everyone's contact information for a working-group list, (3) prepare an agenda and organizational meeting book, and (4) help management organize and prepare a comprehensive due diligence presentation. The leads also wanted to compile a first draft of the Form S-1 that could be distributed at the meeting. The S-1 is the formal name of the marketing prospectus that is filed with the SEC for IPOs. The draft would require reviewing, revising, and cutting and pasting the company's last PPM and S-1s from similar recent deals.

The organizational meeting was held in a large conference room at PEMCO's law firm. It was a packed house, with three or four representatives from each of the five underwriters, the two law firms, and the company's accounting firm. Management and a couple of PEMCO's board members also attended. The meeting began at eight o'clock in the morning. The meeting was co-chaired by the MDs from Burnham and ILB. As bookrunner, Burnham took a more prominent role.

The first order of business was introductions, with every attendee noting their name and affiliation. The organizational books were then distributed. The books contained four sections: meeting agenda, timeline, due diligence request list, and working group list. A separate draft of the latter was also circulated for comments and revisions. The group walked through the agenda and the proposed transaction timeline. The terms of the proposed offering were also discussed.

As previously mentioned, the team was targeting a $125 million IPO. Of this, half would be primary stock issued by the company and half would be secondary stock sold by a group of existing shareholders. This group would include Larry, Jerry, the seed round investors, the strategic investors, and Smart Capital. Larry and Jerry would be selling only a small percentage of their holdings. None of the VCs would be selling (recall, Smart was a hedge fund and later-stage investor). The primary/secondary split for the deal had been discussed at the bake-off. Most underwriters agreed that, in light of PEMCO's success, all of the investors could sell in the deal so long as the overall percentage of selling amounted to less than 50 percent of the offering and that the executive team's selling was limited to just a fraction of their holdings.

Secondary selling in an IPO had once been rare and frowned upon by investors. Under normal conditions, in today's market, this has changed. Investors now accept, if not favor, it. Such selling creates additional public float without unnecessarily diluting the issuer (i.e., having the issuer sell more stock and raise more capital than required for its business needs). It also helps remove "overhang"—the term for stock held by early stage investors after an IPO that is certain to be sold into the market sooner or later.

The percentage of the company that the $125 million offering would represent was not discussed, nor was the number of shares to be offered. These were matters of valuation. Although the underwriters had discussed valuation ranges during the bake-off, valuation would not be finalized for purposes of the S-1 until much later in the process.

PEMCO's deal would have a customary 15 percent "green shoe," or over-allotment option. Named after the company whose offering legitimized the structure, a green shoe entitles the underwriters to purchase 15 percent more shares than noted in a deal in order to stabilize the share price, if necessary, after a deal begins trading (here, 15 percent of $125 million). The option can be exercised by the underwriters at the sole discretion of the bookrunner within 30 days of an offering. FINRA, which, among other things, reviews and has rules concerning underwriter compensation in public securities offerings, forbids the use of over-allotment options that exceed 15 percent. The 15 percent option is exercisable in the same security and at the same share price as the original transaction.

Though they do not yet have them, underwriters actually sell the shares covered by the green shoe at the time of an offering. This creates a large short position and provides the underwriters with proceeds from the sale that can then be used to buy shares in the open market if the aftermarket trading price dips below the offering price. When such purchases are made, this demand stabilizes and helps create an artificial floor in the stock price. If stabilization is necessary, the open-market purchases cover the underwriters' short position. If it is not necessary, the underwriters cover the short position by exercising the over-allotment option and the company receives the proceeds from the original sale. Green shoes can include both primary and secondary shares. Often, they are composed of secondary shares because investors pay less attention to the "shoe" and are not troubled by insider selling when a deal trades up.

Contrary to popular belief, green shoes do not generate gains for underwriters when a share price increases after a deal. Underwriters sell the position at the IPO price at the time the IPO is originally allocated. Therefore, they only receive the gross spread on the 15 percent when a green shoe is exercised.

In connection with the IPO, the underwriters would require PEMCO and all of its shareholders to sign "lock-up" agreements. These agreements contractually prohibit companies and their shareholders from selling shares or otherwise obtaining liquidity for them via option contracts, short sales, or the like after a public offering. The duration of these agreements can vary but generally last for one hundred eighty days in IPOs and ninety days in follow-on offerings. Public investors, and thus underwriters, demand lock-ups to prevent supply from hitting the market and driving prices down after a deal prices. Lead underwriters are empowered to provide early releases from lock-ups though this is rare except when done in connection with a subsequent underwritten offering that occurs prior to the expiration of the contract.

As part of the offering discussion, the topics of stock listing and ticker symbol were raised. The company had already considered these matters. Selecting where to list a stock for trading is not an easy decision. The two market leaders for domestic growth companies, the New York Stock Exchange and the Nasdaq Stock Market, are both great choices. Selected exchanges outside of the United States, such as the London Stock Exchange, have also proven to be good choices and have gained traction with issuers over the past few years. PEMCO's board concluded that the Nasdaq, with its long history of supporting growth and technology companies, was the right fit for the company. They had already reserved the Nasdaq ticker "PERP" and would apply for the listing.

A Briefing on Stock Exchanges

Fundamentally, there are two listing options for public stocks—traditional stock exchanges and the over-the-counter (OTC) market. Exchanges possess three elements: (1) member firms, (2) specialists, and (3) a physical space for trading and price discovery. The OTC has no physical space and has modified versions of specialists called "market makers."

Notable stock exchanges include the American Stock Exchange (AMEX) and the New York Stock Exchange (NYSE or "Big Board"). There are also sizable exchanges found in foreign markets and those that deal in securities and assets such as futures, options, and commodities. Exchange members hold "seats" and are entitled access to the physical space (commonly called the trading floor) to execute trades for themselves and their clients. Historically, these seats were purchased by members. With recent organizational changes, including a public listing by the NYSE, seats are now licensed annually on most exchanges.

On the trading floor, trades are executed at locations specifically designated for each stock. Floor brokers employed by member firms meet at these locations, known as stations, and "cry out" buy-and-sell interest for stocks in terms of price and number of shares. Other floor brokers respond and trades are made. This approach is referred to as the open outcry model and is intended to create an efficient, liquid market with transparent price discovery devoid of collusion and manipulation. A specialist is assigned to each stock by the exchange. The specialist monitors activity in the stock, logs sales and purchases, and stands ready to buy or sell for its own account if no natural counterparty exists for an interested buyer or seller. There are several firms dedicated to being exchange specialists. When a company decides to list, it interviews several specialists and presents a short list to the exchange which, in turn, selects one for the company.

An increasing percentage of trades completed on exchanges such as the NYSE are done electronically. Smaller orders no longer need human interaction. "Bids" (offers to buy) and "asks" (offers to sell) are wired directly to the stations on the floor and matched with natural buyers and sellers. This has led to a reduction in the personnel and the size of the trading floors used by the exchanges.

The OTC market operates without a physical location. Its participants are connected electronically and conduct business in a virtual trading environment. The most notable network and quotation system is operated by Nasdaq. Another entity, the Pink Sheets, also provides electronic quotations and other financial information for the OTC securities market. Bids, asks, and trades are posted in real-time to those connected to OTC networks.

Rather than specialists, member firms in Nasdaq serve as "market makers." Members request this role for OTC stocks that they seek to trade with and for their clients. For each designated stock, a market maker is obligated to post a bid and an ask. This is known as being "in the box." The firm must honor these postings for positions of at least 100 shares. The highest bid and lowest ask among a stock's market makers is known as the "inside market."

Market makers are familiar with the trading activity in a stock and earn compensation by trading positions in it for their clients. A stock can have several market makers. Generally, any firm providing sellside research on a company will also be a market maker in the company's stock. It is worth noting that firms and investors can trade shares over OTC networks without being market makers.

As with the exchanges, an increasing percentage of the Nasdaq's trading volume is completed without any human involvement. Better technology has allowed member firms to automate many trading and market-making tasks. It has also enabled the Nasdaq to deploy networks that match buyers and sellers without member involvement. Originally, these networks addressed only small positions for retail investors. They are now enabling larger institutional trades. Networks of this sort are a response to the "off exchange" trading opportunities that have emerged for exchange- and Nasdaq-listed stocks. Electronic communications networks (ECNs)—sometimes referred to as electronic trading networks (ETNs) or in certain instances "dark pools"—and other services offered by third parties allow buyers and sellers to trade with lower intermediary costs. Institutional trading activity across these platforms has ballooned, particularly in large capitalization, highly liquid stocks. This has also led to consolidation activity between the exchanges and entities providing these platforms.

The exchanges and the Nasdaq operate by receiving fees from several sources. Companies pay them up-front fees and annual fees for stock listings. Brokerage firms pay them fees for memberships and trading rights, and others pay them for access to trading and trading data.

Companies must qualify to list their securities. They must possess certain size and profitability characteristics and must comply with certain disclosure obligations. These demands vary by exchange. Within the Nasdaq, there are different tiers for listing. The highest and most difficult to obtain is the Global Select designation.

Initial listing requirements are more stringent than the requirements to maintain a listing once it has been granted. When a company fails to comply with its ongoing listing requirements, it is generally given a probation period to rectify its issues. If it fails to do so, its stock is de-listed. When this occurs, companies seek to list on an exchange or Nasdaq tier that has less rigorous standards. When no listing is possible, stocks trade on the Pink Sheets, a quotation service without listing requirements that historically has been composed primarily of so-called penny stocks.

Previously, the exchanges and Nasdaq (through its affiliate, the National Association of Securities Dealers or NASD) were self-regulatory organizations sanctioned by the SEC with responsibility for setting conduct standards and policing the behavior of their members. These functions are now conducted through the Financial Industry Regulatory Authority (FINRA), an organization formed for such purposes by the NASD and NYSE in 2007.

There has been significant debate about the merits of listing with an exchange or the OTC market, especially the NYSE versus the Nasdaq. This has included several academic studies regarding market efficiency. To date, there does not appear to be a definitive answer on which is superior. As such, the selection for most companies boils down to industry affiliation and comfort level with the trading model. Companies usually list where their high-profile public peers are found. Beyond this factor, management teams tend to favor either a centralized or a decentralized trading apparatus. Some executives like having a single specialist that is the pivotal clearing point for trades. Others prefer a model with several firms providing this function, believing that the competition improves pricing and liquidity. The Nasdaq and the NYSE, which house the majority of U.S. stock listings, each have about 3,000 listings.

Having covered the parameters of the offering, the organizational meeting turned its attention to the timeline. The goal was to market and price the transaction in late May or early June. A four-month transaction was aggressive but possible. They would spend six weeks drafting the S-1; file the document with the SEC in mid-March; receive comments from the SEC in mid-April; respond to the SEC's initial and further comments until mid-May; and then conduct the road show and price the deal—hopefully before Memorial Day. Throughout this time, the parties would also conduct any necessary due diligence and prepare other required materials such as revisions to the company's charter and bylaws. Specific dates were put on the calendar for the first few drafting sessions.

Besides the emergence of a difficult market, the real threats to the schedule were the financial audits and the SEC. PEMCO's fiscal year for accounting purposes was the calendar year. It would need three years of audited financials in the S-1. Two of these were already done; the most recent year was not. Audits for calendar fiscal years are generally available in mid to late February. If the accountants were not able to adhere to this, timing might slip. In addition, they would need unaudited financials for the first quarter (ending in March). These would be dropped into the document after the SEC comments in April. Any delay in these could also derail the schedule.

Figure 12.1. Timeline for an IPO.

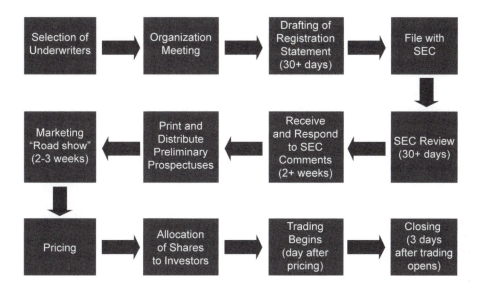

The SEC review process can be a wild card in deal timing. Upon receiving an S-1 filing, the SEC assigns a team to review it to assure that it adequately discloses all material information concerning the filer. This team compiles a list of comments regarding the S-1 that they aim to deliver to the issuer within 30 days of filing. Comments can vary from minimal to extensive and sometimes take longer than 30 days. Most comments are easy to address and simply ask for clarifying language. Others are more difficult and require documentation and support concerning matters such as accounting practices. Once a filer receives comments, an amended S-1 and response letter need to be prepared and filed with the SEC. These may produce further comments. Company counsel may also have direct conversations, albeit sparingly, with the lead SEC reviewer to clarify points and address open issues. In the past, it was common to receive only one or two rounds of comments. Today, filers may receive three or four rounds. Working through comments with the SEC can take weeks or months.

After the timeline was covered, the working group touched upon a litany of other diligence and logistical matters concerning the company. They discussed important personnel changes, pending contracts, and outstanding litigation. They briefly reviewed the list of due diligence materials that the underwriters and counsel would need to examine prior to filing. This effort would help protect the underwriters from liability by assuring that PEMCO was accurately described in the S-1 and that the business was not fraudulent or otherwise involved in wrongdoing. Underwriters' counsel also raised the topic of the "comfort letter" that would ultimately be delivered to the underwriters. Prepared and signed by the accountants, this document further shields an underwriting group from liability by noting that financial information contained in a registration statement corresponds to a company's audited and unaudited financials statements and other financial records.

The company was also warned by counsel against talking to the press, employees, and others about the deal. Known as gun jumping, such discussions are now permitted with greater latitude than in the past but may still expose a budding issuer to unnecessary liability or delays in an IPO.

Finally, the group discussed the status of PEMCO's takeover defenses. There are a number of structural protections a public company can have to protect against unwelcome advances and takeover interest. Notable defenses include:

1) **Staggered board.** With this structure, directors have staggered terms, generally three years in length, so that only a portion of the board is elected annually. This can prevent a hostile party from quickly gaining control of a board of directors and thereby a company.

2) **Poison pill.** Triggered when a party amasses a certain percentage of a company without prior board approval (generally 15% or more but sometimes less) and formally known as a "shareholder rights plan," a "poison pill" distributes extra shares to existing shareholders (excluding the amassing party), thereby increasing the shares outstanding and driving up the price an acquirer would need to pay for the entire business.

3) **Blank-check preferred.** Preferred stock authorized by a company's articles of incorporation that can be crafted and issued pursuant to the wishes of the board is referred to as "blank-check preferred." This stock can be sold to a new investor with any rights and preferences the board deems to be in the best interest of the company. Such shares can be issued to a desirable suitor to fend off an undesirable suitor.

4) **Supermajority vote.** Rather than requiring a simple majority vote, a company's articles of incorporation may require a supermajority vote (typically two thirds or more) for significant decisions such as a sale of the company. This provision places greater power in the hands of minority shareholders to defend against the agendas of majority shareholders.

5) **Limits on written consent.** To circumvent the board and other procedural roadblocks, shareholders, including potential acquirers, sometimes seek to act by collecting the written consent of other shareholders. This ability can be limited by the bylaws and articles of incorporation of a company.

6) **Dual-class common stock.** One way to assure that founders and existing shareholders maintain control over a company is to give them special rights and powers. A dual-class stock structure addressing voting authority accomplishes this goal. Founders are given ten or more votes per share for their stock, whereas public shareholders receive common stock with the traditional one vote per share. Usually, these separate classes are referred to as Class A and Class B Common Stock.

Defense measures are relatively easy to put in place when a company is private. Once public, it is much more difficult, given the required shareholder support. By and large, institutional investors frown on these protections, believing they do more to serve entrenched insiders than shareholders. Boards and management teams argue to the contrary. They claim such protections are necessary to guard shareholder interests. With them, they say better deals can be negotiated and opportunistic suitors can be stopped from raiding companies that are undervalued in the market.

Some investors refuse to buy IPOs and public stocks that are laden with overly protective defenses, particularly dual-class common stock structures. In light of the importance of the topic, the discussion of PEMCO's defense profile was tabled for another day when it could be discussed in greater detail with a smaller group, including representatives from the underwriters' equity capital markets departments (ultimately, they agreed to put in place all of the defenses except the dual-class common stock).

The discussion concerning the deal, timeline, logistics, and selected diligence items took about ninety minutes. The rest of the day was devoted to the management presentation. Delivered by senior executives responsible for each facet of the company, ranging from operations to finance, the presentation was intended to aid in due diligence and preparation of the S-1. Each section of the presentation lasted about an hour and was peppered with questions from the audience. The day concluded around 4 P.M.

The subsequent four weeks were harried. All parties worked feverishly to complete their assigned tasks. The accountants worked with the CFO and finance department to complete the year-end audit. Underwriters' counsel conducted extensive diligence of the company's documentation, including material contracts, stock purchase agreements, and minutes from board meetings. They also prepared the documentation that they were responsible for providing, such as the underwriting agreement and the lock-ups. Company counsel completed their own diligence and drafted their designated materials, including revised versions of PEMCO's article of incorporation and bylaws. The investment bankers arranged diligence calls with PEMCO's key customers, toured the company's operations, and ran background checks on the executives.

A subset of the group led by mid-level bankers from the lead underwriters met once or twice a week to work on the S-1. One or two representatives from each of the underwriters, the underwriters' counsel and the company's counsel attended these drafting sessions. PEMCO's CFO, general counsel, and CEO (sometimes) also participated. All parties were provided drafts of the latest version of the S-1 before the meetings and were expected to arrive with comments in hand. Progress was slow and tedious, as to be expected when following the age-old tradition of drafting S-1s by committee. Despite the process and the frequent grandstanding of bankers seeking to impress the client with their input, a well-crafted document was in place by early March, a little more than a month following the February 1 organizational meeting.

Along the way, the CFO, with guidance from the CEO, COO, and board, revised and refined PEMCO's financial projections to reflect the latest expectations for the business and the added costs of being public, including increased accounting fees and premiums for directors' and officers' liability insurance. Public companies typically have three sets of projections and budgets: (1) those developed and used by executive teams to set their own internal goals, (2) those developed by executive teams that are submitted to boards to establish a company's "official" goals and budgets, and (3) those used to guide investors and "manage" the expectations of Wall Street. These range from most (#1) to least (#3) aggressive.

Critical to the process, the underwriters would do due diligence upon and test PEMCO's #3 projections. These projections would also serve as the foundation for numbers ultimately prepared by research analysts and used by public investors to assess the company and its IPO. It would be critical that the company meet or exceed the numbers it, and by association, the research analysts, set out for at least the first two quarters following the IPO. Failing to do so would be unacceptable to the market. It would undermine confidence in management and the company and drive investors to abandon PEMCO for other opportunities.

After much back-and-forth, PEMCO's projections were finalized with assumptions and conclusions that withstood scrutiny from the bankers. With this completed, the CFO arranged an "analyst day" in early March for the research analysts from the underwriters. Similar to the presentations held at the organizational meeting a month earlier, this day included a review of PEMCO's operations, strategy, and financials. It also provided an opportunity for the analysts to interview and question key executives. This was done as a group event to conserve time, although each of the analysts was able to follow up individually on open items and questions.

During the pre-filing phase of the transaction, another group from the underwriters also became involved with PEMCO and its founders—those from private client services (PCS). PCS professionals are basically sophisticated stockbrokers who work with wealthier individuals and have a broader suite of services and products at their disposal to offer their clientele. Examples include:

- They work with executives and large shareholders on issues concerning their stock holdings and other wealth-management topics.
- They help their clients devise liquidity and asset diversification plans and guide them on investment decisions.
- They help their clients with tax and estate planning with the assistance of on-staff attorneys.
- They provide their clients with access to proprietary investment vehicles, such as special hedge funds, offered by their firms.

Like bankers and others involved in selling securities, PCS professionals are required to be licensed as Series 7 registered representatives.

PCS is a high-touch, highly competitive business. Clients typically interview and have ongoing discussions with PCS teams from several firms prior to selecting one. Teams often include two senior brokers, who work as partners, and a few assistants. The name of the game for PCS is asset accumulation. Rather than offering trading commission-based compensation structures that encourage PCS brokers to churn client accounts, most brokerage houses pay their PCS professionals based on total assets under management. The commissions and "payouts" typically vary by asset class in the accounts. For instance, the payout for money placed in hedge funds may be higher than that for money placed in cash-management vehicles such as money-market funds. These differences correlate to the profitability of the asset classes for the firm. In addition to working with wealthy individuals, PCS teams may also work directly with corporate treasury departments, helping them manage cash positions and stock buybacks. After conducting a mini–bake-off to select PCS representation, PEMCO, Larry, and Jerry selected the team from Burnham. This was not a surprising selection. The bookrunning lead manager has a distinct advantage in such competitions.

By the second week in March, the group was ready to make the final push to file the S-1. To date, the document had resided with company counsel, who had turned all edits from the drafting sessions and distributed revisions to the working group. It was now time to transfer the S-1 to a financial printer. There are only a handful of sizable financial printers in the market. These entities have offices, complete with conference rooms for hosting large groups, located throughout the country. Virtually all public filings that result in a physical document are completed and submitted to the SEC at a financial printer. Financial printers earn six-figure fees on IPOs—the fourth-largest deal expense behind the underwriters, lawyers, and accountants—and have account representatives who call on companies and legal firms for business. Having received bids from the major players, PEMCO's CFO selected the financial printer for the company. Company counsel sent them the document electronically and booked some time at their Silicon Valley office.

The working group met at the printer on a Tuesday morning. It had been six weeks since the organizational meeting. Their goal was to file on Thursday. To do so, the underwriters needed to receive filing approval from their commitment committees no later than Wednesday; the lawyers needed to collect and prepare exhibits to be filed with the S-1, such as copies of PEMCO's material contracts; the accountants needed to obtain filing consent from colleagues at their national office, who were responsible for reviewing the client team's audit work; and the S-1 itself needed to be cleaned up and finalized. The latter included conforming the document to the "style guide" of the bookrunning lead manager (all investment banks have a particular format they follow for client marketing materials, such as prospectuses, to create a consistent look and feel). Unlike most deals, everything went according to plan. Everyone worked around the clock, taking only occasional breaks for snacks, meals, and turns at the pinball machine provided in the break room at the printer (of course, everyone was constantly checking and sending e-mails from their cell phones as well).

The CCMs were uneventful, for the most part. PEMCO's business was doing very well, its projections seemed reasonable, and the research analysts continued to be supportive of the company and the deal. The committees were enthused about the transaction and again congratulated the banking teams on winning the business. The only two issues were preliminary valuation and the lock-ups.

Valuation in an IPO does not need to be decided until just before the preliminary prospectuses are printed and the marketing process begins. Still, most banks like to know that their thoughts on the topic are more-or-less aligned with those of the client prior to filing an S-1. This helps avoid future conflicts and embarrassments. The issue, however, is that companies always have valuation expectations that exceed the views of their underwriters and no underwriter wants to fall on the sword and take point on clarifying the matter before it becomes absolutely necessary (remember banks can be kicked off deals before they price, though this is rarely done after the marketing phase begins). As a result, most deals file with somewhat vague valuation understandings. Committees and bankers get comfortable with this situation by acknowledging that valuations depend upon market conditions and the trading characteristics of comparable companies at the time of marketing, not filing, and that, ultimately, the decision rests with investors, not themselves or the issuer.

PEMCO's valuation opinions were rich. The board and the executives expected to market the deal with a forward earnings multiple that exceeded all of the comparable companies. Management and the board believed this was supported by the company's growth rate, financial characteristics, and market opportunity. All of the underwriters agreed in principle and gave a green light to the filing. A few, however, did have reservations on the specifics.

The lock-ups were a minor matter. The underwriters had requested that all existing PEMCO shareholders sign six-month lock-ups prior to filing. Several of the seed-round investors had failed to comply. Although frustrating to the company, the underwriters, and the other shareholders, no one could force the holdouts to sign. They could only threaten to not proceed with the deal unless the agreements were executed. This was a hollow threat. Underwriters demand lock-ups but do not scrap deals on account of a few stubborn shareholders. So long as the company, the executives, and the shareholders representing the vast majority of shares outstanding signed, the deal would proceed.

The S-1 was submitted electronically to the SEC on Thursday before the evening deadline. It was filed silently, without an accompanying press release. Still, the financial news services picked it up and added it to their daily roster of notable blurbs. The document contained only the anticipated deal amount. It did not specify the number of shares being sold, nor did it contain a completed ownership table showing the shares and percentages held by each party. These would be added after receiving SEC comments and just before printing the preliminary prospectus (that used during the marketing process).

As far as the IPO was concerned, the next thirty days were quiet. PEMCO's executives returned to running the business and the bankers, the lawyers, and the accountants turned their attentions to other clients and transactions. The research analysts from the underwriters started work on their own financial models for the company and the lead managers began preparing the presentation that would be used by management for investor meetings during the marketing road show. The presentation would cover PEMCO's operations, products, strategy, market opportunity, and financial profile (excluding projections). Containing 25 to 30 PowerPoint slides, road-show presentations are designed to be delivered in less than thirty minutes, generally by the CEO and CFO.

On the thirty-second day after filing the S-1 (the thirtieth day was a Saturday), PEMCO received comments from the SEC. These were provided in a letter that was then circulated to the rest of the working group. A conference call was arranged afterward to discuss them. Fortunately, the comments were not extensive. There were just 55 of them; they sometimes run to more than a hundred. Most would only require minor modifications to the document or supplying the SEC with back-up material to support a claim. A couple of the comments were troublesome. They pertained to PEMCO's accounting and, more specifically, the application of certain policies for recognizing revenue and expenses.

The team spent five days, a couple of them at the printer, revising the S-1 and preparing the response materials for the SEC. The document was also modified to include first-quarter financial statements that had been prepared hurriedly by the accountants. The team then filed the first amendment. It was mid-April. Some of the team followed up on the filing with a call to the SEC examiner. The accountants, with the lawyers, wanted the opportunity to discuss PEMCO's accounting policies and to clarify items in the response. The examiner wanted to review the response before this discussion, so a conference call was set up for the following week.

The SEC call went surprisingly well (though the SEC can be reasonable, accounting matters are always tricky). The examiner indicated that he had what he needed and that the second round of comments would be sent shortly. The second comment letter arrived the next day. This time it was very short and none of the comments appeared problematic. The decision was made to print the preliminary prospectuses (also called "red herrings" or "reds" for short) on the next filing. While there was a risk that the SEC would have an issue with the round-two response, which could require a recirculation (printing and sending out another version of the red to prospective investors), in the opinion of the lawyers, this was unlikely given the nature of the comments.

A Briefing on Sellside Research Analysts

Research analysts are employed by investment banks as part of their brokerage operations. Most "cover" companies contained within a specific industry that is of interest to a bank's brokerage clients. Coverage entails preparing and publishing ongoing views and analysis regarding a company's operations, strategy, performance, and prospects. It also includes detailed financial projections prepared by the analyst and usually a buy, sell, or hold recommendation, though the recommendation itself is rarely a focus for institutional investors. Coverage generally begins with a comprehensive "initiation of coverage" report, which may encompass several related companies. Research reports are provided electronically to clients and also physically when requested.

Research analysts develop their perspectives by becoming experts on a company and its industry. They spend most of their time reviewing public filings; tracking press releases; attending trade shows; listening to earnings calls; interviewing management teams; analyzing trends; and talking to competitors, suppliers, distributors, customers, and other relevant industry players. All of their writings, models, and commentary are distilled from information gleaned from these activities. In essence, they are financial detectives seeking to separate fact from fiction and hope from reality in understanding a company's prospects. Many of the best maintain a good rapport with their companies without letting it cloud their judgment and critical thinking.

Aside from their analytical duties, research analysts spend time with brokerage personnel and clients. They provide frequent updates on their coverage internally to stockbrokers and institutional salespeople, particularly when there are notable developments. At many banks, this is done at research meetings held for the benefit of these parties once or twice a day. At larger firms, research analysts give similar presentations that are broadcast throughout the organization to reach far-flung brokerage offices. These broadcasts are conducted over a network of audio feeds into the trading floors and offices (the broadcast mechanism is commonly called the squawk box). Given the dozens of analysts and hundreds of companies under coverage at a given bank, these updates are critiqued, prioritized, and coordinated by a research product manager or other senior brokerage representative beforehand. Research analysts also respond to e-mails and telephone calls from in-house salespeople and traders regarding companies under coverage.

Research analysts engage with brokerage clients as well. They place outbound calls and e-mails regarding developments within their coverage names. They reply to client inquiries and conduct their own road shows to visit with important investors in order to discuss their stocks and opinions. These visits are made to cities with large concentrations of institutional investors, such as New York and Boston. Analysts also arrange "nondeal" road shows for their coverage companies to meet with investors. In addition, they help coordinate and direct conferences held for the benefit of investors to showcase interesting companies and ideas. Many firms restrict access to their research analysts, research reports, and investment conferences. Only clients who generate brokerage commissions that exceed certain levels are given passage to these individuals, materials, and events.

Many institutional investors direct their trades and commissions based on the outcome of internal votes regarding brokerage firms. Portfolio managers and other investment professionals at large institutions vote quarterly or annually on firms according to the relative service and support they have received from across Wall Street. The efforts of research analysts play a vital role in obtaining votes. Even when they have no formal voting mechanism in place, institutions drive trading activity and brokerage revenues to firms based upon thoughtful and credible research.

Another important measure for research analysts is the polling conducted by entities such as Greenwich Associates and *Institutional Investor* (*II*) magazine. Annually, *II* asks institutional investors, large and small, across the country, to vote on their favorite research analysts in a number of defined industries. The results, which are published and known as the *II* rankings, can significantly influence an analyst's compensation at larger firms. The rankings are less relevant at firms that do little or no business with the smaller and more obscure investors included in the polling process. The *II* rankings are more subjective than those compiled by some other organizations, such as *The Wall Street Journal* and StarMine, which are based on criteria such as accuracy of earnings predictions or the results of investment recommendations.

The job of research analysts and their role within investment banks have changed over the past several years. Research always sat on the other side of the proverbial Chinese Wall from their investment-banking colleagues. Legally, they were never permitted access to nonpublic information concerning companies. That being said, they often maintained an active dialogue with investment bankers, attended meetings with bankers, and served as active proponents on investment banking transactions such as IPOs. This is no longer the case. Under the current rules, research analysts and bankers cannot attend meetings together and cannot even interface without a legal observer present. Even with an observer, dialogues are limited to discussing the merits of a proposed transaction (assuming this does not encompass confidential nonpublic information), due diligence on a transaction, and general industry trends. All other business-related communications are forbidden.

With respect to transactions, research analysts cannot participate in marketing a deal though they can respond to questions from potential investors and educate their firm's salespeople regarding an issuer and its industry. Known as "teach ins," these internal tutorials can include views regarding future financial performance and earnings.

The path to becoming a research analyst differs from that of an investment banker. It involves more of an apprenticeship with a senior colleague. The career progression follows the title chain from associate to MD (there is typically no junior title of analyst). Associates report directly to specific senior level analysts and help gather information, analyze data, build financial models, and draft reports for them. Many associates are hired out of top business school programs. Others are hired directly out of industry, particularly in areas requiring strong scientific and technical knowledge. Research assistants—department personnel with administrative and secretarial duties—also play an important role and often perform rudimentary tasks otherwise assigned to associates. Research assistants are usually hired out of college and are frequently promoted to associate after a couple of years on the job.

The duration between titles for a research analyst is similar to that found in investment banking, with three years as an associate, three years as a vice president, and two-plus years as a principal (sometimes also called a senior vice president or director) before becoming an MD. At the midpoint of this progression or shortly thereafter, research analysts are given the opportunity to cover their own stocks. In doing so, they may assume responsibility for some companies previously covered by their bosses or they may be asked to identify and pursue new coverage names. Once independent, research analysts are no longer judged and compensated according to just the opinions of their superiors. Their success is determined by the trading volumes and commissions generated in their stocks, votes they obtain from institutional accounts, and the views of institutional salespeople and retail stockbrokers. Each of these speaks to their value and is presumed to correlate to the quality and accuracy of their research. Research analysts may experience faster career advancement than the timeline noted earlier when they get high marks, are covering a hot sector, or receive a "battlefield promotion" prompted by the departure of a more senior research analyst. Research analysts are compensated with salaries and yearend bonuses that vary by seniority and productivity levels. Historically, these compensation packages were commensurate with investment banking, but this has changed in recent years due to the regulatory environment and the diminished economics of the brokerage business.

Senior research analysts can develop valuable franchises that are recognized by both investors and issuers. Once attained, many maintain this position for several years, overseeing large teams of subordinates to do so. At the same time or afterward, successful research analysts often pursue job opportunities with the buyside at mutual funds, hedge funds, venture capital firms, and private equity firms. Others pursue roles of greater authority and prestige within the brokerage industry, either at their own organizations or at competitors. They become directors of research, with responsibility for the direction and personnel of the department. They may also assume the role of investment strategist, advising clients on macro considerations in the market and helping guide asset-allocation decisions.

Research analysts, particularly those without graduate degrees, are expected by most firms to become Chartered Financial Analysts (CFAs). Awarded by the CFA Institute, the CFA designation requires passing the lengthy and grueling Level 1, Level 2, and Level 3 CFA examinations, each of which are administered sequentially over a three-year period. The CFA Institute is a global organization consisting of more than 80,000 investment professionals in more than 120 countries. Its charter is to "lead the investment industry by setting the highest standards of ethics and professional excellence and vigorously advocating fair and transparent capital markets." As with their investment-banking colleagues, research analysts are required to have the Series 7 and Series 63 securities licenses and the Series 24 if they serve in a managerial capacity. In addition, and depending upon whether they have a CFA designation, sellside research analysts are also required to have Series 86 and 87 licenses.

The role of research and the value of those providing this service have changed over the past several years. Research analysts are not as important to the flow of information as they once were. Moreover, they are not positioned to produce the same level of revenues for their employers. Prior to the internet, the proliferation of computing resources, and the adoption of Regulation FD (short for "Fair Disclosure"), which forbids companies from providing nonpublic information to some investors but not others, research analysts provided a critical link to information and analysis on public companies that were difficult, time consuming, and often impossible to obtain otherwise. After these technological and regulatory developments, information and better analytical tools could be found at everyone's fingertips and companies could no longer provide special insights to their favorite analysts. Accordingly, research commentary has become less important to investors, although the access many top-tier research analysts have to senior executives provides them with special perspectives that are still valued.

As for generating revenues, research analysts are now prohibited from helping firms win and execute banking transactions. They must focus on trading and brokerage commissions for their livelihoods. However, income from these activities has collapsed. Electronic trading platforms, not to mention regulatory issues facing institutional investors who pay for research with trading commissions and fail to disclose it appropriately, have driven down commissions. In addition, the commission dollars generated by research must now be shared with a second, independent source of research when the stock involved concerns a company that the investment bank intends to pursue for business.

To address these new realities, most investment banks have dramatically downsized their research departments or have at least reduced overhead in this area. Some investment banks have also experimented with "unbundling" compensation for research and trading. Under some of these arrangements, institutional investors pay a fixed fee for access to an investment bank's research and then execute trades wherever they see fit based strictly on best execution and lowest commission rates. Under other client commission arrangements, an institutional investor elects to only trade stocks with a few firms and has the ability to direct a portion of its commissions to separate firms for the research value they provide. Requesting that a brokerage house allocate a portion of the commission from a trade to a separate firm for its research is known as a "soft dollar" arrangement.

CHAPTER 13

Initial Public Offerings: Valuation and Marketing

➤ The details of how IPOs are valued by underwriters.

➤ The details of how IPOs are marketed by underwriters.

➤ The role of the institutional sales department within an investment bank.

There was a tremendous amount of work that the bankers needed to complete before filing the next amendment to PEMCO's Form S-1 and giving the order to print the preliminary prospectus. Among other things, they needed to finalize the road-show presentation, resolve any outstanding issues with the underwriting agreement, provide the printer with mailing labels for investors, and obtain final commitment committee approvals. The first and most important item, however, was agreeing upon a price range for the stock to be offered. This would be placed on the cover of the prospectus. In other words, the time for the valuation discussion had arrived.

Determining valuation in an IPO requires obtaining finalized earnings models from the research analysts and applying their estimates to multiples derived from the trading characteristics of comparable public companies. The research numbers are shared with potential investors and used in their valuation assessments; thus they are critical. Ideally, research estimates from all underwriters are similar to each other and in line with the issuer's expectations. Material discrepancies can cause conflict and confusion. In building their models, research analysts look to issuers for guidance and often receive copies of internal projections (note that this is only the case in IPOs; existing public companies do not share this type of information). Research always applies a "haircut" to management's outlook to adjust for the optimistic bias of executives and the importance of investor psychology. Research analysts, like the stocks they follow, are rarely punished for underestimating future performance. But they can be battered when their "numbers" are too high and a company fails to meet expectations—even when performance is strong on an absolute basis. The buyside likes positive surprises and rewards issuers and analysts who can be trusted to deliver them.

Deciding upon the right multiples and marketing range for an IPO is more of an art than a science. Bankers first find an appropriate pool of comparable public companies. These are generally businesses within the issuer's industry. When no such companies exist, bankers look to analogous industries for guidance, namely those possessing similar growth rates, market opportunities, and financial profiles. Once the set of comparables is determined, the bankers compare their characteristics with those of the issuer. Those with the closest similarities are used to determine the appropriate multiples. Slight premiums or discounts may be applied based on differences in margins and growth rates.

Generally, valuations are set based on price-to-earnings multiples (the "P/E") for the next calendar year, or the same calendar year when deals are done early in the year. Another metric considered by bankers is P/E to growth rate, also known as the PEG ratio. An old rule of thumb is that a company should trade in line with its growth rate. For example, a company with a 25 percent long-term growth rate—growth that can be sustained over five-plus years—should trade at 25X forward earnings. Bankers, research analysts, and investors may also consider other multiples, such as enterprise value to revenues or cash flow, when assessing an IPO valuation depending on the industry and other circumstances.

The ECM department works closely with banking in determining comparables and multiples for IPOs. Taking into account their exposure to other deals, ECM can provide a more objective view than investment bankers on how investors will consider an opportunity and how they can be guided to think about valuation. ECM helps construct the case that will be used by an underwriter's sales force to discuss the matter with potential buyers. In this pursuit, ECM interfaces with its counterparts at the other underwriters on a deal to ensure their messages are aligned. Research is also solicited for their valuation input.

As noted previously, issuers usually take a more aggressive stance on valuation than underwriters. Often, they take the highest estimates and apply them to multiples cherry picked from the pool of comparable companies. PEMCO was no exception. In fact, it wanted a multiple that was higher than any of the comparables on the basis that it possessed a superior operating model and growth rate. This argument was not unprecedented, nor was it altogether unreasonable.

After several days of discussion and debate accompanied by exhaustive analysis, the bankers and the company agreed on the valuation that would mark the midpoint of the range that would be placed on the cover of the preliminary prospectus and would be presented to the underwriters' commitment committees. It struck a balance between PEMCO's desire for a strong valuation and the underwriters' desire to not scare away potential investors before they had a chance to meet management and hear the company's story. The underwriters felt strongly that the price range on the cover be reasonable enough to lure in buyers and drive up demand for the deal. The underwriters argued that creating this demand would set the stage for PEMCO to achieve the best valuation and possibly price above the high end of the marketing range. Without luring adequate demand, the deal

Table 13.1 PEMCO Comparable Companies Analysis

Company	Margins		Growth Rate	P/E Multiple		PEG Ratio	
	Gross	Operating		CCY	NCY	CCY	NCY
CompOne	40%	10%	15%	17x	15x	1.1x	1.0x
CompTwo	50%	15%	25%	25x	20x	1.0x	0.8x
CompThree	65%	25%	25%	35x	28x	1.4x	1.1x
CompFour	60%	15%	35%	40x	30x	1.1x	0.9x
PEMCO	67%	20%	50%	TBD	TBD	TBD	TBD

Margins for current calendar year. CCY and NCY refer to current calendar year and next calendar year.

could price below the range and would be considered "broken" by otherwise interested investors.

The proposed midpoint had a P/E multiple that was higher than any of the comparable companies for the current calendar year—50X. But, it had a P/E multiple for the next calendar year that was less than the two leaders—25X—and PEG ratios for both years that were less than all of them except the industry laggard—1.0X and 0.5X. Given PEMCO's superior growth rate (better than all) and margins (better than all but one), the valuation looked reasonable. The valuation and its position relative to the comparables also took into account the price discount expected of IPOs. Generally between 10 percent and 20 percent, this discount is built into an IPO's pricing and is intended to reward investors for risking capital in newly minted public companies with no trading history. After pricing, the underwriters expected PEMCO to trade up to or slightly above the P/E levels of CompThree and CompFour (28X and 30X next-calendar-year earnings, respectively).

Prior to going to their commitment committees, the team also had to decide on a price range for the prospectus cover. They knew the midpoint valuation but needed to translate it into a stock price with latitude on both sides for the low end and high end of the range. There are no hard rules on stock price ranges.

Table 13.2 Preliminary Midpoint for PEMCO's IPO

Next Calendar Year Earnings	$40 million
Current Calendar Year Earnings	$20 million
Agreed Upon Multiple for NCY Earnings	25x
Implied Multiple for CCY Earnings	50x
NCY PEG Ratio	0.5x
CCY PEG Ratio	1.0x
Proposed Valuation	$1.0 billion

Earnings based on consensus estimates of the research analysts.
PEG ratio based on 50% long term growth rate.

Table 13.3 Proposed Price Range for the Preliminary
Prospectus

Price Per Share	$12.00	$13.00	$14.00
Implied CCY P/E	46x	50x	54x
Implied NCY P/E	23x	25x	27x

Most deals are marketed with ranges in the mid-teens to low teens and $2 spreads (e.g., $13 to $15 or $14 to $16). Smaller deals tend to have lower dollar ranges to provide more shares and greater liquidity for the market (e.g., a company would issue twice as many shares at $8 each than at $16 each). Such deals often have single-digit ranges. Once a range is determined, typically an issuer must conduct a stock split or reverse stock split to align the shares outstanding with the valuation. For example, a company with a proposed midpoint of $10 a share and a $300 million valuation would need to adjust its post-offering shares outstanding to 30 million via a split. Accordingly, issuers sometimes lean toward price ranges that require less-complicated splits.

In PEMCO's case, the team decided upon a $12 to $14 range. With a $1 billion post-money valuation at the $13 midpoint, there would need to be roughly 77 million shares outstanding after the IPO (76,923,077 to be exact). To keep things simple and to conform to standard industry practice, the team rounded the number of shares to be issued to 9.5 million, resulting in a $123.5 million offering instead of the previously discussed $125 million. Half of the 9.5 million shares would be sold by existing shareholders so the existing shares outstanding needed to be split to 72,173,077 (i.e., 76,923,077 less 4,750,000).

Each of the underwriters held their CCMs on Thursday, the day before PEMCO was scheduled to file its amendment and "print the reds." As before, the committees wanted a complete update on banker due diligence and company developments. Fortunately, PEMCO was doing very well. Its core business was exceeding prior expectations and its new initiatives in the automotive sector were gaining traction. The company had even secured a design win for a next-generation hybrid from a leading vehicle manufacturer. Most of the time in committee was spent discussing valuation. All of the committees signed off on the proposal though one of the co-managers had been particularly troubled by it. Its research analyst believed the valuation to be too rich. The committee knew this view could create an issue during marketing—not to mention after the deal, when the analyst initiated coverage—but ultimately got comfortable with proceeding. Rightly or wrongly, the committee figured that the deal and its success would be driven primarily by the leads, not by them or their analyst. Besides, a failure would not reflect *that* poorly upon them as a co-manager, and the deal would give them a fee and a high-profile "print."

With committee approvals behind them, the next priority for the underwriters was to finalize the road-show schedule. This is driven by the bookrunning lead manager or, more specifically, the bookrunner's ECM department. Working closely with management and the lead bankers, the "desk," as the ECM department is often called, set forth a detailed agenda of travel and meetings for marketing the deal.

IPO road shows typically last eight or nine business days and are contained to a dozen U.S. cities with high concentrations of institutional investors. They may also include two or three extra days for meetings in Europe when a story holds broader appeal. Each road-show day is filled with back-to-back one-hour meetings with institutional investors. These "one-on-ones" are supplemented by a number of larger group meetings held during breakfast, lunch, or dinner in certain cities. It is common for an issuer to have at least forty one-on-ones and half-a-dozen group meetings during an IPO road show.

A couple of days before a road show begins (sometimes less), management presents to the sales departments at the underwriters. Known as the "in houses" or "kick-offs," these presentations enable institutional salespeople (and possibly retail brokers) to learn firsthand about the opportunity and to ask questions of management regarding the business model, strategy, products, and operations. To prepare for the deal, the research analysts also conduct "teach ins" to educate sales on the issuer and the financial outlook for the business. Following these presentations, salespeople contact their clients about the offering and attempt to set up road-show meetings.

It is worth noting that salespeople serve as investment screens for their clients and thus may be reluctant or unwilling to set up meetings when a deal is questionable in order to protect their relationships. At times, this can result in significant internal conflict within a firm, which may be addressed by increasing the payouts, or commissions, salespeople receive for finding buyers and placing the deal. Meeting requests are submitted to the ECM desk. Based upon past experience and reputation, some investors are accepted for one-on-ones and some are not. Larger institutions generally get their meetings. Others get to share a nice meal and a question-and-answer session with some of their competitors at a group presentation.

A road-show coordinator from the bookrunner's ECM department handles all logistical matters for the two-week ordeal, including transportation (limousines and first-class seats or private planes), hotels (four- and five-star accommodations), dining (when time permits), and other special requests from the issuer ("please be sure to have Tootsie Rolls and Dr. Pepper in the car at all times"). The coordinator also sends out updated schedules daily and is constantly in contact with those traveling. The road-show team includes the presenting executives and one or two bankers from the bookrunner and possibly the co-leads. Bankers from other underwriters attend only group functions, space and time permitting.

PEMCO's red herrings were printed on a Friday in late April. They were then sent directly by the financial printer to several thousand institutional investors pursuant to mailing labels provided by the underwriters. Boxes of them were also delivered to the underwriters. These copies would be used internally, sent to other investors, and carried on the road show.

The final schedule for the in-house sales-force presentations and the road show was as follows:

Week One
Monday	Burnham and ILB in-houses
	Co-managers would join by
	videoconference
Tuesday	Travel
Wednesday	Geneva, Zurich, Paris
Thursday	Stockholm, Amsterdam
Friday	London, Glasgow

Week Two
Monday	Baltimore, Philadelphia
Tuesday	New York City
Wednesday	New York City
Thursday	Boston
Friday	Chicago, Milwaukee,
	Minneapolis

Week Three
Monday	Houston, Kansas City
Tuesday	Denver, Salt Lake City
Wednesday	San Diego, Los Angeles
Thursday	San Francisco, Pricing
Friday	First day of trading

A handful of conference calls for notable investors located in other cities such as Dallas, Seattle, and Portland were also sprinkled throughout the schedule.

The in-houses went well. Having completed several dry runs with the bankers beforehand, management had the story down cold—a tremendous improvement from the choppy and awkward first few attempts. In addition, the sales forces were aware of the buzz on the Street about the deal and were excited to be involved. Being able to show clients "hot deals" helped their relationships and their business. With favorable comments in *Barron's* and the IPO blogs, several institutions had already submitted meeting requests to the leads.

The co-managers had been a little frustrated that their in-houses had not been made in person. In the interest of time, the co-managers had been piped via videoconference into the presentation held in Burnham's auditorium. While they were able to ask questions and absorb the substance of the presentation, it was not the same as seeing management face-to-face. Body language and speaking tones can provide valuable clues in assessing management's confidence and the risks and strengths of a story.

Videoconferencing has become increasingly common for co-managers and sometimes comes as a relief to bankers. The salespeople at lead managers, specifically the bookrunners, bear the ultimate burden for getting deals done. They set up the meetings, collect the orders, and build the "book" of demand. Co-managers play more of a support role in deals, providing clients with additional input and perspectives. As such, some salespeople do not pay much attention to co-managed deals and choose not to attend their in-houses. Seeing an important banking client stand before an empty audience at an in-house can be extremely embarrassing and frustrating, particularly given claims made in the bake-off about institutional focus and commitment. To ensure against this outcome, bankers often recruit any able body they can, whether or not related to institutional sales, to fill audiences at in-house presentations.

In addition to the videoconferencing for the co-managers, the presentation at Burnham was recorded. It would be made available to prospective institutional buyers over the Web through the services of an internet media company. Interested viewers would require a password from the underwriters to access it. Usage would be tracked and monitored.

The seventeen days following the sales-force presentations were an exhausting blur of meetings and travel. PEMCO's road-show team included the CEO, the COO, and the CFO. Together with their banker escorts from the lead managers, they spent the weekdays rushing from institution to institution and the weekends recuperating. The schedule was packed full, barely leaving enough time for transportation between the venues. By the end of the first week, everyone began hearing the presentation over and over again in their heads, whether awake or asleep. They also started to mix up meetings, questioning in their heads if points had already been made or still needed to be made. Starting each day at 7 or 8 A.M., the challenge to keep things fresh, clear, and energized was especially acute in the late afternoon or, worse yet, during investor-attended dinners.

Although the names and faces of the cities and accounts constantly changed, the daily routine throughout the road show seemed the same—meet first thing in the hotel lobby, check out, jump in the limo, arrive at the first institution, wait in reception, move to a small conference room, open up the laptop, present for 30 minutes, respond to questioning for 30 minutes, shake hands with the investor's representatives, jump back in the limo, repeat with other one-on-ones, fly to the next destination, drive to more one-on-ones, have dinner, and check in at the next hotel. The monotony of this schedule was broken up by a handful of group meetings. Held at hotels and restaurants, including New York's famous 21 Club, these accompanied a meal and ranged in size from five to fifty investors, primarily smaller institutions.

The tone of the one-on-ones and the personalities of the portfolio managers and investment professionals from the institutions varied from meeting to meeting. Some investors were warm, friendly, and engaging. Others were cold, antagonistic, and aloof. Surprisingly, many had done very little work on the company prior to attending the one-on-ones, choosing to get a feel for management prior to exerting the extra effort. Despite this, most were very astute and asked thoughtful, pointed, delving questions. Their experience showed. Fortunately, management had been prepped by the banking team beforehand on questions that might be asked, and was prepared for most of the inquiries.

At the end of each day, Burnham's ECM desk held a conference call updating the road show team on the deal's progress. They discussed notable market developments, changes to the schedule, feedback from the meetings, and the status of the order book. The last topic was what the team wanted to hear most. As the road show advanced, the team had started making predictions regarding which one-on-ones would result in orders. This proved to be more difficult than first thought. In the end, some of the most upbeat meetings produced nothing whereas some of the real downers generated substantial demand. Tone, it turned out, was a function of personality and not interest. Likewise, the act of taking a meeting and spending an hour with management did not necessarily correlate to interest. Some investors used the opportunity simply to gain market intelligence for their other investments.

Orders for the book trickled in slowly for the first week. This was typical. Investors needed to do their homework. They spoke with salespeople, research analysts, customers, suppliers, and competitors. They made their own assumptions and built their own models. The level of analysis conducted by the buyside was much higher than the company would have witnessed during the technology bubble. When every IPO was a winner, it was all about getting an allocation, not determining whether you wanted one. Even though PEMCO was thought to be a hot deal, investors were cautious.

Another point of focus for investors was the status of the order book. They wanted color on the number of orders, gross demand, price sensitivities, and notable investor requests to better assess the opportunity and where the stock might trade. Looking to please their clients, salespeople tried their best to ferret out this information, all of which was highly guarded by the bookrunner's ECM desk. Specific information on the book was not provided to the co-managers and only shared selectively with the bookrunner's own deal team. ECM wanted the book to contain real orders, not "fluff" from "flippers" looking to pile into a hot deal. ECM wanted the ability to fairly price the transaction and place it into hands with true interest in PEMCO. This would enable the deal to be successful and serve the company's longer-term interests by creating a more stable shareholder base.

When the roadshow concluded, the members of the management team were ready to get back to their day jobs. It had been an interesting but draining rite-of-passage. Aside from a few travel snafus caused by one or two lost limo drivers, everyone agreed that it had gone well. They had seen over one hundred and twenty institutional investors, including sixty in one-on-ones. Management had also gotten to know Burnham's team much better. The road show had been a bonding experience that had strengthened PEMCO's tie to the firm and its bankers. It was now time to price the deal.

A Briefing on Institutional Sales

Institutional sales is divided into two distinct groups—research sales and trading sales (more commonly known as sales trading). Individuals from both groups are assigned responsibility for servicing institutional accounts, namely mutual funds and hedge funds. Within these institutions, research salespeople cover portfolio managers and their investment teams, who make buy and sell decisions for funds based on the analysis of companies, industries, and markets. Trading salespeople, on the other hand, cover traders at these accounts. Buyside traders execute trades for their organizations to effectuate the buy and sell decisions of portfolio managers and to make necessary adjustments to funds to compensate for capital inflows and redemptions.

Research sales is rewarded by its client base for providing good ideas and thoughtful analysis. Trading sales is rewarded for providing clients with strong execution on trades. Both groups are judged and compensated according to the trading commissions they generate.

As the name suggests, the primary product sold by research sales is a firm's research. Research sales screens the views and analysis of analysts in search of actionable investment ideas for their clients. As part of this, this group receives all published research reports and unpublished research notes produced by its research department and attends research meetings offered before the market opens and throughout the workday. Research salespeople are expected to make "research calls" to their clients on noteworthy items.

Given the breadth of companies covered by many firms, some investment banks have subsets of research sales professionals dedicated to particular sectors, market capitalizations, and securities (e.g., technology research sales, small capitalization research sales, or debt research sales). Other firms have taken the opposite approach in light of shrinking commissions and the diminished economics of brokerage operations. These firms have combined all research sales functions. Their salespeople are responsible for providing institutional clients with the firm's full spectrum of equity and debt research ideas. This approach poses some challenges, however, because it requires covering a much wider range of individuals within each institution (e.g., portfolio managers running small capitalization stock and debt funds are different and have little in common). Research sales is responsible for selling IPOs and stock offerings underwritten by the firm.

A firm's trading capabilities is the "product" sold by trading sales. Trading sales professionals, commonly called "sales traders," help their clients to buy and sell large stock positions. They work with clients to get the best price and to find liquidity for stocks with limited trading volumes. To achieve these goals, sales traders work in unison with a firm's position traders. Combined, these two groups constitute a firm's trading "desk." In fact, sales traders consider themselves traders rather than institutional salespeople even though their primary job function is relationship-based sales.

Discussed further in Chapter 15, position traders make buy and sell decisions on behalf of an investment bank. They coordinate "cross" trades between clients by aligning buyers and sellers. They also put firm capital at risk by directly buying stocks from clients and selling stocks to clients. The long and short positions created from these trades are managed by the position trader, who works aggressively with sales traders to find offsetting trades and

Figure 13.1. Institutional brokerage flowchart.

also moves positions anonymously over electronic trading networks. In many cases, larger trades for clients, particularly those involving less liquid stocks, are not executed all at once. Working with the position trader, a sales trader may agree to execute part of a client's trade at an attractive price with his or her firm serving as the counterparty. This at-risk trade will be done in exchange for a larger order that the position trader will then "work" on a risk-free basis to generate a commission. In some situations, sales traders may bypass position traders entirely and direct client trades over internal "black box" trading systems. Such systems are offered at lower commission rates and are driven by proprietary algorithms that are designed to electronically trade a position throughout a day at a favorable price. Not surprisingly, the use of technologies like these have begun to blur the lines between sales traders and positions traders. Sales traders now make trades and, for survival, position traders have started to extend their role to building relationships with the buyside.

The flow of activity between the primary constituents within a brokerage operation can be depicted as follows:

Institutional sales is an apprenticeship job. Most salespeople are hired out of college as sales assistants. They gather, analyze, and distribute research and information for senior salespeople. As they progress, they develop relationships of their own with certain accounts and are given other accounts to pursue. If successful in generating business, their account package is broadened to include larger commission-producing institutions. The title progression in institutional sales follows the assistant-to-managing director path found in research. Many investment banks pay salespeople a percentage of the commissions they generate from their clients along with a modest salary. These "payouts" constitute the majority of their incomes. Some firms do not use commission-based compensation structures, preferring a salary-plus-bonus approach instead.

Institutional sales is a high-touch profession. Salespeople are in constant dialogue with clients via the telephone and e-mail. They also spend substantial time with them face-to-face, much of which involves wining, dining, and attending sporting events. For this reason, the account packages for most salespeople are geographically concentrated. Ultimately a salesperson's success is determined by relationships and the respect and trust of clients. As with research analysts, many institutions vote upon institutional salespeople and use these votes to determine where to allocate their commission dollars on Wall Street. In light of the relationship element of the job, institutional sales professionals must strike a careful balance between serving the interests of their clients and their firms. Conflicting agendas can be evident when pricing a trade or selling a questionable securities offering.

As mentioned previously, the business of institutional brokerage has changed over the past several years. The internet and better technology have opened the doors to better and more readily obtained information on public companies. Technology has also enabled even large, complicated trades to be made electronically with good pricing and small commissions. Despite these headwinds, institutional sales commissions still amount to billions of dollars annually. With more than 6,000 publicly traded companies in the United States alone, institutional clients still appear to value service providers who can help them screen and find attractive investment opportunities as well as produce liquidity for volatile and difficult-to-trade stocks.

CHAPTER 14

Initial Public Offerings: Pricing, Trading, and Other Thoughts

➤ The details of how IPOs are "priced" and allocated to investors.

➤ The role of retail stockbrokers within an investment bank.

➤ Noteworthy variations to the traditional IPO path: online offerings, the use of shell corporations, and others.

PEMCO's order book had grown substantially over the last three days of the road show. It now stood at six times "oversubscribed," meaning that there were orders for six times as much stock as contemplated on the cover of the offering. Included in the demand were a large number of "10 percent" orders from top institutions. Ten-percent orders refer to those requesting 10 percent of the shares offered and are generally the largest orders submitted by institutions, although, occasionally, there is one for 15 percent or 20 percent.

The book of interest was solid but there was price sensitivity. The market had grown choppy, particularly for IPOs, and there had been a couple of curiously timed press releases from competitors that helped undermine PEMCO's story (a common last-minute challenge for many budding IPO issuers). Investors had reflected price limits in their orders. For this reason, the team, earlier in the week, had decided not to increase the range on the offering as originally hoped. Increasing the price range above a certain level would have required filing an amendment to the S-1 with the SEC. The underwriting team still had some flexibility regarding the size and price of the deal. By increasing the offering price or number of shares offered, an issuer, as a general rule, can raise 20 percent more proceeds in a deal than stated on the cover of the prospectus without filing an amendment beforehand.

A "pricing call" was scheduled for 4:30 P.M. on the final day of the road show. Participants for the conference call would include the bankers and ECM representatives from the lead managers, PEMCO's road-show team, and two of

PEMCO's directors. The directors, along with the CEO, constituted PEMCO's "pricing committee," which would have final say over accepting or rejecting the offering proposal presented by the underwriters. Prior to the call, the banking team and underwriters' counsel conducted a final due diligence call, commonly referred to as the "bring down" call, with management and the company's accountants to determine whether there had been any developments over the past three weeks that could negatively impact the business or would need to be disclosed to potential investors. As expected, the call was uneventful, revealing nothing noteworthy. The day before, the team had also submitted their request for the deal to become "effective" with the SEC. This would be necessary to price.

In the final hours leading up to the pricing call, Burnham's ECM desk had worked aggressively to gather any color they could regarding orders in the book. They checked on which orders corresponded to one-on-one meetings and asked the salespeople to inquire with their clients about price, aftermarket intentions, and work they had done on the deal. To structure the deal correctly and make the right proposal to PEMCO, the bookrunner needed to be able to separate the orders of genuine investors from those of opportunists. Or, as they say, the desk needed to separate "the buyers from the liars."

The pricing call occurred as planned. Burnham's ECM desk led the discussion, first congratulating management on a job well done and then walking them through the details of the book and other market factors germane to the pricing such as how the broader indexes and comparable public companies had performed during the road show. Management and PEMCO's pricing committee asked a number of questions throughout the discussion. In the end, Burnham proposed a deal at the high end of the range—$14 a share. Burnham also proposed that the deal be left at 9.5 million shares and not upsized. This proposal had been discussed beforehand with the co-lead to assure a consistent message. Given the circumstances, ILB concurred with Burnham's recommendation. PEMCO's pricing committee requested some time offline to discuss the proposal. After fifteen minutes, the group reconvened on the call. PEMCO agreed to the terms.

Burnham notified the co-managers and provided details on the "layout" of the deal. Proceeds to the company and the selling shareholders would amount to $13.02 per share. The 7 percent gross spread was $0.98 a share. This gross spread was further broken down into three components: management fee, underwriting fee, and the selling concession. As was customary, management and underwriting would each be roughly 20 percent of the gross spread and the selling concession would be the remaining 60 percent. Here, Burnham noted management, underwriting, and selling concession as $0.19, $0.19, and $0.60 per share, respectively.

The management fee compensates the managing underwriters for their work on the deal. It is divided among the managing underwriters in accordance with the originally agreed-upon fee split. The underwriting fee is intended for the entire underwriting "syndicate." Along with the managing underwriters, this may include other firms invited to participate in the deal. Done more for tradition than to share risk, the practice of syndicating deals, even IPOs, has died out over the past several years. Most deals do not include other underwriters, leaving the managing underwriters to divide the entire underwriting fee according to the original splits. When other firms are involved, the managing underwriters still receive and divide roughly 80 percent of the underwriting fee with the remainder going to other members of the syndicate after all underwriting expenses, including those for underwriters' counsel and the road show, are paid. Interestingly, when syndicates are formed for deals, non-managing underwriters only receive a check for their participation. They do not receive any stock to sell except when there is some special arrangement supported by the issuer.

The selling concession is intended for the underwriters who actually sell the deal. Shares in an offering are directed to two types of investors—institutional investors and retail investors. The selling concessions associated with these shares are sometimes called the institutional "pot" and the retail "pot." Unless otherwise agreed, the institutional pot is divided among the managing underwriters pursuant to the original fee split. The institutional shares themselves are allocated to institutions at the sole discretion of the bookrunner. The retail pot is a different matter. The bookrunner allocates the retail shares among the managing underwriters based on historical practice. Large retail-focused underwriters receive large retail designations from the pot and smaller, institutionally focused firms receive small retail designations. The selling concessions for the retail shares track these designations. Underwriters are free to allocate their retail designations as they chose. Usually 10 percent to 30 percent of an IPO will be set aside for retail investors; the remainder for institutional investors.

To further complicate matters, a "reallowance," typically $0.10 per share, must be noted in the prospectus. This amount is paid out of the selling concession on shares that an underwriter chooses to allow another firm to sell. In effect, the reallowance is a reseller's fee. Despite the disclosure obligation, deals are not distributed using these arrangements. The bookrunner wants to have total control over the institutional allocations and co-managers have no interest in sharing their portions of the retail pot with other firms.

With the terms finalized, Burnham's next task was to set the institutional allocations. Its ECM desk had done all it could to "scrub the book" and understand the orders it contained. Now it was time to specify the shares each order would receive, if any. It was a complicated process that involved many considerations, both for the issuer and the bookrunner. Burnham wanted long-term holders for PEMCO. This helped the deal, the company, and thus the bookrunner's own reputation. But Burnham also knew that some shares needed to be "flipped" to create liquidity in the aftermarket. In deciding who would get what, the desk had to consider their experience and the firm's relationships with the different institutional investors.

Ultimately, all the investors were "cut back" on their requests and many were "bageled" (i.e., given nothing). The largest allocations went to a few top mutual funds and hedge funds that had been vocal about their interest in PEMCO and had a history of holding their positions. Smaller allocations were mixed between longer-term holders and some firms that were expected to flip their shares. Burnham had given the flipper shares to important clients, many of which were hedge funds that paid the firm for its "prime brokerage" services—prime brokerage provides administrative and back office support to hedge funds in exchange for fees and trading activity. Flipping is a low-risk way to make money. After all, underwriters price deals to trade up in the aftermarket and stand ready to purchase shares when they fall below the offering price in order to stabilize the market. Giving a flip is a good way to reward good customers.

While Burnham was working on institutional designations, all of the managing underwriters were allocating their retail designations. The approach for distributing such shares varied by firm. Most investment banks distribute such shares to their top-producing brokers for sale to their top-producing clients. Although there are usually policies that punish retail flippers by denying them access to future deals, it is expected that many of these sales result in flips. Underwriters sometimes also allocate retail shares to institutional clients. This practice is frowned upon by bookrunners, who want complete control over institutional designations, but is unpreventable given the drive banks have to reward important clients.

A Briefing on Retail Stockbrokers

There are several hundred thousand retail stockbrokers housed in more than 170,000 broker-dealer branch offices in the United States. Employed by brokerage firms, they work with individual investors, or retail accounts, to identify and select investment opportunities appropriate to the financial profile of each account. Unlike registered investment advisors, retail brokers do not serve in a fiduciary capacity to their clients and rarely have decision-making authority for investments. Nevertheless, they are obligated to understand and maintain a record of their clients' investment objectives and to provide and execute securities transactions accordingly. Retail brokers carry a Series 7 license, as is the case with other Wall Street professionals transacting business in securities with clients.

Retail brokers come from a very wide range of backgrounds. Whereas some join the profession directly out of college, many pursue the position after other careers. The latter approach can be fruitful to a new broker who has developed a suite of relationships elsewhere that can be used to seed an account base. Brokers are paid based on the commissions they generate from their accounts. Commissions are paid by clients for transactions involving mutual funds, stocks, bonds, and other securities. Generally, retail brokers must maintain a certain production level and receive a fixed percentage of production. This percentage is tiered and often escalates at higher production levels. In a shift to court wealthier clients and thwart a churn-and-burn mentality, some firms tie compensation structures to the amount of client assets in an account base, rather than trading commissions.

Retail brokers are part investment advisor and part salesperson. To be successful over the long-term, they must build and maintain a large portfolio of accounts. This requires gaining the trust and respect of clients. They must understand financial instruments and guide clients to worthwhile strategies and investments. They must also be able to win new clients.

Some junior retail brokers apprentice under established senior brokers. Beyond learning the ropes, these positions allow junior brokers to assume an account package upon their mentor's retirement. Transitions of this sort typically involve a *de facto* buyout in which the senior broker continues as a named representative on the account and receives a portion of the commissions for several years (the approach is similar to the buyout of a dental or medical practice). Commission-splitting arrangements like these must be on file with the broker's employer.

Retail brokers are supervised by managers possessing Series 24 securities licenses. Managers must monitor the activities of their brokers to assure appropriate behavior given the circumstances and investment objectives of clients. They must also take steps necessary to assure appropriate and accurate record keeping and reporting. For the most part, retail brokers operate as small, independent businesses. The manager is focused on compliance and production. So long as these two goals are met, retail brokers are free to conduct their affairs as they see fit.

Discount and online brokerage firms have significantly changed the landscape for retail brokers. In the past, anyone looking to transact in securities more-or-less had to do so through a retail broker and pay the corresponding commission rates in the process. This is no longer the case. Online brokerage services now offer significantly lower transaction costs and an attractive alternative for many individuals. This has increased the number of retail investors on an absolute basis but has also cannibalized traditional retail accounts. In response to this dynamic and the pressures on stock trading commissions discussed earlier, brokerage firms have shifted the focus of their retail brokers to wealthier clients seeking deeper financial advice and higher service levels.

The evening of PEMCO's pricing, a subset of the working group reconvened at the financial printer to file the post-effective pricing amendment with the SEC. This document would be used to print the final prospectus that would be delivered to all buyers in the deal.

The underwriters and the issuer (on behalf of itself and the selling shareholders) also executed the underwriting agreement, a document that now contained the terms of the transaction. In addition, the underwriters received a signed copy of the comfort letter from the accountants. The underwriters now technically owned the shares offered in the deal and would hold them until ownership transferred to the new investors.

As a practical matter, there was very little risk in this proposition. The order book contained more orders than the deal could supply. Investors in the book were expected to take whatever was given to them subject to the price and size parameters of their orders. Failing to do so could result in irreparable harm to the investor's reputation and dealings with the Street.

The deal would officially close with the shares and money trading hands three days after the first trade (this "settlement date" is the customary "T+3" referenced in brokerage parlance). The first trade would occur the morning after the pricing. Only a catastrophic change to the company could unwind the transaction at this point. Only a few IPOs have been cancelled and unwound after pricing and these occurrences were prompted by unlucky events like a critical company factory burning to the ground the day after the offering.

PEMCO's IPO was allocated to 80 institutional accounts. The list of recipients is known as the "pot list." Twenty percent of the deal was set aside for retail investors. This landed at several thousand accounts. Even though the green shoe (i.e., the over-allotment option) had not been exercised, the shares constituting the shoe were allocated as part of the institutional pot. As noted previously, this would give the underwriters a short position that could be filled with shares purchased in the open market if the stock traded below the offering price—a process referred to as market stabilization. The shoe was 15 percent of the offering, which was standard. In rare instances, the lead underwriter may over-allocate the deal and create a short position larger than the 15 percent contractually provided for in the option. Known as going "naked on the shoe," this is done when a deal is almost certain to need stabilization due to weak demand or choppy market conditions.

Table 14.1 PEMCO's IPO Share Allocation

Shares Offered		Shares Allocated	
Transaction	9.500	Institutions	9.025
Green Shoe	1.425	Retail	1.900
Total	10.925	Total	10.925

PEMCO's management team and pricing committee were invited to Burnham's office the next morning to see trading "open" in the company's stock. This, along with any necessary stabilization, was done by the bookrunner. Before opening the stock, the position trader assigned to cover PEMCO's stock worked with Burnham's salespeople and ECM desk to gather all initial buy and sell orders. ECM knew where and how the stock had been allocated. It knew which big orders had been cut back and which likely flippers had been allocated stock. ECM engaged the institutional sales force to target clients accordingly in order to line up buyers and sellers. The institutional pot list had not yet been shared with the other underwriters to help ensure that any orders flowed through Burnham's desk. Once the list of prospective buyers and sellers was accumulated, a price was determined for the opening. This price took into account the demand and supply as well as price levels indicated by all interested parties.

Trading opened around 11 A.M. Eastern time, roughly 90 minutes after the broader market had swung into action. The next several hours were frenetic.

The stock opened at $16, bounced as high as $19, as low as $15.50, and finally closed at $16.25 ("sixteen spot two five" in traders' parlance). A total of almost 20 million shares traded hands. This was typical. Most IPOs trade two to three times as many shares as offered in the deal on their opening day. Much of this volume is driven by shares that trade hands several times. Seventy percent of the trades had come across the bookrunner's desk. The other 30% had gone through a combination of: (1) electronic trading networks that matched buyers and sellers and (2) other brokerage firms, including the other underwriters, that had registered to be "market makers" in PEMCO stock. Nasdaq market makers must maintain bid and ask quotes in their designated stocks and stand ready to purchase or to sell shares at those levels.

A deal's bookrunner has the best information on sources of supply and demand and can therefore provide the most efficient market for buyers and sellers. Institutional investors understand this but sometimes choose to trade their positions elsewhere for other reasons. One of the most notable is to avoid scrutiny. An investor that voiced an intention to be a long-term holder in order to get a big allocation and later decides to sell will often trade through other channels so as to not be discovered.

PEMCO's IPO priced on Thursday, opened for trading on Friday, and closed the following Wednesday—three business days after the trade date. The company and the selling shareholders received their proceeds at the closing, net of the underwriters' gross spread. "Billing and delivery" for the shares to new shareholders was also conducted by the bookrunner at this time (this included all of the original buyers, even though they might have already sold their positions). PEMCO's Registrar and Stock Transfer Agent recorded and documented ownership changes. Physical stock certificates were provided to the new owners, though many purchasers elected to have their shares registered under a nominee name of the Depository Trust Company (DTC). DTC is basically an electronic storage and clearing house for securities that enables brokerage firms and other institutions to efficiently move securities and settle trades electronically. PEMCO's stock had also been assigned a "CUSIP" number by Standard & Poor's CUSIP service bureau. A CUSIP is required for all newly issued securities and is the tool by which all securities are identified for administrative purposes within the brokerage community.

PEMCO's stock continued to perform well during the week following the offering. As such, the bookrunner decided to exercise the over-allotment option (better known as "exercise the shoe") early and not wait until the end of the thirty-day option period. It had previously been decided and disclosed in the red herring that the shoe would be divided between the company and the selling shareholders 50-50 just like the original deal. The parties held a subsequent closing for this part of the transaction. With this completed, the bookrunner, on behalf of the underwriters, was able to close out the 15 percent short position it had created when the stock was originally allocated.

In the final analysis, it had cost PEMCO over $13 million to become a public company. Among other things, legal expenses were $1.2 million, accounting $1.3

million, and printing $200,000. The underwriting fees amounted to $10.7 million. Unlike most of the other fees, those paid to the underwriters had been contingent on the deal closing. Pursuant to the terms of the shareholder agreements from PEMCO's various private financings, the company had covered the offering expenses for the selling shareholders, except for the underwriting fees. All of the offering expenses would not impact PEMCO's income statement and would not impair its second-quarter financial results. Transaction expenses of this sort only impact the shareholders' equity account on the balance sheet.

After closing the IPO and the over-allotment option, PEMCO's ownership was as shown in Table 14.2.

Table 14.2 Initial Public Offering

	Pre-IPO Ownership	Shares Sold	Post-IPO Ownership	
			Shares	%
Larry	16.1%	500,000	11,094,605	14.3%
Jerry	16.1%	500,000	11,094,605	14.3%
Seed Investors	3.6%	1,262,500	1,314,079	1.7%
Alpha & POC	26.3%	-	18,945,433	24.4%
Beta	16.4%	-	11,818,341	15.2%
Carto	12.3%	-	8,877,288	11.4%
Strategics	3.1%	1,200,000	1,019,322	1.3%
Smart	6.3%	2,000,000	2,546,904	3.3%
Public Investors	0.0%		10,925,000	14.1%
Total*		5,462,500	77,635,577	

*PEMCO issued a total of 5,462,000 new shares. Excludes shares to be issued under stock options.

The bookrunner took out a quarter-page advertisement in *The Wall Street Journal* commemorating the transaction. This "tombstone" followed the bookrunner's format and noted the company, the ticker, the underwriters and the deal's total shares and proceeds with the green shoe. A month later, the co-leads organized a "closing dinner" for the entire deal team to celebrate the transaction. It was held in a large, private room of a swank San Francisco restaurant. Complete with excellent food and expensive wines, toasts were made, stories and jokes were shared, and management received a few high-end keepsakes (engraved pens from Tiffany's). All attendees were also given a specially prepared "lucite" to commemorate the transaction (in essence a large plastic paperweight displaying a small copy of the tombstone). Pursuant to the never-ending quest among junior bankers to create interesting and clever lucites (or deal cubes or deal toys as they are also known), the banking analyst and associate at the bookrunner had devised a large transparent Lucite encasing a small globe surrounded by miniature perpetual energy machines. Etched on the front was a copy of the tombstone.

While the globe theme was nothing new for deal cubes, it played well to the audience.

OTHER OBSERVATIONS ON INITIAL PUBLIC OFFERINGS

PEMCO's IPO followed a conventional path and timeline though its brief description lacked many of the issues, drama, and delays often found in deals. When considering an IPO, companies may contemplate other approaches to becoming public based on their unique circumstances. Notable variations include the following:

Dual-track Process

A company may choose to entertain acquisition offers during an IPO. When an IPO is undertaken with the intent to generate interest from potential acquirers, the approach is referred to as a "dual-track" process. The offering creates publicly filed documentation that can be used to quietly seek a buyer and enable interested parties to assess the business. The IPO also provides a "threat" to interested parties that a business will no longer be available for acquisition, at least not at the same price. If pursuing a dual track, a company must have the qualifications to go public and be prepared to complete the offering if a satisfactory acquisition offer does not surface before pricing. Generally, the lead manager is selected to work as the company's sellside advisor. Other underwriters are kept in the dark and may expend substantial time and energy on the IPO before seeing the company disappear in a transaction for which they receive no compensation. In light of the market and regulatory challenges previously discussed for smaller public companies, many IPOs over the past several years have involved dual-track processes, with several being sold in the process. Assuming an attractive price is on the table, being acquired has been the preferred exit strategy for many private companies.

Online Offerings

The explosive growth of the internet was accompanied by the advent of the online IPO. The first such offering was completed by, of all things, a small brewery located in New York City (Spring Street Brewing Co.). Advocating the distribution power of the Web and the fairness of opening up IPOs to investors otherwise excluded by Wall Street's traditional approach of allocating shares to institutions and large brokerage clients, a couple of investment banks emerged in the late 1990s to offer online offerings to interested companies. A few companies took the bait and conducted online auctions for their IPOs.

The marketing and pricing process for most of these involved "Dutch auctions" whereby interested investors submitted orders indicating a number of shares and a share price at which they would be willing to buy the IPO. The deals were completed at the highest price containing the sufficient number of shares to close. Those investors indicating that price or better received shares at the ultimate offering price. As a side note, the Dutch auction pricing structure is often used in public tender offers conducted for public company acquisitions and stock repurchases.

While holding much promise, the online offering model has been a disappointment. Even Google struggled with the approach, pricing its online IPO far below original expectations. Google subsequently abandoned the model for its follow-on offerings. Each IPO is unique, requires investor education and, in essence, must be sold. The internet offering model as currently constructed fails to deliver what is necessary to produce truly successful transactions.

Shell-corporation Reverse Mergers

There are public companies with limited to no real operations. Referred to as "shell corporations," these entities are offered for sale to private companies considering an IPO as a means of becoming public without the fees and expenses associated with a traditional offering process. They are also offered to businesses that do not have the qualifications to pursue a normal IPO but seek liquidity for shareholders. When a shell corporation is purchased, the buyer merges into the public entity, thus becoming its operations and identity.

Going public through a shell corporation is good in theory but bad in practice. It may save money in the short run, but it does not provide the right tone and framework to lure the interest of institutional investors and such investors remain the dominant source of capital in the market. Shell-corporation deals are viewed with suspicion and considered by many to be the realm of "pump and dump" penny stockbrokers. Companies with the option of taking the traditional IPO path are well advised to do so if they want to create the right impression with investors. Underwritten deals are also accompanied by research and trading/market making commitments. Both can be critical to educating investors, providing liquidity, and generating investor interest in a story.

Blank-check Companies

Over the years, there have been a number of publicly offered vehicles, the sole missions of which have been to acquire yet-to-be identified businesses. These entities raise pools of "blind" capital and are commonly referred to as "blank-check" companies. Recently, the structure of choice for these vehicles has been the special-purpose acquisition company or "SPAC." SPACs are formed and taken public to buy businesses, usually within a stated industry. In essence, they are well-capitalized shell companies. Generally, they are headed by a notable business personality or buyout specialist who is tasked with finding and buying an attractive business with a combination of cash from the IPO and company stock. The acquisition, assuming it is approved by the SPAC's shareholders, becomes the primary operation of the public entity. Being acquired by a SPAC can enable a private company to become a public one while providing full or partial liquidity for its shareholders in the process.

Carve-outs and Spin-offs

IPOs are sometimes conducted for subsidiaries of existing public companies. Their purpose is to allow the smaller entity to grow without being encumbered by the parent because of issues such as lack of capital, management distractions, and competitive concerns. They are also done to unlock shareholder value. While buried within a larger organization, a division may not be valued by public share-holders in the same fashion as stand-alone competitors. For example, if public comparables for a division trade at 30X earnings and the parent only trades at 12X earnings, the parent's board of directors may look to take the division public to eliminate the discrepancy, thereby creating value for shareholders and allowing the business to access capital at more attractive rates. Once public, the parent may retain shares not sold in the IPO, or may distribute them to its shareholders in a tax-free manner. When the goal is to distribute the shares, which could also have been done without an IPO, the offering is conducted to establish trading, research, and value before the shares land in the hands of the parent's investors.

Personal Observations on IPOs

1. *IPOs come in waves.* If you see a successful IPO, others are sure to follow from the same industry. With input from investment bankers, executives and private investors track new-issue activity within their industries very closely. When financing windows open up and the public demonstrates its appetite for certain opportunities, several companies invariably jump into the fray to exploit the demand. This is especially true when a pioneering transaction occurs. If a first-of-its-kind IPO does well, similar businesses are quick to follow suit. Frequently, the first company maintains a leadership position in the minds of investors and outperforms the followers. Other times, a follower with better characteristics can cause investors to swap out of the pioneer and into it.
2. *If given the option, only a fool would not use a traditional underwriting process.* Other choices might be less expensive in the near term but not in the long term. A traditional process creates the broadest exposure and strongest ongoing support for a company and its stock. These factors translate into more interested buyers, higher stock prices, and lower-cost capital.
   Although the traditional IPO process is inefficient, it works. The multi-month ordeal can be tremendously time-consuming and draining. It is not efficient—not even close. The first half entails armies of

bankers, lawyers, and accountants sitting around conference rooms debating everything from the composition of an offering to the use of every single word in the prospectus. The second half involves weeks of investor meetings and umpteen miles of travel throughout the country (if not the globe). There are ways in which the overall process could be more focused and absorb fewer resources but, as it stands, it usually accomplishes its primary goals. It allows the underwriters and other sellside professionals to gain a thorough understanding of a business, disclose it appropriately for investors, and uncover issues and problems that need to be rectified or revealed. It also provides the opportunity for a broad group of public investors to learn about an investment, engage directly with management, and do their homework before buying a newly issued stock.

3. *When selecting underwriters, bigger is not always better.* When considering an IPO (or other public securities offering, for that matter), many prospective issuers instantly gravitate to selecting a bulge bracket firm to lead the transaction. They do so because they believe that bigger firms will provide them with more credibility, greater distribution resources, and stronger aftermarket support. Although a few firms can provide a certain prestige, the assumptions just noted are wrong as often as they are right. What matters is focus and expertise. A firm with the right combination of both can be every bit as effective as a larger or more established firm in selling and supporting a company. In fact, some are more so because their reputations hinge upon the success of every one of their deals and client references.

4. *High-flying IPOs rarely defy gravity forever.* Even those that ultimately become huge, successful public companies often see their stock prices collapse at some point during their maturation process. The pattern is common: A company with a huge market opportunity and tremendous growth prospects goes public. Its stock trades up after the deal to valuation levels far beyond the comparables and continues to climb as, quarter after quarter, it puts up financial performance that exceeds market expectations. But then the growth slows and the stock price craters—maybe not below the IPO price but still far below its peak. Momentum investors ditch the stock and value-types step into it. Earlier investors make money and later investors lose money. When a stock is shooting to the moon, an issuer and its inexperienced investors should prepare themselves for this inevitability. It is almost guaranteed to happen.

5. *IPOs are not well suited to retail ownership.* Except in rare circumstances involving well-known consumer brands, IPOs are best left to institutional investors. They are risky and require substantial investor education before sound purchase decisions can be made. Attempts to democratize the process, as well as management efforts to push retail distribution, overlook these facts and also ignore that

retail investors ultimately benefit from successful IPOs via their mutual fund holdings (the largest buyers of IPOs). Most retail investors who do prosper in IPOs do so at the expense of the issuer, mutual fund investors, and other institutions serving broader constituents. They are the flippers who buy shares, hope for a price pop, and immediately sell them, putting downward price pressure in the market.

CHAPTER 15

Public Investors and Life as a Young Public Company

> ➤ How existing public companies interface with investors and other stock market constituents.

> ➤ The role, activities, and careers of trading professionals on the sellside and buyside.

> ➤ How companies prepare and conduct quarterly earnings calls with investors.

> ➤ The role, activities, and structure of institutional investors in the securities market—namely mutual funds and hedge funds.

As PEMCO closed out its second fiscal quarter and first six weeks as a public company, the company's stock continued to rise. By June 30, it reached $18.50, a 32 percent increase from the IPO. As evidenced by the typical post-offering decline in average daily trading volume, the stock now rested primarily with longer-term holders. For the most part, these investors would stick with the stock, and possibly add to their positions, so long as the company met or exceeded expectations and the stock continued to perform.

The names of the investors and the size of their current stakes were not known to the underwriters or PEMCO. All of these constituents were now aware of the original institutional allocations but none of them was aware of the subsequent ownership changes, at least not with any certainty. PEMCO's stock registrar was willing to disclose information it had on registered owners to the company but most of the institutional ownership was held via DTC, which was not at liberty to divulge such data. Through DTC, the company could only communicate with shareholders via required mailings such as the proxy statement and the annual shareholders report.

The trading desks of the underwriters had purchased and sold positions for many institutions, but this information was not shared between them or with the company. PEMCO's CFO had developed a dialogue with the position traders at each firm responsible for market making in PEMCO's stock. The traders had given the company some color on trading activity but were not permitted to divulge specifics. They would not even provide these details to their own investment bankers, fearing the bankers might succumb to client pressure and relay the information. Trading activity for clients is confidential, nonpublic information. Therefore, commentary is limited to statements such as "a large existing holder has been reducing its position" or "a new investor has been accumulating stock."

A Briefing on Trading

The term "trader" is often used by the press to refer to anyone who makes money buying and selling securities or other assets. The term is used to describe celebrity hedge fund managers and buyout experts alike. By the *Webster's* definition, this is correct. By the nomenclature of Wall Street professions, however, it is not. Traders are a narrower group of professionals employed by sellside and buyside firms. They buy and sell securities for their clients or organizations and have an expertise in achieving the best prices and managing risks in doing so. They are liquidity experts who, in fact, may have no role or a limited role in determining what to buy or what to sell. They are focused on when and how to make a purchase or sale.

Trading across Wall Street is divided by security type. There are stock traders, bond traders, convertible traders, options traders, futures traders, commodities traders, currency traders, and so on. Technology improvements and advances in financial theory have expanded most of these markets and opened new ones over the past decade. Better analytical tools and computing speeds now enable improved risk management and profit pursuit in dealings with simple as well as more complicated financial instruments. That being said, some markets remain more efficient than others—they have more history, more players, and are better understood.

The activities of traders are tailored to the dynamics of their particular markets. Within the sellside (i.e., trading within the brokerage division of an investment bank), for instance, stock traders operate in a more volatile and liquid market than do bond traders. Most stocks trade tens of thousands of shares every day and have listing affiliations that provide real-time pricing data. They also have individual characteristics that can cause prices to move significantly on any given day. Because of these factors, sellside stock traders move their positions quickly and try not to hold inventory. Many bonds, on the other hand, trade infrequently, have no real-time price quotation system, and are valued based upon the broader credit market. In addition, they trade in thousand-dollar increments (a bond trading at par or 100 means it trades for $1,000) and are primarily for institutional investors. As a result of these factors, bond traders, with the aid of sophisticated risk-management tools, maintain an inventory of positions from which they sell positions and buy positions.

With respect to stocks, brokerage floors have two trading groups aside from the sales traders discussed in Chapter 13—listed traders and OTC traders. Listed traders work in exchange-listed stocks and function through affiliated floor brokers on the relevant exchanges. They may also execute trades electronically on or off the exchanges. OTC traders work primarily in Nasdaq stocks and conduct all of their trading electronically—over the Nasdaq network or otherwise.

Known as position traders, those within these two groups are assigned stocks for which they have trading responsibility. These assignments come from the head of trading. Stocks within an industry are often influenced by the same news and market events. As such, the stock roster for most position traders (commonly called a "list" or a "pad") is tied to specific industries. Successful senior traders gain a feel for and develop a strong understanding of supply and demand dynamics for stocks within their industries.

Position traders make buy and sell decisions on behalf of an investment bank in response to client orders generated by sales traders and research salespeople. Some decisions involve risk-free "cross" trades between third parties whereas others put firm capital at risk and involve buying and selling positions for the firm's own account. The long and short positions created from these trades are managed by the position trader. A position trader's "book" of at-risk trades generally operates at a loss. The objective of position traders is to have low "loss ratios"—losses that fall below the commissions generated by the orders. Position trading should not be confused with the proprietary trading operations found at many investment banks that, in effect, are internally operated hedge funds designed to make money on stock positions themselves (i.e., not for facilitating client trades). Position traders in Nasdaq stocks also serve as the market makers for such stocks.

Buyside traders execute trades on behalf of institutional investors. Large buyside institutions such as mutual funds and hedge funds employ traders who serve the liquidity needs of their funds. Smaller institutions have more limited trading operations and may outsource the trading function entirely to firms that specialize in this area. The primary mission for buyside traders is to obtain the best execution for their trades. To achieve this goal, they: (1) trade through sellside traders, (2) trade through electronic networks, (3) trade on exchanges directly, (4) trade directly with other institutions, and (5) basically do whatever is necessary to purchase or sell a position at the best price.

In the context of trading, the buyside also includes business entities with ties to the underlying assets of particular securities, namely futures. For example, energy and commodities producers have legions of traders in the futures market who write and trade contracts that are designed to protect the economic value of their production. Likewise, large consumers of these products and services have traders who assure predictable supply and pricing for their future needs. Along similar lines, corporations with distribution and supply arrangements throughout the world actively trade in currencies to stabilize their revenues and expenses.

For stocks, one of the key measures used by buyside traders to guide their execution strategies is the daily volume weighted average price, or VWAP. Calculated by dividing the gross dollar amount of all trades in a stock during a given day by the total number of shares traded, buyside traders seek to buy at or below this level and sell at or above this level. Because large purchases or sales can drive stocks up or down, buyside traders often work with sellside traders to execute trades relative to the VWAP over the course of one or more days. Many brokerage firms have programs that do this automatically through electronic networks for larger, more liquid stocks.

Like most jobs on Wall Street, there is no school to teach the practical skills for becoming a trader. Although there are courses on financial engineering and game theory, trading is a learned profession. Most traders are hired out of college or business school and apprentice under more senior traders. Young recruits generally have strong quantitative backgrounds, particularly for positions concerning more complicated financial instruments. When hired, a prospective trader first serves in an entry-level position, performing data input functions on the trading desk. After one or more years of this (sometimes less), one becomes a trading assistant and is assigned to sit next to and to learn from a senior trader while continuing to perform mostly clerical tasks. Career progression beyond this point depends upon success and senior-level attrition.

On the sellside, a trader can advance from trading assistant to becoming a full trader in as few as three or four years. Once anointed, a new sellside trader is typically given a handful of "names" to trade. The trading list is expanded when the trader has proven himself or herself and more securities become available through departures or realignments on the trading desk. Compensation is dictated largely by the commissions generated in their al-lotted names and their loss ratios. As for the buyside, the career track for traders varies but generally follows a similar progression. Compensation and promotion hinge upon effectiveness and, more specifically, the ability to con-tain trading costs (i.e., commissions) and to find buyers and sellers with the best terms. It is worth noting that changes in technology have automated many of the functions previously performed by would-be traders. As a result, firms have significantly downsized their trading desks, and the career choice to becoming a trader is now much less available and much less predictable than in the past.

As part of their trading efforts, the buyside and sellside also hire serious academics with degrees like PhDs in mathematics and financial theory. These individuals work as teams to develop complex trading models, algorithms, and strategies to manage risk and generate profit. Such efforts are proprietary and treated as closely guarded secrets.

Investors were free to discuss their holdings with PEMCO and several had done so in their post-offering discussions with management. The underwriters and the company's IR firm had encouraged PEMCO to re-engage and open a dialogue with the institutions that had been allocated shares. The company had wisely accepted this advice and contacted each institutional investor using information provided by the bookrunner and business cards and notes gathered during the road show. Most investors were receptive and, in fact, had been looking to establish further communications with the company.

Although helpful in tracking ownership, commentary from investors must be taken with a grain of salt. Investors are under no obligation to reveal the truth about their holdings and sometimes mislead companies to gain information. Institutional investors only need to disclose their positions accurately in filings with the SEC. These filings occur when any entity or individual accumulates a position equaling 5 percent or greater in a company. Certain institutions must also file to disclose their ownership stakes at the end of each quarter. This must be done within forty-five days of the end of the quarter. Given the delay, the utility of these filings for companies, the sellside, and the buyside is limited.

The retail ownership of its stock was even more opaque to PEMCO. The original retail allocations were not disclosed to the company and individuals are not required to file any documentation regarding their stakes (except those involving 5 percent or greater positions). Even the stock registrar would not know most of the retail owners. Retail positions are generally held in "street name." Brokerage firms aggregate all shares held in retail accounts under their custody and hold these shares in their names. Individual owners retain voting authority over these shares and receive proxy statements and other shareholder mailings through the firms.

Along with ownership, PEMCO began tracking the trading activity of its underwriters and other brokerage firms during this time. Willingness to commit capital to trading in order to provide liquidity to public shareholders had been an important consideration in selecting the underwriters. PEMCO wanted to know whether its bankers were following through on their commitments. PEMCO was provided a monthly statement from Nasdaq noting which firms had been responsible for trading its stock. PEMCO also consulted other sources for this information, including AutEx, a service that reflects trading data voluntarily submitted by market makers. There were discrepancies between the AutEx and Nasdaq figures. PEMCO later learned that, in the battle for market share and bragging rights, some traders are guilty of submitting exaggerated trading data.

Shortly after the IPO, research had been initiated on the company. It began with two investment banks that had not been selected to underwrite the deal. The research was comprehensive, thoughtful, and positive. Both analysts had published reports of thirty-plus pages. Their actions made a favorable impression on management and the board. If and when PEMCO conducted another transaction, these firms had improved their chances of being involved.

The underwriters were not allowed to initiate research coverage until forty days after the IPO. Three followed this schedule. Of the remaining two, one initiated two days later. The other would not initiate for several months, much to the chagrin of management. Three of the four timely reports were also received favorably by the company. They were thorough, well written, and generally shared management's perspective on the story and opportunity. They also contained "buy" ratings and twelve-month price targets in the $20s. The fourth report contained a "hold" rating. Published by the analyst who had voiced concerns over valuation at the time of the final commitment committee meetings, the report placed a price target on PEMCO stock below its current levels. Though they suspected this might occur given the earlier discussions with the analyst, management was not pleased.

By early July—roughly two months after the IPO—the company had six firms covering the stock. This put PEMCO well ahead of most public companies, well over half of which currently have no research coverage or only one covering firm. Fortunately, the revenue and earnings estimates contained in all of PEMCO's research reports were consistent. They varied modestly but not enough to cause confusion in the market or set expectations that the company was concerned about meeting.

Inconsistent estimates can be a real problem, particularly when one or two analysts have numbers far ahead of the Street's "consensus" numbers. These create false hope and can reflect poorly on a company's ability to provide appropriate guidance. Investors are critical of the latter, albeit unfairly, since a company can only do so much to influence opinion within the legal parameters of today's fair disclosure regulations.

Leading up to initiation of coverage, the research analysts had contacted and quizzed PEMCO's management on questions regarding strategy, operations, market opportunity, and business model. PEMCO was free to comment on matters in the public record but could not reference nonpublic items such as its performance in the current quarter (ending June 30). This would be publicly released in late July or early August. To prevent inadvertent disclosures, many public companies avoid analysts and investors and even refuse to attend investment conferences near the end of a quarter until earnings are released. During these times, executives and other corporate insiders are prevented from buying and selling stock pursuant to internal "black-out period" policies.

Once the research reports were prepared, they were submitted to internal editorial and compliance groups at the investment banks to assure that they contained proper support and disclosures. Among other things, the reports needed to state: (1) whether the firm had done or intended to pursue banking business with the company, (2) ratings on other companies referenced in the report, and (3) the firm's mix of buy, sell, and hold recommendations. It is worth noting that different firms have different rating systems. Some are simple and contain just buys, sells, and holds. Others are much more detailed and reference characteristics such as the speculative nature of a stock.

Once completed and approved for release, the research reports and their contents were presented by the analysts to their respective sales forces. They were also distributed electronically to interested clients at each firm. Beforehand, the ratings and earnings estimates were publicly announced and posted to research tracking services, including First Call, Nelson's, Zacks, Multex, and I/B/E/S (Institutional Brokers' Estimate System). Research opinions and the mere act of initiating or updating coverage can have market-moving consequences. As such, there cannot be a preferential release of this information. Analysts and companies carefully guard even the existence of pending research.

PEMCO released its second-quarter earnings after the market closed on August 1, well within the window required by the SEC and the Nasdaq listing rules. A week beforehand, the company issued a press release noting the date and indicating that management would hold a conference call to discuss performance at 5 P.M. Eastern time on the day of the earnings release. The conference call could be heard over the internet via a link on the company's Web site. It could also be accessed directly with a toll-free telephone number. Those dialing-in would be permitted to participate in the question-and-answer session with management following prepared comments.

Leading up to August 1, the CFO, internal accounting team and outside auditors had worked diligently to prepare the financials. The numbers would not be audited but would be "reviewed" by the outside accounting firm—audits typically only occur for year-end numbers. Management wanted to make sure they were accurate, particularly given current guidelines requiring a CEO and CFO to sign off on the accuracy of the financials. If there were problems with the numbers, the signatories could be held personally liable to investors. PEMCO's audit committee—comprised of selected members of the board—also held a conference call to review the quarterly earnings release.

The earnings release was put out on the newswires at 4:30 P.M. Eastern time, after the market had closed. It contained a summary balance sheet and income statement comparing the current period to that of the prior year. It also contained a brief discussion of notable business developments and trends as well as the business outlook. Management had worked with its IR firm and lead bankers on the release. They had all debated what future guidance to include, if any, and settled on expected revenue and earnings per share for the next quarter and the current year. Management would provide a narrow range of expectations for these figures. This was a common approach (though, increasingly, public companies are reluctant to give meaningful guidance for fear of being mistaken and facing shareholder lawsuits). PEMCO filed its earnings release with the SEC on a Form 8-K (the form for disclosing material developments). It would file its 10-Q encompassing more detailed quarterly financials shortly afterward.

Thirty participants dialed into PEMCO's earnings call, including investors, research analysts, and even some of the company's investment bankers. More joined over the internet. All had PEMCO's earnings release in hand and all wanted to hear firsthand what the company had to say about the quarter and the outlook for the future.

The call went well. PEMCO had exceeded financial expectations for the quarter. It had done so in terms of both quantity and quality. The company had beat the Street's projections on an absolute basis and had done so by growing sales and maintaining margins rather than benefiting from an unusually low tax rate or other one-time accounting benefit. The underwriting team was happy, and relieved. The bankers believed this would occur but could not be sure until it "hit the tape."

The company had a broad line of PEMs in the market. Sales were brisk, and PEMCO continued to gain traction with new design wins and OEM partners. Though the company's first foray into the automotive market was not yet available to consumers (the car would be released very late in the year), PEMCO had secured two more vehicle design wins. These were mentioned on a no-names basis during the call.

The call lasted about an hour. The question-and-answer period was uneventful. Other than a handful of detailed questions concerning margins, product mix, and future direction, it was mainly punctuated by congratulatory comments from well-wishers. When it was over, the research analysts with coverage on PEMCO prepared some remarks. They also tweaked their models and made upward revisions to their revenue and earnings predictions to reflect the quarter's performance. These would be shared with their sales forces, clients, and the market before the next day's open. PEMCO's stock traded to an all-time high of $21 on August 2.

The rest of August was relatively uneventful. Besides a few calls and meetings with investment bankers, PEMCO had very little interaction with Wall Street during the month. This was to be expected. August is notoriously slow in the capital markets. Most players disappear for the month's final two weeks and begin checking out beforehand. Trading is light and few financings get done. It was a welcome break for PEMCO's management team. They relished the time to regroup and focus on their business.

A Briefing on Institutional Investors

Several types of institutions invest in public securities. Those responsible for the bulk of this activity are mutual funds and hedge funds. Investing the capital of individuals and other institutions such as pension funds and foundations, these two fund categories have combined assets amounting to over $14 trillion. Not all mutual funds and hedge funds buy IPOs; in fact, most do not and prefer the characteristics of more seasoned securities.

Most mutual funds are part of larger fund "complexes" or "families" that contain a number of funds dedicated to different investing strategies. The largest complexes have funds addressing separate geographies, industries, securities, and market capitalizations. Smaller organizations are usually dedicated to a particular sector (e.g., technology) or investing style (e.g., growth, value, income, growth and income, or growth-at-a-reasonable price—GARP). Mutual funds may acquire securities without a publicly traded market. Given the challenges of valuing such securities and obtaining liquidity for them, however, this practice is not very common.

Individual mutual funds within a complex or, in some instances, a few closely related funds, are managed by distinct investment teams. These teams usually contain one or two portfolio managers (PMs) and several junior staff, namely buyside analysts. The PMs are responsible for all of a fund's investment decisions. Within the parameters of a fund's charter, PMs have final say over how capital is deployed. They work closely with their teams to identify opportunities, analyze companies, and monitor existing and potential investments. All of these players interface directly with companies as well as institutional salespeople and research analysts from the sellside. Some organizations are structured with separate research departments dedicated to servicing all of the funds within a complex. These research departments loosely mirror those found on the sellside, with individuals dedicated to covering and providing insights on different companies, industries, and financial products.

As a general rule, there are two fundamental investment approaches for mutual funds. Most are run by stock pickers who focus on finding and buying individual stocks that are deemed to be attractive because of their fundamental characteristics (business model and opportunity) or their technical characteristics (how they trade in the market). Others are indexers who buy pools of stocks that are intended to mirror the performance of the market or a particular index. The most notable of these include S&P 500 index funds. By-and-large, indexers purchase stocks without any consideration for their underlying businesses. They simply follow the composition of their noted index or use other, primarily quantitative, screens to compose portfolios. Some mutual fund managers hold themselves out as stock pickers but secretly behave as indexers—the so called "closet indexers."

Momentum investing, whether or not admitted, has become a common investment strategy for stock pickers. Rather than looking at a company's long-term potential, momentum investors focus on catalysts that can drive near-term performance. Every quarter, they try to identify companies that are likely to exceed earnings expectations or other noteworthy performance metrics. Knowing that such events fuel investor interest and higher stock prices, they spend time on these rather than examining relative valuations and fundamentals. They also quickly abandon stocks that fail to perform. Many stock pickers have adopted a momentum strategy in response to the behavior of their own fund investors. Without strong quarterly performance, finicky fund investors move money out of funds. They do not take a longer-term perspective and, as a result, neither do their fund managers. Self-preservation does not allow it.

As a related theme, many fund managers are guilty of "window dressing" their portfolios. This practice entails selling poorly performing stocks and buying strongly performing stocks just prior to the end of a fund's public reporting period. Done for marketing purposes, the reallocation allows a fund manager to disclose an attractive set of holdings instead of stocks that suggest questionable judgment and investment practices.

Beyond the investment-management side of the business, mutual fund organizations have client-services personnel who are responsible for courting and supporting fund investors. Some staff call centers and sales offices to aid and lure retail clientele. Others work closely with institutional investors and distribution partners that receive compensation for selling the funds to their clients. Both of these groups require direct attention and sophisticated sales efforts, complete with face-to-face meetings and presentations demonstrating the strength and stability of the fund offerings. Many pension funds, foundations, endowments, and similar institutions allocate capital and outsource investment decision making to portfolio managers within mutual fund complexes. Depending on the size of the allocation, this capital is either added to existing mutual funds or managed separately. Distribution partners include retail brokerage firms, retirement account administrators, and registered investment advisors (sometimes known as licensed financial consultants). Because of their interest in protecting their clients and reputations, distribution partners carefully examine the funds they recommend and must be convinced of the merits of an investment. Such partners generally maintain a small recommended list of funds in each fund category and are solicited by client-service professionals from several fund families.

The career progression and backgrounds of those in the mutual fund industry are similar to those found on the sellside. Investment-management personnel are usually hired out of top-tier universities and business schools and apprentice in a fashion akin to sellside research analysts. Some are also hired into the industry from the sellside, usually from research departments at investment banks. Depending on the firm, senior-level attrition rates, and their own investment acumen, investment-management professionals can become junior portfolio managers in as few as five or six years. Those in client services follow a path similar to sellside institutional salespeople. They possess varying backgrounds and first serve to support senior account executives and then receive their own client packages after a few years.

Mutual funds operate as either open ended or closed ended. Open-ended funds allow new investors and directly receive and invest capital when an investor makes a purchase. When sales or "redemptions" occur, open-ended funds must fund them out of cash reserves or by selling securities. The quoted price for an open-ended mutual fund refers to the "net asset value" (NAV) of the securities and cash in the fund divided by the number of fund shares outstanding. Closed-ended funds are different. After receiving a certain amount of capital, they close themselves to new investors and then trade like stocks. When fund shares are bought and sold, the mutual fund is not involved. Money changes hands between buyer and seller. The trading value for such shares may be higher or lower than the actual NAV for such funds.

Most mutual funds are open-ended. Even though larger funds can be harder to manage, particularly those focused on less liquid securities, larger funds receive more fees, thus creating an economic incentive for managers to leave them open to new investors. The incentive structure for distribution partners also favors open-ended funds.

Closely related to closed-ended mutual funds are exchange-traded funds (ETFs). ETFs blend the characteristics of closed-end funds and open-ended index funds. They trade like stocks and track indexes like the S&P 500 or narrower, more exotic targets, such as stocks in a particular industry or the price of certain commodities. ETFs operate with relatively low expenses and contract or expand according to investor redemptions or inflows. Their daily composition is driven by computer algorithms that make purchase and sell decisions based on strictly defined considerations. Given their benefits, the ranks of ETFs have swelled in recent years.

Mutual funds are closely regulated and governed by the Investment Company Act of 1940, the Investment Advisers Act of 1940, and other securities laws. Funds are required to make periodic disclosures to their investors regarding their management, investments, performance, fees, and expenses. Funds must also provide this information to prospective investors. Along with disclosure obligations, mutual funds possess legal limitations regarding their actual investments. Historically, they were not permitted to use leverage to acquire securities (i.e., buy on margin) and could not "short" securities (i.e., sell borrowed securities on the belief that their values will decline and can then be replaced by securities purchased at lower prices). These limitations were designed to protect investors and ensure liquidity for fund redemptions. Most mutual funds can still not perform these functions. However, there has been an easing of the rules and a handful of newer funds are beginning to deploy so-called 130/30 or 120/20 strategies. Both of these use margin and shorting. In the case of a 130/30 approach, a fund will short $30 of stocks for every $100 of invested equity. It will then take the proceeds of the $30 short to purchase an additional $30 of stock, thereby resulting in a $130 long position and a $30 short position.

Mutual funds are overseen by boards of directors responsible for guarding and protecting the interest of fund investors. According to the Investment Company Act of 1940, at least 40 percent of a board's members must be independent (there are several initiatives to raise this percentage to above a majority). These directors cannot be employees of the fund's investment advisor or principal underwriter. Most mutual fund families are governed by a single board and managed by a single investment advisor retained by the board to operate all funds within the family. The investment advisor employs all personnel associated with the funds and oversees administration and all day-to-day activities. It is typically affiliated with the principal underwriter for the funds, which is responsible for distributing the funds to investors (directly and through separate broker-dealers). The organizational structure of mutual fund companies is not readily evident to investors. As a practical matter, the identity of a fund family is that of the investment advisor. PMs and certain employees may leave or be asked to resign but investment advisors almost never change.

Hedge funds are more loosely regulated and are not constrained by the same investment limitations as mutual funds. Structurally, they are similar to private equity and venture capital funds. Funded by institutions and wealthy individuals, they are limited partnerships. The disclosure obligations and the ability of investors to build or liquidate positions are dictated by the terms of the partnership agreement and not by regulations contained in the securities laws. Generally, investors can redeem hedge fund positions only once a quarter with thirty-plus-days prior notice. Some hedge funds limit redemptions to once a year or longer. In theory, this allows them to take a longer-term approach to investments than their mutual fund counterparts. Hedge fund operators usually receive a 1.5 percent to 2 percent management fee on funds under management plus a 20 percent carry on profits of a fund. A few funds have as much as a 3 percent management fee and a 50 percent carry. Hedge funds are active investors in public securities and, subject to the objectives outlined in their formation documents, may also invest in options, private securities, commodities, currencies, derivatives, real estate, art, or whatever. They can also use leverage and can short securities. Hedge funds have great latitude in their investment tactics and, as such, are widely considered, at least theoretically, to be better investment vehicles than mutual funds. As a result, their ranks have swelled over the past decade. There are now more than 8,000 hedge funds controlling over $2 trillion.

Most hedge funds rely upon their ability to use leverage and short securities in order to generate returns and "alpha," a term referring to investment performance that exceeds a fund's benchmark, such as the S&P 500 or some other relevant index. They also short securities to hedge investments and reduce volatility. For each dollar invested in a hedge fund, most usually invest in a combination of long and short positions. The relative size of each creates either a "net long" or a "net short" exposure for the fund. A set of positions, for example, might be $1 of equity being leveraged to invest in $1.20 long and $0.80 short for a total gross exposure of $2 and a net long exposure of $0.40 ($1.20 minus $0.80).

Shorting requires access to securities that can be borrowed in large quantities. This access requires strong relationships with large brokerage firms. Under standard arrangements, brokerage firms hold custody over securities in client accounts and are permitted to lend those securities. Along with other investors, hedge funds borrow these for short sales. In doing so, they must comply with margin requirements. These dictate that sufficient equity be in place to cover losses if a shorted security increases in value.

A big fear for those who short is the dreaded "buy-in." If the securities borrowed by a short seller are sold by their rightful owner, the short seller must replace them immediately irrespective of whether the stock has gone up or gone down. This can be done with the broker making a substitution with other shares that are available to be borrowed or with the broker stepping into the market to purchase the shares and close the position on behalf of the short seller. The short seller does not know which securities in the brokerage house's custody it is borrowing. Identical securities within "the borrow" held by a broker are fungible. Given this, hedge funds do everything they can to ensure that someone else, and not them, is hit with a buy-in when inventory declines. Larger fee and commission generators tend to be the most protected in these situations.

Shorting, at least when done on margin, is a form of leverage. Returns are produced in part by borrowing other people's money. Many hedge funds use leverage aggressively for both their long and short positions to supercharge their equity returns. Any returns above the cost of the borrowed capital inure to the benefit of a fund's investors. Of course, leverage works both ways. Placing a big, highly leveraged bet on the wrong investment can destroy performance and wipe out equity. Several hedge funds and their investors have experienced such collapses. Month after month, a fund puts up great performance and then, bam, it has a 20 percent down month.

Hedge funds obtain their leverage from investment banks, traditional banks, and, more recently, bond financings—whatever method provides the least-expensive capital.

Hedge funds are spearheaded by a diverse group of money managers. Most share three traits—investor relationships, strong reputations, and investment acumen. Many are defectors from mutual funds seeking less short-term performance pressure and more attractive compensation packages (the "2 and 20" fee structure in hedge funds compares favorably to the relatively low expense ratios used to compensate managers in mutual funds). Others are former employees of other hedge funds who decided to go it alone. Some also hail from the sellside—successful private client brokers, research analysts, traders, and institutional salespeople. The career path is generally less structured and defined than those found in other institutions on Wall Street. It is driven primarily by the ability to produce returns and make money for clients.

Large hedge fund organizations often operate several funds and are organized similarly to mutual fund complexes—complete with investment teams, research departments, and trading personnel. The operation of smaller funds may be limited to only a handful of investment professionals. Most smaller funds rely upon the "prime brokerage" operations offered to them by larger investment banks for office space, trade execution, record keeping, and administrative support. These services are provided for fees and allow the banks to gather securities in custodial accounts that can be lent to other clients on margin for additional fees. They also create a captive audience for products like margin loans. Some hedge funds are affiliated with mutual fund complexes and investment banks.

Related to hedge funds and worth mentioning are "funds of funds," which pool assets from smaller accredited investors and invest in hedge funds, venture capital funds, and private equity funds. Funds of funds screen for good fund investment opportunities, monitor ongoing performance, and allow smaller investors to access funds that would otherwise require much larger minimum investments (often $1 million or more versus as little as $100,000 for a fund of funds). For these services, funds of funds typically receive a 0.5 percent management fee and a 5 percent carry on profits (above the fees paid to the underlying funds). Like their targeted investments, these funds are structured as limited partnerships and reside outside the scrutiny of many securities laws.

CHAPTER 16

Follow-on Offerings and Liquidity for Insiders

➤ The primary public financing options available to newly minted public companies: follow-on offerings, convertible securities offerings, and others.

➤ The financing path most often pursued by newer public companies to raise capital and provide liquidity to pre-IPO shareholders: the follow-on offering.

➤ The typical timing and process for conducting a follow-on equity offering or other marketed and registered securities offering.

PEMCO's Wall Street activities shifted back into high gear following Labor Day. PEMCO had been invited to participate in two investor conferences in September, each sponsored by one of its underwriters. Management had also been invited by a research analyst to participate in a two-day non-deal road show to visit with investors in New York City. The company accepted the invitations. The CEO and CFO would attend the conferences and the CFO would do the road show alone. Although these events would be distracting, PEMCO wanted to broaden its exposure to investors and support its new partners. Management understood that well-attended investment conferences and non-deal road shows help investment banks improve their standing and commissions with institutional clients.

The investment conferences were multiday events showcasing notable companies to institutional investors. Participation, as a speaker or attendee, was by invitation only. The formats of the two conferences differed slightly. At one, PEMCO was asked to make its standard investor presentation (basically an updated version of the IPO road-show presentation) and, at the other, was given the opportunity to make some general comments followed by questions and answers. The presentation times were roughly 30 minutes each. Both conferences had several concurrent speaker tracks that began early in the morning and finished

Figure 16.1. Funding progression—Follow-on offering.

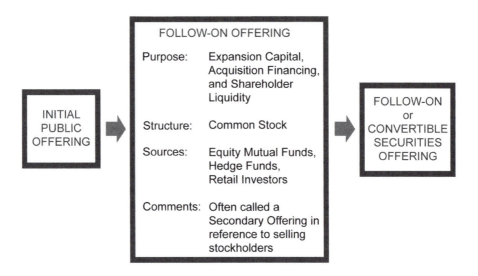

late in the day. One conference was held at a ritzy hotel in San Francisco; the other at a luxury golf resort in Scottsdale.

PEMCO management attended each conference for a day. Besides their formal presentations, they spent the conference days behind closed doors in one-on-one meetings with interested investors. These meetings were similar to those that occurred during the IPO road show but lasted only 30 minutes each. Investors often seek to ferret out sensitive information during these discussions. As such, management had to be particularly careful not to divulge material nonpublic information and violate the "selective disclosure" prohibitions contained in fair disclosure securities regulations.

Two of their meeting slots were filled with visits from their investment bankers. It had been more than three months since the IPO in May and PEMCO's stock had continued to do well. It was up 57%—hovering around $22. With the lock-up agreements for its investors expiring in less than three months, bankers had started approaching PEMCO about another financing. Most discussed the idea of a straight-forward follow-on offering composed primarily of selling shareholders with a few shares from the company (in light of the composition this is also known as a secondary offering). This was a common transaction for companies with IPOs that had traded well. The deal would allow for an orderly disposition of shares that were at risk of being "dumped" into the market. Lock-up expirations concern investors and for good reason. They can disrupt supply and demand and drive down prices, particularly for less liquid public stocks.

A few bankers raised the idea of completing a combination deal involving both a secondary offering and a convertible note offering. Under these proposals, the common stock deal would be for selling shareholders and the convertible deal would raise money for the company.

A convertible offering can be an attractive financing option for a public company. As with conventional debt, "converts" require the issuer to pay interest, but they generally have interest rates (known as "coupons") far below straight debt and can result in less shareholder dilution than a common-stock offering. When a stock increases, such securities are entitled to convert into common stock at prices above those found when the security was issued. This difference is referred to as the "conversion premium." For example, a $50 million convert issued at a 25 percent conversion premium for a stock that trades at $40 would convert at $50 per share (resulting in the issuance of 1 million shares instead of 1.25 million). Of course, the stock has to trade up for there to be a conversion; otherwise the instrument must be repaid like normal debt. Convert investors like the opportunity to participate in a company's upside while receiving a coupon and having the downside protection of a debt or debt-like instrument. These investors are also guarded by "call protection" provisions that limit the right of an issuer to force conversion or redeem a convertible instrument prior to the expiration of a fixed period of time, typically three years. The legal document describing the contractual terms of a convertible or debt security is called an "indenture."

Despite their benefits, convertible offerings rarely occur so soon after an IPO. Buyers deploy hedging strategies for such securities (i.e., transactions involving the company's underlying common stock) that require larger public floats than those possessed by most young public companies. Moreover, convertibles are debt until converted and most young, growing companies do not possess the cash flow characteristics to support or risk large debt loads.

Management raised the idea of a financing with a few of the board members, namely the VCs whose firms would account for the majority of the selling. The board had transitioned to a quarterly meeting schedule but individual directors still maintained an active dialogue with management. It was agreed that a financing was warranted to address the issue of shareholder overhang. They convened a special telephonic meeting and informally approved the project. It would be a traditional follow-on offering and would include two million shares from the company and ten million shares from selling shareholders. The company had no immediate needs for capital and did not want to dilute the shareholders but believed it had to include some shares in the deal. Doing otherwise would be unusual. Besides, it never hurt to have a little extra cash on the balance sheet, particularly when a company had deep-pocketed competitors like traditional energy vendors. Two million shares seemed reasonable. The overall deal was in line with market precedents at roughly 15 percent of the shares outstanding—according to its bankers, a post-IPO deal of 10 percent to 20 percent was typical. If they participated, pre-public shareholders would be locked up for an additional 90 days after the offering.

PEMCO's more experienced board members had seen what happens to companies that fail to take a proactive role in distributing secondary shares after an IPO.

Often, it is not pretty. When a stock price goes up, individual holders sell their shares immediately, and VCs distribute their shares to their own investors—the LPs—who also quickly make sales. At best, all of this selling activity drives down a stock price temporarily. At worst, it has a longer-term detrimental impact. Public shareholders can perceive poorly managed secondary selling as reckless and the byproduct of weak leadership, thereby squelching confidence and interest in a company.

Unlike PEMCO's prior transactions, there was no formal bake-off to select underwriters for the secondary offering. The board considered several factors and simply made its picks. With input from management, it took into account PEMCO's relationships with the banks and more specifically: (1) contribution in the IPO, (2) trading performance, (3) research, (4) post-IPO banking dialogues, and (5) other support, such as conferences, non-deal road shows, and helpful introductions. They settled on Burnham and ILB as co-leads, again. For co-managers, they stayed with Deutsche Credit and RSF and added Silverman & Co., one of the firms that had launched research after the IPO. Silverman had also done a good job trading PEMCO's stock and had attentive bankers. PEMCO decided to drop Feeman from the deal. It had not devoted trading and banking resources to the company and was the firm with the problematic research analyst.

Management shared the board's thoughts on the follow-on offering with the co-leads but did not officially mandate them for the assignment. PEMCO said nothing to the prospective co-managers. It was early October. The company wanted to release its third-quarter earnings before officially informing its bankers of the deal and the underwriting selections. This would allow PEMCO not to reference the transaction in the earnings press release (failing to do so could be considered a material omission if a deal was formally mandated) and would allow the research analysts employed by the underwriters to comment freely on the quarter following the release. Once mandated on a deal, bankers must notify their compliance departments, which, in turn, monitor activity in the affected stock and limit certain trading and research activity. This compliance activity occurs even when all information pertaining to the proposed transaction is contained to just the investment bankers.

Management scheduled the Q3 earnings call for the third week in October. The full underwriting team would be notified two days later, after their research departments had time to publish their commentary and update their projections. PEMCO would file the offering, along with its quarterly report, on Form 10-Q a week later. Assuming the transaction was not reviewed by the SEC (the SEC does not typically review transactions when a company has been reviewed on another matter shortly beforehand), PEMCO would launch the deal in the first week of November and look to price by mid-month.

PEMCO's schedule worked as planned. Its earning release and subsequent conference call were similar to those held for Q2 in August. The news was good and well received. The company had again beaten expectations. It had also exceeded the market's "whisper" numbers—unpublished performance predictions and rumors that circulate on Wall Street. Allowing time for research commentary,

Figure 16.2. Public Offering Flowchart.

* Trading for new shares begins day after pricing with closing 3 business days later.

PEMCO officially notified its underwriters about the deal and invited them to participate. The all-hands organizational meeting was held the following day. It included the same cast of characters from the IPO except, of course, the dropped and added underwriters. PEMCO's stock was trading at $24.

The chronology of events in PEMCO's follow-on offering would be similar to that found in the IPO, albeit with the prospect of certain stages being less time-consuming.

The process leading up to filing the registration statement with the SEC was, for the most part, a condensed version of the IPO experience. It included commitment committee approvals, due diligence reviews, drafting sessions, and preparing legal documentation. The most notable difference was soliciting the selling shareholders. Some were approached confidentially before filing. Others were given notice after filing. Pursuant to the terms of their shareholder agreements, potential sellers were entitled to ten days' written notice before having to make a decision to participate. PEMCO and the team hoped to get feedback sooner. They would need responses from all affected parties prior to completing the selling shareholder table for the marketing prospectus.

The deal filed nine days after PEMCO's earnings release. The document was a revised version of the Form S-1 from the IPO, mostly with updated financial information. It, too, was a Form S-1. The company would not be able to use the simpler SEC form for more mature issuers—a Form S-3—until it had more history as a public company. The primary difference between the two forms is the extent of information that must be included. S-1s must address a heavy list of disclosures required by SEC regulations whereas S-3s have fewer disclosure requirements and simply refer potential investors to other public filings that contain more detailed information. S-1s are a lot more work.

PEMCO's stock dropped about 10% on the filing. Buyers stepped out of the market to learn more about the transaction, and institutional investors interested in buying stakes deferred their purchases, believing they might be able to get allocations in the deal. Accumulating a position beforehand would only serve to increase the share price. If the deal looked like it would be significantly oversubscribed, pre-deal buying might be warranted. Until the road show was underway, however, it was too early to make that call.

The SEC took five days to get back to the company with its decision not to review the deal. PEMCO was free to proceed but now needed to lock down the selling shareholders. Each had been provided with notice of the deal at filing. Most had responded and wanted to participate. The company had not yet heard from POC Ventures, one of the Series A investors. After a direct inquiry, PEMCO learned that POC was contemplating not joining in the deal. Instead, POC was weighing the benefits of a distribution to its LPs after the original lock-up expired. Even though a distribution could drive down a stock price, some venture capitalists favor this approach due to their compensation structures. As previously discussed, VC firms receive 20 percent of the profits from their investments. The profits are calculated at the time of a cash or stock distribution. For stock distributions, VCs keep shares representing the 20 percent profit. If a stock subsequently declines, it does not impact the number of shares the VC receives; it only impacts the value of these shares. Depending on the situation, a stock distribution may be a better outcome for the VC than selling the stock and then making the cash distribution to its LPs.

After pressure from management and, more importantly, the VC board members, POC agreed to sign on to the deal. POC would pursue a liquidation strategy similar to that of the other VCs. It would sell a portion of its holdings in the transaction and retain the other shares for a distribution at a later date. Subject to lock-ups or other contractual limitations, VCs have wide latitude in making stock distributions. They can do so at their first opportunity or they can try to time the market and distribute shares when they reach higher prices to maximize their profit participation.

After aggregating all of the selling interest, it was decided that the selling shareholders would each be entitled to sell roughly 15 percent of their holdings. For marketing purposes and the "optics" of the deal, the cofounders agreed to sell only 10 percent of their holdings. While acknowledging the need to diversify, investors like management teams to be as exposed as possible to a company's stock. The debate concerning management versus financial sponsor liquidity in a secondary offering can often be very contentious. VCs and private equity firms— referred to as the financial sponsors of a company—often pressure founders and management teams to limit their selling in order to help the deal and enable more of their own selling. This pressure is frequently supported by contractual rights in shareholder agreements that permit financial sponsors to sell more. This can lead to resentment among management teams who carry the daily burden of making a company and a deal successful.

The difference between the cofounders' 10 percent and 15 percent would be divided among PEMCO's other sellers. The green shoe for the transaction (i.e., the over-allotment option enabling the underwriters to stabilize the market, if

Table 16.1 Follow-on Selling Shareholder Table*

	Pre-Deal Ownership	Shares Offered	Post-Offering Ownership	
			Shares	%
Larry	11,094,605	1,109,460	9,985,144	12.5%
Jerry	11,094,605	1,109,460	9,985,144	12.5%
Seed Investors	1,314,079	229,664	1,084,415	1.4%
Alpha & POC	18,945,433	3,311,127	15,634,306	19.6%
Beta	11,818,341	2,065,513	9,752,829	12.2%
Carto	8,877,288	1,551,500	7,325,789	9.2%
Strategics	1,019,322	178,149	841,173	1.1%
Smart	2,546,904	445,127	2,101,777	2.6%
Total	66,710,577	10,000,000	56,710,577	

*Excludes impact of the overallotment option and assumes issuance of two million primary shares.

necessary, after the deal) would be the standard 15 percent and would be composed of all secondary shares (i.e., shares to be sold by pre-IPO shareholders rather than PEMCO) if exercised. The deal's layout would be as follows:

With the selling shareholder list finalized, PEMCO filed an amendment to the S-1 and printed the red herrings (i.e., preliminary prospectuses). These were distributed to the underwriters and prospective investors. The road show then kicked off with presentations to the underwriters' sales forces. The road show lasted nine business days and covered the same U.S. cities as the IPO. In the interest of time, it did not include Europe. The schedule was similar to the IPO and encompassed one-on-ones and group meetings with many of the same investors. The meetings were also similar but placed a greater emphasis on post-IPO developments, including the company's financial performance, new products, and customer wins. When the road show concluded, the book was three times oversubscribed and the stock had traded back above the price found at the time the Form S-1 was filed. It was $25 on the day of pricing.

A 3X book was commendable for a follow-on. Unlike IPOs, the stock in follow-ons has public trading history and deals rarely experience significant pops after pricing. As such, follow-on books contain only those investors that truly want to purchase and hold a stock ("own a story" in Wall Street parlance). These investors indicate what they want to own in their orders and expect to get allocated most of it. By-and-large, follow-ons do not contain the opportunists and speculators found in IPOs.

The pricing call was uneventful. The underwriters offered $24.75 a share. This was $0.25 below the last sale but above the filing price. The underwriters had encouraged PEMCO to not be greedy and to leave the $0.25 on the table to reward investors for their support and participation over the past six months. PEMCO's pricing committee agreed to the proposal. The deal would have a 5.25

Table 16.2 PEMCO Follow-on—Final Fee Splits

			Selling Concession*	
	Management	Underwriting	Institutional Pot (80% of total)	Retail Pot (20% of total)
Burnham	30%	30%	30%	30%
ILB	25%	25%	30%	25%
Deutsche	20%	20%	15%	20%
Silverman	15%	15%	5%	20%
RSF	10%	10%	20%	5%

*Retail figures represent percentage of retail shares provided to the respective underwriters for distribution.

percent gross spread (i.e., underwriting fee). This had been agreed to before the organizational meeting. Rounded, this amounted to $1.30 a share.

Bigger deals for more mature companies can see gross spreads at 4 percent or lower, but 5 percent to 5.5 percent was in line with the market for deals akin to PEMCO's. Some issuers reward underwriters with an extra 25 basis points (0.25%) for deals that get completed above predefined levels. The company had contemplated this structure but decided against it, concluding it would be unnecessary. The board did agree, however, that an incentive-based fee was worthwhile when dealing with the splits between the underwriters.

A few of the underwriters had proposed that a "jump ball" be used to determine the underwriting splits and PEMCO was supportive. Recall, the gross spread is divided into three parts—management (20%), underwriting (20%), and selling concession (60%). With a jump ball, management and underwriting are predetermined and run along the same lines as in an IPO, but the selling concession is different. The selling concession for the institutional pot is divided according to the wishes of the institutional buyers. When this structure is used, salespeople lobby their clients aggressively to get jump-ball designations. Caps, typically 50 percent to 60 percent, are placed on the amount of the "jump" that can go to lead underwriters in order to prevent them from taking all of it since buyers always designate the leads for their full percentage to assure that they are not at a disadvantage when it comes to receiving an allocation. Jump-ball arrangements presume that firms that do a good job educating the market about a company and a deal are rewarded accordingly. While rare in IPOs, jump balls are popular in follow-ons and favored by firms with a strong sales, trading, and research presence in a stock. The selling concession for the retail pot in a jump-ball scenario is decided in the same fashion as in an IPO. The bookrunner allocates retail shares to the underwriters in accordance with historical precedents and the underwriters capture the respective selling concessions.

After the designations were tallied, the final fee splits for PEMCO's transaction were as shown in Table 16.2.

As typical for follow-ons, no underwriting syndicate was used in the transaction. The only parties to receive compensation were the managing underwriters. Each would be provided with its share of the gross spread by the bookrunner approximately three months after the transaction closed. The delay would provide time to receive and settle all expenses incurred by the underwriting team during the deal, including attorney fees, road show costs, and out-of-pockets for travel, meals, parking, and ancillaries.

Before and after the pricing call, the company, bankers, lawyers, and accountants undertook the same steps they did in the IPO. They requested effectiveness from the SEC for the S-1 and completed a bring-down due diligence call. Afterwards, they updated the S-1 and filed it with the SEC. The bookrunner's equity capital markets desk allocated shares to institutional investors in the book and each underwriter allocated its retail designations. The final prospectus was provided to the buyers with their purchase confirmations. Roughly sixty institutions were given stock. Half of these were new investors.

The next day's opening of the stock was much less suspenseful than in the IPO. There was an established market and thus more clarity on where the stock was likely to trade. Because the company had not pressed to get the absolute highest price ($25 vs. $24.75), the tone of investors was expected to be positive. In many respects, the biggest risk was that of the broader market. If news hit the tape that could negatively impact PEMCO's industry, it could put downward pressure on the stock. To help minimize this risk, the underwriters had attempted to time the deal when no notable market event was scheduled. On the day of pricing and the first day of trading, no competitors or market moving companies were scheduled to release earnings and no potentially harmful economic data were scheduled to be released.

PEMCO's stock opened at $25 and stayed within a tight trading band all day. It closed at $25.25. With extra shares in public hands, volume was heavier than usual. This was also influenced by existing public shareholders looking to sell. Interested sellers had delayed pulling the trigger after the filing. They waited until after pricing when demand flowed back into the market and the underwriters stood ready to stabilize the stock at the issuance price, if necessary. Immediately following a deal is a good time to unload shares without impacting price.

The next day, PEMCO's stock traded to $25.75 and trading volume died down. The bookrunner's ECM desk decided to exercise the green shoe early. The closing for the over-allotment would be done concurrently with the closing of the main transaction. The total transaction contained 13.8 million shares. It amounted to almost $342 million. Because they accounted for the entire shoe, the selling shareholders received $277 million after the 5.25 percent underwriting fee. PEMCO received $47 million. Having turned profitable in the second quarter, the company's cash balance now totaled more than $150 million. Its market capitalization was roughly $2 billion.

The closing dinner was upgraded from the IPO. This time it was held in Scottsdale, at the Phoenician. Larry and Jerry had taken up golf with their new found riches, a sport popular with their VCs. The leads were anxious to keep them happy and, with $18 million in underwriting fees, they could afford to do so.

Personal Observations on Public Investors

1. *Investor psychology is as powerful as a company's fundamentals to a stock's performance, at least in the short term.* How investors perceive a company's performance and how they perceive the likely reaction of other investors to such performance are the two factors that drive stocks. A business's absolute performance and the actual impact of accomplishments and failures on its prospects are secondary. In part, this is why companies that show strong performance but miss "whisper" numbers see their stock prices punished. It is also why companies that have disappointed investors with poor results will trade at a discount to their peers even after they have regained their financial footing and performed well. The phenomenon of investor psychology creates investment opportunities for those with longer-term perspectives.

2. *Momentum has become the name of the game.* Increasingly, public institutional investors—namely mutual funds—have taken a momentum approach to investing. This is true for at least those that actively pick stocks. They buy and sell based on near-term catalysts and trading expectations for companies. They do so because their own investors are impatient and judge them on a quarterly basis. This has enabled private equity funds and certain hedge funds (both of which have substantial limitations on investor redemptions) to make attractive investments in companies that are likely to see near-term challenges but longer-term successes.

3. *There is little "hedge" in most hedge funds.* Contrary to what most investors would assume from their name, the primary function of most hedge funds is not to "hedge" investors against market declines and losses. It is a misnomer. They should be called something like "leveraged funds" or "fully flexible investment funds." While hedge funds may use investment strategies designed to reduce certain risks and, as a class, they have shown less volatility than the public stock market, most funds are designed to produce returns, not preserve capital. Investors want returns and hedge fund managers get paid to produce them, typically by using a hearty dose of leverage. In most cases, the big paydays for managers come from their profit participation fees (20%) not their management fees (2% of assets).

4. *With adequate disclosures, the law should continue to be eased to allow mutual funds to deploy many of the same investment strategies as hedge funds.* There has already been a significant blurring of

the lines between the activities of other Wall Street players. Among other things, investment banks now make private equity investments, private equity firms now have M&A advisory practices, commercial banks now have brokerage operations, and hedge funds now participate in syndicated loans. Hedge funds appeal to institutions and wealthy investors because of the breadth of investment tactics they can use to generate returns, most notably the ability to short stocks and use leverage. Their drawbacks are their high fees and lack of liquidity. Mutual funds, on the other hand, are liquid, have relatively low fees, and are available to the masses. Allowing them to do what hedge funds do (or at least much of it) would seem to provide the best of both worlds. We have started to see regulatory easing on this issue with the emergence of 130/30 and 120/20 funds.

5. *Sellside research and trading are still valuable, at least in smaller capitalization stocks.* For less liquid and less understood stocks, these traditional brokerage house offerings are still valuable for investors. Perhaps not as much as a decade ago before the proliferation of the internet, widespread computing, and new trading networks, but valuable nonetheless. They help improve the flow of information and remove friction that hinders market efficiency. In making this point, however, it is necessary to note that this is not always fully appreciated by the buyside. Brokerage commissions are easily quantified and reducing them is a measure of success for buyside traders. Therefore, some buyers seek to trade where commissions are the lowest, not necessarily where execution and input are the strongest.

CHAPTER 17

Acquiring Businesses: Targeting Opportunities to Fuel Growth

➤ How and why companies source certain acquisition opportunities.

➤ The negotiating process and notable terms for a public company acquisition.

➤ The definition, purpose, and structure of "PIPE" financings.

After the follow-on, the remainder of the year was quiet for PEMCO, at least as far as Wall Street was concerned. There were no more investor meetings or conferences. The CFO had hired a head of investor relations prior to the deal. Previously a research associate from the sellside, she was now responsible for daily dealings with the Street and coordinating investor events with senior management. She had fielded questions from investors and research analysts in December but nothing more.

The lack of investor-related distractions allowed management to focus on closing out a successful year. They spent their time expanding the product line, nurturing existing customers, developing new customers, and helping with the launch of the company's first design win in the automotive sector—a PEM-powered subcompact. The car, known as the PEMobile, was released in early December to an enthusiastic reception.

Although successful, PEMCO's experience with its automotive initiatives had revealed some weaknesses at the company. Most notable was the lack of design expertise. The company had proven it could morph its alternative energy technology to meet the needs of different markets. However, the company had not been as capable at packaging its products to best meet the demands of its OEM customers. It had fumbled on important integration details several times. This had almost cost the company some important contracts, not to mention product delays and financial shortfalls.

To rectify the situation, PEMCO had been actively searching for a new team to run this aspect of its engineering operations. The company had also been approached by several investment bankers about acquisition opportunities. Most of these discussions involved face-to-face meetings and presentation books listing potential targets and acquisition rationales. Some ideas were presented without these formalities and were simply outlined in emails. Given their time constraints, management preferred the latter approach from bankers they knew well.

The company was shown a wide range of ideas. Bankers were anxious to help PEMCO spend its cash and use its richly valued stock. Some ideas were smart and creative; others were idiotic. The company valued them all—at least most of them. Management did not have the bandwidth and expertise to sort through the multitudes of public and private companies that could be a good fit for PEMCO. The bankers provided the resources and a channel to do so.

To help in this effort, the company decided to hire a business development person who was tasked with finding and assessing strategic opportunities, including business alliances and acquisitions. Management considered several people for this role. Among them was a mid-level investment banker from ILB and a vice president of business development from a large commercial battery manufacturer. They settled on the banker, a common choice for younger growth companies. The banker had done a good job on PEMCO's deals, had subsequently presented some good ideas, understood the M&A process, and knew how to interface with management teams, VCs, and other bankers. The company had never worked with the other party and, rightly or wrongly, perceived him to be less current on new technologies and changes in the energy landscape. PEMCO lured the banker away with an attractive stock option package but a reduction in current income.

By early January, PEMCO started to seriously assess purchasing another business to fill its design hole. It had not been able to find a pool of sufficiently qualified new hires for this function and believed an intact team from a closely related business might be the best answer. Such a team would need to learn about PEMCO but not how to work together. Without providing specifics on their internal issues, management had shared their interest in this area with a few investment bankers and several ideas had surfaced.

After reviewing the options, management became increasingly interested in one company, Energy Integrators Corporation. EIC worked with battery and component manufacturers to sell and integrate their solutions into OEM products. Like several players in the semiconductor sector, EIC was part distributor and part design and integration firm. It had a good reputation and strong relationships with many top OEMs. It was also public and financially troubled.

PEMCO had also carefully considered a similar business named Holland All Service Holdings. Headquartered in Europe, Holland All Service was large and successful and had a $700 million market capitalization. Its shares were listed on the Amsterdam Stock Exchange and the NYSE via American Depositary Receipts (ADRs). ADRs permit shares listed on a foreign exchange to trade domestically. This is accomplished through a special legal construct created by the issuer and a domestic custodian bank. Foreign shares are placed with the custodian bank, which, in turn, issues a depository receipt for them that is then listed on a domestic exchange. The issuer pays for the listing and the ADRs trade in lockstep with the shares traded on the foreign exchange (more-or-less; minor discrepancies and arbitrage opportunities sometimes emerge in daily trading). In some situations, dual listing can also be accomplished by directly listing the actual shares on both exchanges. Foreign corporations expend resources for ADRs and dual listings to broaden their access to capital. Studies indicate that this listing strategy can improve a company's cost of capital, particularly when the foreign exchange is second tier. PEMCO chose not to pursue the Dutch company given its size. Management was also concerned over the logistics of executing the acquisition of a foreign public company, especially as its first foray into M&A.

EIC had a market capitalization of $70 million. Its revenues and margins had been unable to support its overhead, particularly the expenses required to be public. It had posted a loss for each of the past three years and had depleted its cash balances to under $3 million. The company needed to do something. It was rumored that EIC was considering a PIPE financing.

PIPE is the acronym for "private investment in public equity" (sometimes the word "entity" is used in place of equity). PIPEs involve the issuance of convertible securities (notes or preferred stock) or common stock (possibly with warrants) by small public companies to small investment consortiums, usually one or two institutional investors. They are publicly announced upon closing and not during marketing. They do not require a prospectus or any prior public filings. PIPEs are typically pursued by public companies that need capital but do not possess the financial characteristics to raise debt or the profile to raise equity through a traditional follow-on offering. With very few exceptions, debt requires cash flow and traditional public equity deals require a $30+ million raise and a $150+ million market capitalization. PIPEs are sometimes completed by larger companies that, for various reasons, want or need to raise capital without it being disclosed beforehand. Most PIPEs range in size from $5 million to $20 million. They must involve less than 20 percent of an issuer's outstanding shares or are required to receive shareholder approval prior to closing under stock-exchange rules (a lengthy and untenable proposition for financially needy companies with unstable share prices).

PIPE issuers generally hire investment banks to agent such transactions. A number of larger banks and boutiques have expertise in this area and maintain an active dialogue with the market's most active PIPE investors. Hopeful agents pursue and pitch potential issuers aggressively. Calling efforts are generally spearheaded by industry bankers with support from PIPE specialists contained within ECM departments. Likely issuers are also targeted by investors looking to secure opportunities before they become agented and marketed more broadly. Issuers sometimes opt for this path, preferring to forgo the lengthier, more involved process of using an agent. Agents usually charge 5 percent to 6 percent of capital raised.

The process for a PIPE is more or less a blend between a private placement and a narrowly marketed, confidential sellside M&A process for a public company. First, an agent is selected. The selection is based upon reputation, relationships, ideas, and the historical calling effort with the company. In order to avoid troubles and leaks from disgruntled losers, rarely is a there a formal bake-off. Once selected, the agent and issuer enter into an engagement letter. These typically have six- to twelve-month terms and provide for compensation in the event of any financing or sellside M&A transaction. The agent then contacts potential investors on a "no-names" basis about the opportunity. Investors are targeted based on past transactions and areas of interest that they have previously indicated to the agent (sectors, deal sizes, etc.). Depending on the situation, ten to twenty investors are approached. These are generally hedge funds, including some that focus exclusively on PIPEs. If interested, these parties are asked to sign NDAs before learning more. The NDAs restrict their ability to release any information about the deal or trade in the issuer's securities prior to the public announcement of a transaction. When signed, potential investors are given the company's name and an information packet of publicly filed documentation and notable research reports. When a potential investor refuses to sign, it may sometimes remain in the process after providing oral assurances that it will keep all information in confidence in accordance with Regulation FD and basically act as it otherwise would have under a NDA (here, certain actions, such as shorting a company's shares and covering the position with shares purchased in a PIPE, remain illegal under federal securities laws). Other than the proposed terms and construct of the transaction, PIPE marketing materials only contain public information. Nevertheless, all materials provided to interested parties are specifically labeled "confidential" to limit potential leaks.

PIPEs can move very fast. Investors are asked to submit term sheets within a week or two of signing the NDA. Often, this is done before the investors even meet management. Typically, investors must rely exclusively on publicly available information, thereby eliminating the need for lengthy due diligence. Bidders, however, have the benefit of a publicly traded stock to use in determining valuation and terms. After a review of the term sheets, a winner is selected (if the company is attractive enough and fortunate enough to have competing proposals). Closing occurs a few weeks later, following confirmatory due diligence. For stock deals, the winning bidder receives shares that must be registered subsequently by the issuer (an obligation that usually must be satisfied shortly after the deal). Shares are sometimes issued pursuant to shelf registration statements already on file with the SEC. If so, these are registered upon issuance. Discussed further in Chapter 20, a "shelf registration statement" is a generic filing that outlines a certain number or dollar amount of shares or other securities that a company intends to issue over the foreseeable future. The document is public and permits an issuer to "draw down" securities registered pursuant to it at any time.

As with most deals, the principal term in a PIPE is price. Common stock PIPEs are almost always done at a discount to the market price of the issuer's shares. The discount may be straightforward, like an offer to pay $18 a share for a stock that trades at $20. It may also involve the theoretical value of warrants issued along with the shares. Many PIPE financings include the issuance of warrants entitling the investor to acquire additional shares of common stock at a set price. This "strike price" may be higher or lower than the price of the shares sold in the PIPE.

When included, the value of these warrants must be included in determining the discount. Terms for a PIPE at $19 per share may be worse than a deal at $18 when the $19 transaction includes warrants valued at an additional $1.50 a share. The value of warrants is generally calculated using a Black-Scholes options pricing model. All-in discounts for common stock PIPEs usually range from 10 percent to 30 percent.

PIPEs involving convertible notes or preferred stock have terms similar to traditional convertible offerings. They have a set coupon and are convertible into shares of the publicly traded stock at some premium to the current price. When the PIPE market was being developed in the late 1990s, most deals involved convertibles. The terms associated with these were often extremely onerous. Many had reset provisions that forced companies to issue more shares upon conversion when stock prices declined. The terms of these "toxic" or "death-spiral" converts produced a slippery slope. The more prices declined, the more shares needed to be issued, and the more shares needed to be issued, the more prices declined.

Issuers and investors have become wiser and no longer permit such terms. The market for PIPEs has become very large and much more efficient. Much of this growth can be attributed to the recent expansion of hedge funds (which have greater flexibility in structuring transactions than their mutual fund counterparts) and the lack of other financing options for small public companies.

PEMCO authorized one of its bankers to approach EIC. The company had decided to use Silverman as its advisor. Silverman was the first to raise the EIC idea and knew EIC's management team. The firm's bankers also knew two of EIC's outside board members. This could be helpful in negotiations, particularly if management resisted opening a meaningful dialogue. Silverman had analyzed the strategic and financial merits of a transaction and was best suited to working with the company.

The approach was made in late January, but PEMCO's name was not used. Silverman wanted to gage EIC's receptivity to takeover discussions before divulging the identity of the potential suitor. Although the party line for takeover targets is almost always "we're open to learning more and doing what makes sense" due to their fiduciary obligations to shareholders, a lot can be gleaned from the tone and body language of management when an actionable idea is presented. A company's true sentiment can range from very receptive to very reluctant when it comes to being acquired.

When a target's management team refuses to engage in discussions with a legitimate suitor, there are a handful of tactics the suitor can deploy to force a discussion. The optimal approach depends largely on the buyer's timeframe and the seller's takeover defenses. A short-term strategy for breaking the silence can be to engage with the target's board, possibly through a "bear hug" letter. Outlining the rationale and merits for talks, a bear hug contains a request for discussions and creates a formal record of the inquiry. Although this approach may not lead to a deal, it generally catalyzes a dialogue. Longer-term strategies can involve proxy contests to obtain favorable representation on a target's board of directors or just becoming (or gaining the support of) a vocal, activist shareholder who can influence other shareholders to apply pressure for action. Subject to certain laws and company defenses, they may also include a public offer to buy all or most of the company via a tender offer—a public solicitation to purchase shares at a set price. Before approaching a target, a buyside advisor will research and prepare a "defense profile" to understand and summarize the takeover defense mechanisms contained in the company's charter and bylaws.

Silverman's initial discussions with EIC went as expected. Management was open to exploring an acquisition, assuming the price and strategic rationale made sense. The company needed a solution to its financial troubles and, as suspected, had already engaged an investment bank to raise money in a PIPE. Marketing for the deal was about to begin. EIC was looking to raise $10 million. From what Silverman had gathered, the financing sounded like a stopgap measure to prevent a near-term meltdown and not a long-term solution to the company's woes. Management seemed tired.

Silverman relayed the information to PEMCO and was given the green light to set up a face-to-face meeting between the top executives as soon as possible. The meeting occurred two days later. To prevent employee rumors and speculation, it was held over lunch at Silverman's Silicon Valley office. The CEO and CFO of both companies were present, as was PEMCO's new head of business development. No bankers attended. The meeting was intended to provide a forum for both parties to discuss their businesses and the merits and challenges of a possible combination. Keeping the meeting small and informal facilitated the flow of information. The bankers advised PEMCO to deflect any inquiries regarding potential terms.

Chemistry between the parties was positive. EIC had heard of PEMCO's unique products and recent successes but knew little of the management team and culture. EIC's management liked what they saw. PEMCO looked to be well positioned for the future with solid vision and direction. It also had a smart and hungry CEO. He was a young but humble straight shooter who seemed capable of leading the charge. As for PEMCO's perceptions, they now understood EIC much better. EIC was not the mismanaged business that they had expected to find. The company's troubles seemed to be driven by its position as a middleman in the market and not by the quality of its team or services. EIC had been squeezed by suppliers and customers that continued to maintain internal design and integration teams that competed with EIC's offerings. While these critical constituents had discussed outsourcing, they had not yet fully embraced it. PEMCO had a newfound respect for EIC's team. The meeting lasted four hours. It had been scheduled for two.

PEMCO was now convinced that a deal should get done. Management needed to confirm its views through further due diligence but believed EIC had the right operations and expertise to address PEMCO's integration and design shortcomings. EIC also had customer relationships that could fuel additional product wins. PEMCO's management had come to accept the notion that, indeed, sometimes it may be better to buy than to build (a perspective many companies within and outside of technology have difficulty embracing due to egos, internal fiefdoms, protectionist agendas, and not-invented-here [NIH] mindsets). In arriving at this conclusion, management also ruled out some of the "walk before you run" combination strategies involving EIC. Forming a joint venture or other closely linked commercial relationship with EIC would not achieve PEMCO's goals. Design and integration services were functions that the company needed to be able to offer internally. PEMCO communicated its opinions to Silverman.

Silverman tailored the feedback for EIC, indicating to the company that PEMCO would be interested in seriously exploring a combination. Silverman encouraged EIC to put its PIPE process on hold, at least for a couple of weeks. EIC was reluctant to do so. Notable delays could harm its financial position and negotiating leverage. They could also compromise EIC's ability to attract acceptable terms from investors later if discussions with PEMCO fell apart. After its management and board of directors debated the topic, EIC agreed to hold off marketing the PIPE for two weeks despite these risks. In exchange for doing so EIC wanted some guidance on acquisition terms as soon as possible. There was no use in delaying the PIPE if PEMCO was contemplating a lowball offer. EIC notified its banker, JV Securities, regarding the discussions. Pursuant to the terms of the PIPE engagement letter, JV Securities was now EIC's M&A advisor.

Silverman and PEMCO developed a set of preliminary terms that they would share with EIC. They wanted these to reflect a purchase price that would be attractive enough to prevent EIC from resuming the PIPE process or from shopping the company to other potential suitors. A company is not obligated to "shop a bid" when its board concludes that pursuing an offer on an exclusive basis is in the best interest of the company. This can occur when the price being offered is at a significant premium to the public share price, there has been limited acquisition interest in the past, and efforts to find a better buyer could undermine or destroy negotiations with the interested suitor. PEMCO also needed a price that could be increased during subsequent discussions. Putting the best and final offer on the table as a starting point is almost always a losing strategy. Egos and human psychology typically require that a negotiating process encompass a back-and-forth and give-and-take in order to produce a positive outcome.

As for other terms, ultimately, there would be a long list that would be included in the discussions. These would pertain to everything from how EIC's employee stock options would be treated in the deal (i.e., would they vest and cash out immediately or be converted into options in PEMCO stock), to how the specific language would read in the acquisition agreement, to the role of management after the acquisition. For now, however, the other main term included in the initial volley would be currency—would the price be paid in cash, PEMCO stock, or a combination of both? Generally, buyers prefer stock deals and sellers prefer cash deals (the primary exception being where sellers seek to defer the taxes from a transaction by accepting stock—cash is always taxable whereas stock may not be). To a buyer, stock can serve as a retention mechanism for important employee shareholders and can help align the interest of all constituents after an acquisition closes. To a seller, cash provides the greatest flexibility—financial and otherwise.

Whether stock is an acceptable currency to a seller, particularly a public company, often boils down to the size of the acquisition relative to the size of the buyer. Larger deals usually involve stock and smaller deals usually involve cash. Companies rarely have sufficient cash resources on hand to fund large acquisitions and thus require stock for such deals. Conversely, small sellers often refuse to accept stock when contemplating an exit with a much larger buyer on the basis that their operations can only modestly impact those of the buyer. The argument goes that without the ability to materially influence the performance of the buyer, it would be unfair to require a seller's shareholders to become shareholders of that buyer since the shareholders' position would be too unrelated to their original investment. There is no bright-line rule on what is too large for a cash deal or too small for a stock deal. That being said, deals equating to less than 10 percent of a buyer's market value generally involve cash for they are typically considered too immaterial to require extensive public disclosure and rarely involve fairness opinions for the buyers.

PEMCO's initial offer for EIC was $90 million, all in cash. Since EIC was public, the deal would not involve an "earn-out" or an escrow. Among other things, both are usually considered too cumbersome to administer in a public deal. To keep a seller's management team focused after a transaction, particularly when a company's financial projections show significant future improvement, deals sometimes require that a portion of the acquisition price be set aside to be paid out in the future based upon achieving certain performance goals. These are called earn-outs. Escrows involve setting aside a portion of the acquisition price to fund liabilities or penalties associated with breaches in the seller's representations and warranties contained in the acquisition agreement. Often around 10 percent of the purchase price, these funds are placed in an escrow account for a finite time period. If unused, they are released to the seller's shareholders after the period expires.

At a 28 percent premium to EIC's market value of $70 million, the initial price was in line with the premiums paid for public companies. These usually range from 20 percent to 30 percent and are calculated based on the pre-announcement closing price of the target's stock. The premium relative to average closing prices over wider preceding timeframes, such as one week, one month, and three months, can also be relevant to sellers, particularly when there have been notable movements in a stock. The preliminary offer was sufficient for EIC to agree to continue the negotiations without pursuing the PIPE or other suitors.

The next three weeks were a frenzied mix of negotiations and due diligence. While agreeing to discussions, EIC had rejected the initial offer as inadequate. The company liked the cash currency but not the price. PEMCO had requested a counterproposal and access to more extensive information on EIC in order to help it better assess a combination and determine value. EIC complied with the information request under a NDA and "standstill" agreement—a document limiting PEMCO's ability to take certain actions, such as acquiring stock in EIC, during the discussions. EIC did not agree to the counterproposal request. At this early stage, it did not want to negotiate against itself. It wanted another volley from PEMCO.

Table 17.1 PEMCO Financial Performance and Revised Guidance*

	Expectations at IPO		Present Guidance			
	IPO Year	Current Year	IPO Year	Current Year Range		
Revenues	$142.0	$255.0	$155.0	$280.0	-	$300.0
Gross Profit	$94.7	$170.0	$103.3	$185.0	-	$200.0
Operating Income	$24.7	$85.0	$33.3	$100.0	-	$110.0
Net Income	$20.0	$50.0	$28.7	$60.0	-	$70.0

*IPO year under present guidance reflects actual performance. Gross and operating margin figures rounded and calculated based upon percentage of guidance provided to the market by management.

PEMCO's second proposal came in at $95 million. Due diligence on EIC had gone well. PEMCO's bankers, lawyers, and accountants had scoured the company's records, contracts, and financial statements. EIC did not appear to have any hidden issues, at least none that was material. PEMCO was comfortable raising its bid modestly, but again the offer was rejected. This time, however, EIC countered at $105 million, a deal with a 50% premium. After more back-and-forth, the parties settled on $100 million. They now needed formal board approvals before signing the deal.

In the midst of the final negotiations, PEMCO was scheduled to release its year-end financials. It was early February. The numbers and conference call were well received. The company had again exceeded expectations and guidance was rosy for the upcoming quarter and year. Initial sales of the first PEM-powered automobile—launched in December—were ahead of plan and the established military and consumer businesses showed no signs of slowing down. Furthermore, the company had a growing list of partners and new solutions across all of its product lines. PEMCO's stock traded up to $27. With just under 80 million shares outstanding, the company had almost a $2.2 billion market capitalization.

After the earnings call, PEMCO finalized its Form 10-K filing. The document contained audited financials for the year and detailed disclosures regarding the company's operations not found in the previously filed 10-Qs. Form 10-Ks are time-consuming to prepare and resemble the Form S-1 found in IPOs. The Form 10-K serves as the foundation for the annual shareholder report that is sent to investors (substantively the same document only with better packaging). Later, PEMCO would also need to file a proxy statement on Schedule 14A containing matters to be voted upon at the company's annual shareholders' meeting, such as the election of board members. The proxy statement would also discuss management's compensation and the performance of the company's stock relative to the market and comparable public companies. The annual meeting was scheduled for May 15. Companies with a calendar fiscal year generally hold them between April and June.

In early January, it looked certain that PEMCO would beat its quarterly guidance for the fourth quarter, and the company considered releasing this information to the public prior to its normal quarterly earnings release. Management decided against it. Although common and arguably necessary for shortfalls in order to avoid shareholder litigation, "pre-releases" are less typical when a company anticipates beating the numbers. They are done when the performance discrepancy is significant or when a company is looking to drive its stock price higher before the formal release to help with matters such as employee retention or a stock-based acquisition. PEMCO fit neither of these descriptions.

PEMCO's management team made no mention of their discussions with EIC during the earnings call. In response to a question, management did note that they might consider acquisitions to fuel growth or satisfy other needs. Requiring further negotiations and board approvals, the EIC deal lacked the requisite level of certainty for specific disclosure. In legal terms, the combination of the deal's probability and the magnitude of its impact on PEMCO if it did occur meant that the possibility of the transaction remained "immaterial."

CHAPTER 18

Acquiring Businesses: Valuations, Fairness Opinions, and the Approval Process

➤ The role of fairness opinions in merger and acquisition transactions.

➤ How fairness opinions are delivered to boards of directors and other constituents.

➤ The primary valuation methodologies used by investment bankers when providing fairness opinions.

➤ The typical process for obtaining shareholder and other necessary approvals in M&A transactions.

The boards of PEMCO and EIC were aware of the discussions between the companies and the progression of terms. Several directors of each company had, in fact, been consulted informally for advice and opinions. With terms mutually acceptable to the management teams in hand, the boards now wanted and needed a more in-depth review of the discussions and the current proposal. They also wanted fairness opinions from each company's respective advisor—Silverman and JV Securities. EIC required one. Selling the company without a fairness opinion would be unprecedented and would greater expose its board to liability for failing to adhere to this common business practice. Strictly speaking, PEMCO did not need a fairness opinion. As noted previously, fairness opinions are uncommon for deals representing less than 10 percent of a company's market value, as was the case with EIC and PEMCO. Having the formal opinion of an investment bank is not needed for a board to exercise "reasonable business judgment" in such situations. Nevertheless, it was PEMCO's first deal and the team wanted to be thorough.

Silverman rendered its opinion to PEMCO and JV Securities rendered its opinion to EIC. The opinions were similar in most respects. Both were delivered by the banking teams to the boards at meetings called specifically to discuss the deal. The teams presented a two-page letter noting that the deal was fair from a financial point of view (sometimes they say otherwise) and set forth the process used to arrive at this conclusion, along with any caveats. The teams also walked the boards through a thick set of materials known as a "board book." The books reviewed the terms of the proposed transaction and briefly described the businesses, their product lines, and the merits and rationales for a combination.

The board books contained an extensive discussion on the price to be paid for EIC and the fairness of it. For the most part, the fairness of price is determined by looking at a combination of comparable financial metrics found in the market. More specifically, investment bankers generally assess fairness relative to following four methodologies. The first three are always addressed in buyside and sellside fairness opinions. If used, the fourth is often found only in the buyside analysis.

1. **Multiples paid in comparable M&A transactions.** Bankers compile a list of transactions deemed to be comparable to the one being proposed. The list is based primarily upon industry and deal size. Transactions on the list are deconstructed to determine the amounts paid according to multiples of past and future revenues, cash flows, and earnings. These multiples are used during negotiations by both sides and in fairness opinion discussions regarding the appropriate value for a business.

2. **Premiums paid in comparable M&A transactions.** Similar to precedent M&A multiples, bankers will compile a list of premiums paid in prior M&A transactions when the deal being proposed involves a publicly traded target. The list of premiums is generally more expansive than the list of deals used for multiples. It contains comparably sized transactions and notes whether the currency involved was stock or cash, since stock and cash deals receive slightly different premiums.

3. **Trading multiples of comparable public companies.** The list of comparable M&A transactions, particularly deals that can be mined for detailed information, is usually short. As such, bankers also look to publicly traded companies to assess the merits of a financial proposal. Being mindful of notable differences such as growth rates and margins, the multiples of comparable companies serve as helpful metrics in determining whether a price is too low or too high.

4. **Discounted cash flow analysis.** Bankers also prepare a five- to ten-year DCF analysis to assess the fairness of price. Because the outcomes of DCFs are highly dependent on the assumptions used in the calculations, they are generally afforded less credence than the metrics noted earlier in fairness discussions.

It is worth pointing out that the methodologies just noted are used to determine fairness for both the buyer and the seller, although the motivations and price considerations for the two differ. For a company that has decided to sell, the goal is simple. It is to receive a fair price and hopefully the absolute best price for shareholders. What other parties have paid and are currently paying for similar businesses provides a good yardstick to make this determination. For a buyer, on the other hand, the goal of an acquisition is to buy a business for less value than it will later prove to be worth—from either an offensive or defensive perspective and with or without cost and revenue synergies. To serve the buyer's shareholders, an acquisition must be additive to the acquirer's business at some point in the future. Other than the DCF, the methodologies noted earlier do not address this question. What others are willing to pay for similar businesses has no bearing on whether a deal is good for a particular buyer.

Analysis of price is summarized in the board book on a sheet commonly referred to as the "football field." Resembling the aerial view of the gridiron, this sheet has horizontal bars depicting the ranges of fair value for a business using the four methodologies outlined earlier. The bars fall between vertical lines of dollar values and range from the lows to the highs in the market. Means, medians, and the value being proposed for a company are marked against these bars. Fair deals generally fall within the bars, preferably at or above the means or medians. Often, a deal is above average according to some methodologies and below in others. This occurs, for instance, when a target's projections show significant growth, in which case the trailing multiples may be high but the forward multiples low. The EIC deal was shown to be fair across all methodologies.

In addition to the methodologies described earlier, a buyer's fairness opinion presentation usually contains an accretion and dilution analysis. The bankers prepare a set of pro forma financials combining the projections of the seller and the buyer that take into account how the purchase is to be funded. Pro forma results for earnings per share are then compared against expected stand-alone results. The deal is considered "accretive" when the earnings per share improve and "dilutive" when they decline. Accretive deals are viewed favorably, though the accretive or dilutive nature of a transaction is not necessarily indicative of fairness (as an aside, accretion and dilution analyses are also used for capital-raising transactions to determine whether a deal will improve or harm expected earnings results based on the anticipated use of the proceeds).

Along similar lines, fairness opinion books for stock-based transactions also include "contribution" analyses. These compare the percentage of the stock the seller receives in the combined company to the financial contribution that the seller's business will make to the combined company's operations. Pro forma financial statements are prepared for past and projected periods to help in this assessment. Contribution to revenues, cash flows, and profitability are taken into account. Sellers want to receive more of a combined company than they are contributing and buyers want the opposite. For example, a seller and a buyer would have differing views on a transaction in which the seller is to receive 20 percent of the combined company but is only contributing 10 percent to projected net income. As with the previously discussed valuation methodologies, it is typical for some components of a contribution analysis to support the seller and others to support the buyer. In the example just given, for instance, the discrepancy may be acceptable to the buyer when the revenue or cash flow contributions from the seller exceed 20 percent.

Prior to the board meetings for the EIC deal, the advisors presented their conclusions and board materials internally to their fairness opinion committees. Rendering fairness opinions entails financial risks. The merits of a transaction and the conclusions of a fairness opinion may be challenged by unhappy shareholders and their lawyers. Becoming embroiled in litigation concerning these matters can be costly and time-consuming. Organizationally, investment banks seek to avoid this scenario even at the risk of losing future fees and harming client relationships. Banking teams, on the other hand, often seek to support the will of those who hired them, be it management, the board, or both. Steered by this bias, bankers have been known to take positions and cherry pick market data that support a desired outcome. The committees at Silverman and JV Securities agreed with the fairness conclusions of their bankers. The premium was the only outlier in the valuation discussions and, at 43 percent, was far from unprecedented.

The committees and the boards also inquired about other notable terms in the transaction. For instance, it contained a provision allowing PEMCO to break off the transaction in the event of a material adverse change in EIC's business. Known as a MAC, this was typical. It also contained a breakup fee to protect PEMCO in the event that EIC changed its position and accepted a better offer. This was a legitimate risk. The acquisition was still subject to shareholder approval and, as fiduciaries, EIC's board members were obligated to consider other offers prior to closing. The breakup fee would make such a move more expensive and unlikely. The proposed fee was 2 percent of the transaction's value. Though not all deals have breakup fees, they generally range from 1 percent to 3 percent. Under the terms of their engagement letter, Silverman would receive half the fee if a breakup occurred—also typical. All of the parties were comfortable with the fairness of these provisions.

Had the PEMCO/EIC deal involved stock, there would have also been a detailed discussion of stock-related considerations, including aspects of the "exchange ratio." This ratio refers to the number of shares of the acquirer that each share of the target receives in a deal. For example, a target that is being purchased for $30 a share, all in stock, by a company with a $60 share price will receive half an acquirer share for every target share—the exchange ratio is 0.500.

Exchange ratios are set before a deal is announced. Because this puts the target's value at risk in the event that the acquirer's stock declines post-announcement, there are often resets for the exchange ratio when the acquirer trades above or below predetermined levels—called a "floor" and a "ceiling" (it is worth noting that resets are not found in merger-of-equals transactions (MOEs) because the parties combining forces are not treated as a buyer and a seller). Between these levels, the seller's value decreases or increases with movements in the acquirer's stock. Below or above these levels, the seller receives more shares or fewer shares. All of these matters, as well as an analysis of historical trading ratios between buyer and seller, are discussed and debated extensively in stock-based transactions.

The transaction was announced the day after the fairness opinions were rendered in late February. Leading up to this point, there had been great secrecy surrounding the transaction. Only those within the companies, their bankers, their lawyers, and their accountants who needed to know about the discussions had been informed about their existence. No one wanted a leak or suspicious trading before the announcement. PEMCO and EIC had been placed on the "watch lists" by the compliance departments of both advisors and Chinese walls had been established within each of the organizations to guard against accidental disclosures. A Chinese wall is the common term for internal policies and pro-cedures designed to limit nonpublic information pertaining to transactions and companies to only specific personnel with necessary access, such as investment banking deal teams.

Like all such discussions, the transaction had been code named by the pursuer's advisors. Silverman had dubbed the deal Project Olympus. PEMCO and EIC were referred to in all written materials as Pan and Echo, respectively. Looking to tap into the faded memories of their college educations, M&A bankers frequently use Greek and Roman themes to identify projects (sports themes are also popular).

Upon announcement, EIC's stock price quickly surged to just under the price PEMCO was offering to pay. The market believed that the offer would not be topped; otherwise, it would have traded higher. The minor discount between the trading price and PEMCO's offer reflected the time value of money and the risk that the deal might collapse. There was no use for an investor to pay the full offer price for EIC's stock today when all that could be gained was getting the same amount back in a few months if and when the deal closed. As the closing date approached, the discount would shrink. During this time, arbitrageurs would trade around their positions to lock in gains produced by the discount.

PEMCO's stock traded flat initially. Its investors read the press release but withheld judgment on the acquisition until they could learn more. Furthermore, investors had nothing to gain from playing the typical arbitrage game of a "paired trade" given that the deal involved cash. Found in stock deals, arbitrageurs de-ploying this strategy short the buyer's stock and long the seller's stock to secure gains.

PEMCO scheduled a conference call with investors to discuss the transaction on the day of its announcement. These calls are universal in larger transactions and PEMCO's team felt a formal call was warranted despite EIC's relatively small size. It was the company's first acquisition and would deplete the company's cash balances. PEMCO's CFO and IR department had fielded several inbound inquiries concerning the deal before the call. In the interest of fair disclosure, they had deflected each of these and referred investors to the scheduled discussion. Including questions and answers, PEMCO's talk on the rationale and merits of the EIC transaction lasted about 90 minutes. The call was joined by most of PEMCO's larger shareholders as well as research analysts with coverage on the company. Several of EIC's larger investors also listened in. Management's comments and responses had been carefully scripted with the assistance of its advisors. PEMCO's shares traded up modestly after the call.

Once terms are agreed to in a public company acquisition, the target's share-holders must be solicited for their approval before the deal can be consummated.

Generally speaking, this can be done in two ways: by obtaining their votes or by obtaining their shares. Votes are gathered by using a proxy statement. Shares are gathered by using a "tender offer." The tender offer process is quicker and thus preferred by many buyers. It also does not involve some of the previously discussed formalities and the drawn out campaigning necessary to secure certain institutional votes. A tender offer entails soliciting some majority of the shareholders to submit, or tender, their shares in exchange for the consideration being offered in a transaction. Shareholders are given 20 business days to accept or deny the offer. If a sufficient number of shares is tendered, the deal closes (holdouts remain as shareholders or can be forced out by the acquirer in a subsequent legal proceeding).

Over the past two decades, tender offers have been used infrequently in negotiated transactions due to past interpretations of the "best price" rule (note that they are also rare in nonnegotiated deals due to the antitakeover protections of most companies). This rule holds that a buyer must offer each shareholder the highest price offered to any other shareholder. Some courts have held this amount to include items like severance payments offered to employee shareholders such as executives, thereby making the tender offer approach too costly in most acquisitions.

Recent SEC interpretations, however, differ on this point. Going forward, it is likely we will see tender offers reemerge as an important mechanism for completing mergers and acquisitions.

PEMCO's transaction had been structured in a fashion requiring a shareholder vote. As a result, the next step for the parties was to prepare the proxy statement to solicit the approval of EIC shareholders. Similar to the documentation process involved in a public offering, the proxy statement was drafted by EIC's management team, lawyers, and bankers. The bulk of the work fell on the attorneys. The proxy statement would be filed with, and likely reviewed by, the SEC before being mailed out. At that point, shareholders would be given no fewer than 20 business days to submit their votes before EIC's formal shareholder meeting to approve or reject PEMCO's offer. Shareholders could also vote in person at the meeting if they chose to do so.

Pursuant to SEC-mandated disclosure requirements, the proxy statement contains all information deemed necessary for investors to make a well-informed decision about the transaction. Among other things, this included a copy of EIC's fairness opinion, details on the negotiation process and transaction timeline, and any nonpublic financial projections provided by EIC to PEMCO.

Along with EIC's proxy statement, the parties needed to prepare a HSR antitrust filing. Required for many mergers and acquisitions exceeding certain threshold sizes, the HSR filing enables the Department of Justice and Federal Trade Commission to review the competitive impact of a transaction on the marketplace and challenge it, if necessary, to protect the interests of consumers. Given its modest scale and the fragmented nature of the integration and design market within power supplies, the EIC acquisition would not face resistance. Once filed, the HSR process, assuming no challenges or "second requests" from

Figure 18.1. Acquisition flowchart.

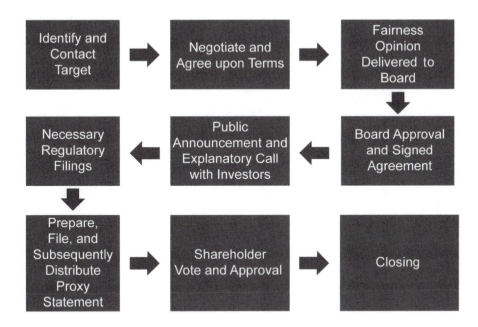

the government for more information, encompasses a 30-day waiting period before a transaction can proceed.

The proxy statement and HSR filing were submitted in mid-March. With the SEC review process and the legally required waiting period for shareholder votes, EIC's final vote was not tallied until mid-May. The transaction was approved. It closed shortly thereafter. The parties had done an effective job at soliciting the support of EIC shareholders and campaigning to win over influential proxy advisors whose verdicts on a deal can significantly sway the votes and opinions of institutional investors.

The acquisition of EIC had been an interesting process and learning experience for PEMCO's management. From start to finish, the primary phases of the transaction could be graphically depicted as follows:

Prior to the closing, members of the transaction team, including company management, bankers, lawyers, and accountants, had been contacted by the SEC. Names of the team members had been provided at the agency's request by PEMCO and EIC. Each team member was presented with a list of individuals. The list noted names and cities of residence. Without further explanation, the team members were asked whether they knew anyone on the list. Fortunately none did. Although not stated, the list contained the identities of people who had suspiciously traded in EIC's stock shortly before the announcement. The SEC was looking for insider trading. The agency follows a similar procedure after the release of news that significantly impacts a company's stock price. The names on such lists can be very surprising. Suffice it to say, not every case of improper trading makes front page news. Most are handled quietly but firmly by the authorities.

Prior to EIC's shareholder vote, PEMCO closed out its first quarter and reported its results. The call and earnings release occurred on May 1. For the most part, it followed the same script as in the past. The news was good. The company beat the numbers, the business looked better than ever, and expectations were raised modestly for the year. The stock hit $30 a share.

The day before the announcement, PEMCO's board had convened its regularly scheduled quarterly meeting to review performance and progress. The meeting brimmed with optimism. Few of the board members had ever seen, much less been involved with, a company that had such demand for its products and successful execution in delivering them. In the course of the discussions, Larry raised an issue that had cropped up with one of the newer and larger PEM models. A couple of the recently launched PEM-powered automobiles had been returned to dealerships with overheating units. The defective PEMs were replaced without incident. With a few thousand vehicles already on the road, all indications pointed to the cause being an anomalous glitch triggered by sloppy installations—Friday afternoon specials, as some would say. The board was unconcerned. Installations were the responsibility of the vehicle's manufacturer, not PEMCO. No further mention of the incidents would be made, especially publicly.

No fewer than three closing celebrations were held for the EIC acquisition in early June. Silverman and JV Securities each held a dinner with their clients. These events followed the standard protocol of good food, good wine, toasts, joke gifts, and lucites containing small commemorative tombstones of the deal. Hoping to foster a new banking relationship, JV Securities also invited PEMCO's management team to their event for EIC. Without any advisors, PEMCO also held a separate golf weekend for the two management teams. PEMCO wanted everyone to get better acquainted and to bond. While taxing, most would argue that getting a deal done is the easy part; making it work is the real challenge. Smartly, management wanted to establish trust and open communication lines in order to smooth EIC's integration process.

Personal Observations on Strategic Acquisitions

1. *Buying a business is easy; making it work is hard.* Acquisition-hungry executives, particularly those from recently minted IPOs with high-flying stock prices, forget this fact. Many get deal lust and lose sight of the post-acquisition challenges to making a combination work, such as dealing with competing internal agendas, retaining employees, and gaining support from customers. Before closing a deal, careful thought and significant energy should be spent on an integration plan and strategy.

2. *Even with the best intentions and strong coordination among all parties, many strategic acquisitions simply do not work.* They fail to achieve results that come anywhere close to justifying their purchase prices. This happens for a myriad of reasons—customers do not cooperate, markets do not grow as expected, products do not integrate well, et cetera. Even when deals work, it seems that they rarely live up to original expectations. In fact, many deals that are hailed for their merits when consummated are subsequently divested or shut down with much "what were they/we thinking" commentary.

3. *All deals are shopped.* In almost all situations (public and private), targets are shopped before a deal is signed. This may occur very quietly and it may occur despite management's protests to the contrary, but it occurs nevertheless. No one should be surprised when a deal "blows up" and "trades away" at the last minute.

4. *Gaining support of a target's management team is critical to a successful acquisition.* A transaction can make tremendous sense strategically to both companies involved but without the support of the target's executives, it is not likely to occur, much less be successful. Though they are tasked with serving their shareholders, CEOs and other senior executives sometimes lose sight of this fact and direct their energies to serving their own agendas. If a deal does not fit their agendas, senior insiders can be great obstructionists—derailing negotiations, harming company performance, and poisoning employee moral. As a result of this fact, many sound business combinations never occur.

5. *The amount of value an investment banker provides as a buyside advisor is highly dependent upon the size of the acquisition and the nature of the industry.* There is no such thing as a novel idea or introduction in larger, more mature industries. The executives know all of the companies and all of the players. Often, they also have large internal business-development teams to find and execute transactions. Here, an investment banker's value is typically limited to providing a fairness opinion and the financing instruments to effectuate a transaction (e.g., coordinating a large bank facility to fund the purchase). Such assignments are often passed around to investment banks without much concern for the quality of their advisory services (some bankers refer to these mandates as "Lazy Susan business"). In less mature industries, especially those with many private companies and a rapidly changing landscape of players, ideas and introductions are valuable. In these situations, investment bankers are justifiably compensated for their traditional role—putting deals together.

CHAPTER 19

Business Difficulties and Stock Drops

➤ How a business crisis can impact operations, shareholders, and stock prices.

➤ The role and prosecution of shareholder class action lawsuits.

➤ How and why some companies with battered stock prices resist takeover attempts and pursue alternative financing options for survival.

It happened a week after the last closing celebration. Larry received a late-night call from PEMCO's general counsel. It was urgent. The company had been contacted that evening by its PEMobile partner, Hybrid Motors. There was another problem with a couple of the cars, this time a big one. During the morning rush hour, one of the first models off the showroom floor burst into flames. Fortunately, the damage was contained to the engine compartment and no one was injured. Upon first inspection, the issue appeared to be a simple electrical fire. When the car arrived at the local dealership for repairs, the mechanics found a different story. The vehicle's PEM had imploded. Other components under the hood had ignited from the heat caused by the event. The twenty-four hours following the call were a nightmare, and the subsequent few months were not much better.

An emergency board call was convened in the middle of the night. A product warning and recall were issued first thing the next day for all PEMobiles and sales of the vehicles were halted. The news caused a ripple effect that immediately impacted sales of PEMCO's other products, as well as discussions with existing and potential OEM partners. Though no issue had ever arisen with the earlier, smaller PEM units, customers feared the worst about the young technology. Although only one other, injury-free implosion would occur before all of the PEMobiles could be recalled, the damage to PEMCO's business had been done. It would take months and months to reclaim the trust and confidence of customers and partners after the problem with the larger units was identified and cured—tasks that PEMCO's engineering team was able to complete within three weeks of the first implosion.

Investors take several approaches in the face of bad news. Some sell first and ask questions later. Others attempt to make informed decisions in order to avoid what could later be characterized as panic selling. Those in the latter category who decide to sell after their assessment either do it quickly or wait for the market to briefly stabilize due to opportunistic buyers. In PEMCO's case, most investors feared the worst and those who did not feared those who did. With the influence that investor psychology rather than company fundamentals can have on a stock, there is much to be said about the old adage "you can't fight the tape." This is particularly true when it comes to generating short-term performance—a requirement for many portfolio managers who are judged by their constituents quarterly. Trading volume went through the roof, with more than 20 million shares switching hands. PEMCO's stock closed at $15 a share and was dragged lower over the subsequent week. It ultimately bounced back to just under $17 when trading volumes subsided. There had been a complete rotation in PEMCO's shareholder base. Momentum investors were replaced by value investors and others interested in distressed situations.

A securities class action lawsuit was filed against PEMCO within days of the stock price drop. The cause of action was fraud. More specifically, the suit alleged that management had provided overly optimistic guidance in the past quarter's earnings release and failed to disclose material information concerning the status of PEMCO's products and business. The suit sought damages for all investors who had purchased the stock since the release. A clever attorney had uncovered evidence of the PEMobile's earlier overheating incidents. Even if this was not discovered, a shareholder suit would have been highly likely. Stock drops of this magnitude draw legal fire. If accompanied by insider selling beforehand, a suit is all but certain.

Shareholder class action lawsuits are big business. Such suits result in billions of dollars annually in settlement and damage awards from publicly traded corporations accused of wrongdoing. A handful of law firms have taken the lead on the majority of these cases. These firms actively monitor the market for stocks that drop precipitously and may be the victim of corporate wrongdoing. In a potential cause of action, these firms jockey aggressively with each other to identify and represent a model plaintiff around whom a court will certify a class action. Each firm then files a suit as soon as possible on behalf of their identified plaintiff, hoping the individual possesses damage and reliance characteristics common to others in the class. Courts weigh a myriad of variables in selecting the final "named plaintiff" and the suit that will serve to represent an injured class. Those plaintiffs and suits not selected become part of the class action.

The firm representing the named plaintiff generally spearheads the suit, as-suming it is qualified to do so and is on the short list of firms approved by large institutional investors to represent them. Although lead firms are not awarded the contingency fees associated with many other torts cases—generally amount-ing to one third of the recovery—they do receive large payouts for the time and resources they commit to cases. Plaintiff lawyers in the cases get paid only if their clients win a case or obtain an acceptable settlement (class action settlements require court approval). Fees are paid out of the damages and are decided by the courts on a case-by-case basis. Fee determinations ultimately involve proposals, submissions, and negotiations between the plaintiff's firm, the plaintiffs, and the court after matters are resolved. Under the American legal system, the plaintiffs and the defense each pay their own legal costs. So even if the defense prevails, it still loses financially. In many foreign jurisdictions, the loser pays the legal costs for both sides.

There has been substantial debate over the merits and abuses of securities class action lawsuits. Some argue that they are an important policing mechanism to protect shareholders, punish wrongdoers, and deter corruption. Others claim that they are too often abused, thereby harming innocent corporations and the competitiveness of the U.S. capital markets. Whereas this debate is best saved for more informed advocates, there is some truth to both positions. Sometimes corporations and their management teams behave fraudulently. Injured investors need legal recourse and should be entitled to it. Other times, attorneys file baseless suits knowing that the defense will settle rather than incur the costs and distractions of a long, drawn out legal battle. These abuses ultimately harm the same investors the law is supposed to protect.

The suit against PEMCO was permitted to proceed and a class action was certified several weeks after the initial legal filings. Despite challenges from PEMCO's counsel, the court was not willing to throw out the suit as a matter of law. There were facts in dispute that could support a fraud claim. These would be left to a jury. Plaintiffs were seeking over $100 million in damages. Investors who had purchased the stock after the earnings announcement and retained ownership until the stock drop were covered by the suit. These buyers had paid an average of $30 a share. Seven million of the roughly 23 million shares in the public float were impacted.

Before the PEMobile implosions, PEMCO had been contemplating a convertible note financing. While the company was starting to generate significant cash flow, it had depleted most of its cash balance with the EIC acquisition. Its cash position had stood at less than $75 million or 3.5% of its market capitalization before the stock price decline. Most emerging growth companies in a similar position (those with an attractive stock price, large market opportunity, and well capitalized competitors) maintain cash positions closer to 10% of their market capitalizations. The board and management believed that a greater financial reserve for future acquisitions or unforeseen difficulties would be prudent. Little did they know at the time how right this perspective would prove to be.

Financially, the company performed well in the second quarter given the late timing of the PEMobile issue. The third quarter, however, was a disaster. By the end of August, it was clear that the company would fall short of the revised guidance provided in its late-July earnings release for the second quarter. Most customers had simply stopped purchasing PEMs due to safety and product liability concerns. Rather than falling 25 percent from beginning-of-the-year expectations, PEMCO pre-released that its revenues were likely to be down 50 percent and the company would be unprofitable. Its stock fell to $10. The company was in a very precarious position. Not only did it not have the financial wherewithal to settle the securities suit, it would not have sufficient cash to fund operations if its business continued to deteriorate. It had a large overhead and now suffered the added costs of funding litigation, nursing damaged OEM relationships, and paying for the recall. By the end of the third quarter, PEMCO's cash balance was down to $55 million. It could only sustain two or three more quarters on its current track.

PEMCO's lawyers were convinced that they could settle the outstanding class action litigation for $50 million. They had dealt with the plaintiffs' counsel before and had a good sense for what it would take to make the case go away. As a percentage of an original claim, settlements often amounted to less, but here it would take more. Plaintiff's discovery in the litigation process had revealed the earlier overheating issues and the board's discussion of the matter in connection with the first quarter's earnings call. Though the comments seemed benign and reasonable at the time, they could look bad in retrospect, particularly when aided by the spin of a silver-tongued trial lawyer. Plaintiff's counsel believed that they had a smoking gun and a winning case. That being said, they were also aware of PEMCO's financial situation and the costs and risks of time-consuming trials and appeals.

PEMCO had few options to fund a $50 million settlement. As a practical matter, it did not have the cash or the debt resources to do so. The company's line of credit and bank relationships required financial metrics that PEMCO no longer possessed due to the current state of its business. Likewise, everyone agreed that attempting to settle directly with stock or freely tradable debt securities was not viable. Such settlements are cumbersome and extremely rare. Because they are difficult to value, plaintiff lawyers do not like them, nor do the courts. PEMCO needed a new investor, but before one could be found another option surfaced.

Common Electric was a leading industrial and consumer products conglomerate with multiple product offerings throughout the energy sector. CE sold everything from small batteries to large power generators. CE was a public company but was controlled by a large hedge fund that owned the largest single position in the company. The fund's founder was credited with turning around CE's fortunes over the past several years. After acquiring his stake in the business, he had become chairman, made several key acquisitions, and transformed CE into a market leader from a market laggard. The founder had a reputation for being highly aggressive and highly opportunistic.

CE had approached PEMCO about a combination prior to the company's IPO but had been rebuffed. CE and its chairman now saw an opening and wanted to reengage. They had done their own homework on PEMCO and concluded that: (1) the product's technical problems had been fixed, (2) the company's legal liabilities were limited to the securities matters, and (3) the company would soon be facing financial challenges. PEMCO's problems were likely to be temporary. The strength of its product, when proven safe, would lure back customers and return PEMCO to its prior success. CE's Chairman firmly believed this and approached PEMCO's CEO accordingly.

Though tactful, CE's overture was not well received by either management or the board. Even with preliminary price talk around $15 a share, a 50% premium to current levels, it fell on deaf ears. The board was required to entertain inquiries but had broad latitude to reject them given that it had not taken steps to sell the company and put it "in play." Exercising reasonable business judgment, PEMCO's board had come to the same conclusions as CE and believed that the company's current troubles would pass. PEMCO just needed time and an injection of outside capital.

Until PEMCO ran out of money, CE was in a difficult bargaining position and its chairman knew it. PEMCO was not a dysfunctional public company with poor management and a large and diverse shareholder base that could be courted by CE's traditional fear-and-greed tactics. Appealing to the public shareholders directly for support would not work here. They held less than a third of the company. A deal would require support from PEMCO's founders and original investors, or at least the latter. The original outside investors still held roughly 45 percent of the company. CE attempted to work on the larger investors directly, including Alpha, Beta, Carto, and POC, but without success. As with the founders, they were not interested in selling out at current levels.

PEMCO's concentrated ownership was similar to many emerging growth companies, particularly in the technology sector. Such companies experience very few takeover battles as a result. Had the ownership been different and more diffuse, PEMCO might have accepted CE's offer but in all likelihood only after shopping it beforehand to secure the best price. Likewise, under this scenario, if there had been serious personality differences between the management teams or disagreements over strategic direction, PEMCO might have targeted and pursued another suitor that could offer similar terms and more aligned thinking. Known as a "white knight," PEMCO could have tilted the discussion in this party's favor and accepted a deal even if the terms offered did not contain the absolute highest price. The best offer determination can take into account other variables. PEMCO's takeover defenses, installed prior to its IPO, would have afforded the company significant time and negotiating leverage to strike a deal to its liking. Of course, an aggressive suitor offering an attractive price for a company with limited alternatives and a broad shareholder base can ultimately win the prize given sufficient time, even against the most recalcitrant management team and board.

With the CE transaction out of the question, PEMCO immediately undertook the process of finding financing and a suitable outside investor. The company would seek a PIPE using an approach similar to that which EIC had contemplated before being acquired. The primary difference would be the group of targeted investors. PIPEs generally involve small syndicates of institutional investors that focus on public securities. They rely exclusively on publicly available information and typically involve no more than $50 million in aggregate proceeds. PEMCO's deal would be different. The company was seeking to raise $100 million and would need to bring the new investor or investors into the nonpublic fray. The investor would want to understand the status of the litigation and would need to be involved in the settlement strategy. If a deep-pocketed investor put money in the business before the settlement was resolved, the plaintiffs were certain to seek more money. A handful of private equity players and hedge funds were best suited to fulfill this role.

PEMCO's PIPE strategy was formulated with the assistance of its lead investment bank. The company had again hired ILB as its advisor and agent, given the firm's continued commitment to the business, relationships with private equity funds, and role in PEMCO's past transactions. The company believed that some of the interested investors from the Series D round could be well suited to the current opportunity.

Before engaging ILB, the board had contemplated an "inside" financing round (i.e., one involving only the existing major investors). The board representative from Carto Ventures had voiced an interest in funding the settlement for an added stake in the business. Several companies with deep-pocketed inside investors had taken this approach to fund operations and restructurings after the technology bubble burst. In PEMCO's case, the idea had been dismissed when the funding discussion turned to a larger round. Carto's current fund was not in a position to write a $100 million check. Counsel had also cautioned the company about undertaking any action that could later be construed as favoring inside interests given the existing shareholder litigation.

ILB and PEMCO developed a short list of targeted investors. It included two private equity firms and three hedge funds. All had sufficient funds, a technology focus, and a history of making large minority investments in public companies. All were approached under NDAs. PEMCO had also considered including the hedge fund run by CE's chairman. He was clearly interested in the company. It was decided, however, that the fund was conflicted and may even be prevented from undertaking the investment due to the "corporate opportunity doctrine." This doctrine prevents senior corporate insiders from independently pursuing opportunities better suited to their companies.

Two of the potential investors were interested in the PEMCO opportunity. Unaware of the prior discussions with CE, one of these parties even encouraged the company to take itself private. PEMCO would only need $400 or $500 million to buy out the public shareholders, fund the settlement, and stabilize the business for renewed expansion. PEMCO's significant insider ownership would simply be rolled over into the private company. The investor argued that the new investment could be funded by an equity syndicate that it would lead, members of which it had already identified and worked with in the past. To strengthen the insiders' position, most of the new equity investment could even be structured so as to be repurchased with debt proceeds once the company returned to profitability. PEMCO's board liked the idea but was not interested in putting the company in play with CE lurking on the sidelines. Pursuit of an insider buyout, commonly referred to as a management buyout or MBO, would provide an opening that would legally enable CE to put up a better offer and win the company. It might also draw other suitors.

After a series of meetings and negotiations, PEMCO settled on Platinum Lake Partners to work with on the investment. Founded by a group of ex-investment bankers and Silicon Valley executives, PLP had established itself as one of the leading buyout and special opportunity players on Wall Street in the technology arena. PLP had a solid reputation for creative solutions and fair dealings. PLP and PEMCO did not formally agree on investment terms as this would have required public disclosure. Rather, the parties agreed in principle on a conceptual framework for the investment.

Working with PLP behind the scenes, PEMCO spent the next several months negotiating its class action settlement. The matter was resolved at year-end, much faster than typical but necessary given the company's deteriorating financial status. A securities class action suit can last years and years. It may also name company directors and officers as defendants. When included, the legal expenses for directors and officers are generally borne by the company and directors' and officers' (D&O) insurance policies funded by the company. Settlements and damages against them are also covered by these sources. Intentionally unlawful acts and certain other acts of malfeasance are excluded from company indemnification and insurance coverage.

At the start of the new year, PEMCO found itself with $65 million in cash—the remains of its prior balance and the post-settlement proceeds from PLP's investment. PLP held a board seat and was now the fifth largest shareholder behind Larry, Jerry, Alpha, and Beta. Its investment was a no-coupon preferred stock that converted into PEMCO common stock at $12 a share. Although it offered no yield (i.e., no dividend payments), it provided PLP with upside opportunity through the common stock and downside protection through the preferred stock's more senior position in PEMCO's capital structure (no-coupon securities should not be confused with zero coupon instruments, which are issued at a discount to face value and accrete to face value at maturity, thereby producing yield to the investor).

In early January, PEMCO's stock rallied to $16. PLP and PEMCO were each winners. The company still had much work to do to win back customers but it was back on track to do so, had capital, and was no longer under the cloud of material and uncertain litigation. Furthermore, the stability helped improve morale and retain employees, many of whom had grown skittish about the company's prospects and were at risk of being poached by competitors. Fortunately, with the stock price trading above the IPO (the point where many had been given stock options) there was no need to reset the "strike price" on the options to current levels to keep the employees motivated. Resetting options to keep employees after a major stock price collapse, though dilutive to shareholders, is a common and often necessary practice.

CHAPTER 20

Financing Considerations for a Maturing Business

➤ The alternatives available to pre-IPO investors for obtaining liquidity when a company matures: registered sales, Rule 144 sales, and unregistered institutional sales.

➤ The characteristics of the primary financing options for more mature businesses in the public securities market: equity-linked financings, debt financings, and others.

➤ The function of rating agencies for debt and debt-related securities.

➤ The use of "shelf" registration statements.

Two years passed before PEMCO reclaimed the position it held before the PEMobile implosions. The company had been public for three and a half years and in existence for nine. Despite serious setbacks, it had survived and was again thriving. Its military and consumer businesses were again expanding and its automobile partners had successfully launched two new PEMobiles, both of which carried new branding and monikers. It had accomplished these feats without raising any additional financing beyond simple bank debt, an amazing accomplishment given the stringent testing requirement now imposed on the company by business partners, consumer protection organizations, and government regulators. As the company matured to and beyond this point, it would or could face a host of considerations involving the capital markets.

SHAREHOLDER LIQUIDITY

PEMCO's inside shareholders would eventually seek to liquidate their positions. As parties who acquired their shares prior to the IPO, their stock was not registered with the SEC. The law provides that public sales of securities must be registered unless the sale fits within specified exceptions. Besides giving it away, parties in this position basically have three options to dispose of stock:

1. **Registered sales.** Holders of unregistered stock can request that the issuer register the shares with the SEC. After being registered, the shares are freely tradable and no longer "legended" (a term referring to the legal language describing transferability limitations, such as the provisions of a lock-up agreement, printed on the back of a stock certificate). Because the registration process can be time-consuming and costly, issuers rarely oblige such requests without being under a contractual obligation to do so. Shares issued in many nonpublic transactions, such as late-stage private rounds and PIPEs, are generally accompanied by a stock purchase agreement entitling the buyer to one or more "demand" registration rights. Barring exceptional circumstances provided for in these agreements, issuers must register shares pursuant to these requests. Registrations usually occur under "shelf" registration statements. A shelf is an "evergreen" document placed on file with the SEC that permits the holders of the registered shares to effectuate sales whenever and however they choose.

2. **Rule 144 sales.** Almost all unregistered sales are made pursuant to Rule 144. Under this rule, unregistered securities in a public company may be sold by the holder, assuming the shares have been held for more than a specified time period, currently six months, and the issuer is current on its informational filings with the SEC. Sales of this sort are executed in the same fashion and to the same buyers as sales of registered securities. Venture capitalists and private equity investors often distribute shares in their public holdings to their limited partners, who then sell the smaller positions pursuant to Rule 144 at their own discretion. The firm's ownership duration is "tacked" onto that of its limiteds to enable compliance with the holding-period requirements. Following a 144 sale, shares are freely tradable by the new owner.

3. **Institutional sales.** The law permits issuers to sell unregistered securities to qualified institutional buyers (QIBs). This provision has been stretched to allow shareholders (institutional or otherwise) to make similar sales. While defined with greater specificity in the rules, QIBs are essentially all large institutional investors, including mutual funds, hedge funds, pension funds, and foundations. Secondary sales of unregistered stock to QIBs are uncommon because the trading limitations follow the stock to the new owner in such sales. When they do occur, the sales prices are discounted to compensate for the illiquidity.

A sale made pursuant to each of the methods just described may be completed through a brokerage firm serving as an agent to find buyers in exchange for a commission—in essence, the same approach found in typical public market stock sales. A sale can also take the form of a "bought deal" in which the brokerage firm itself serves as the initial buyer and then places the shares in one or more subsequent sales to new owners. Bought deals usually involve large positions that can disrupt trading volume and negatively impact price. A bought deal structure allows the seller to shift this risk to the brokerage firm. In exchange, the firm is generally able to buy the position at a discount to the public price. If the firm is able to move the position at a higher price, it books a gain. If the price falls, the firm either loses money or holds the position for a later sale, hoping the price rebounds.

Executives and directors of public companies face special limitations in buying and selling stock. They may be sued by shareholders to relinquish profits generated from closely timed purchase and sale transactions—known as "short swing" profits. They must also comply with company trading policies that generally prohibit stock transactions between the period beginning two weeks before the end of a fiscal quarter and ending shortly after the announcement of financial results. These so-called "window period" or "blackout period" policies are intended to prevent actual and perceived insider trading.

By dint of their positions, topmost senior executives are constantly exposed to sensitive information concerning their companies. To avoid claims of improper trading behavior surrounding the use of this information, many executives with large equity positions put in place liquidation mechanisms known as Rule 10b5–1 programs or plans. Structured and executed by private client departments within brokerage firms, these programs systematize the quarterly sale of securities to enable asset diversification. Pursuant to the terms of the program, an executive sells a set percentage or set number of shares each quarter at a specified time. Once in place, the executive has no input or control over the sales. They occur automatically, whether the stock is doing well or poorly. Despite this lack of control, the press often reports these transactions in their published listings of insider sales. As a result, these listings may not be a good indicator of executive sentiment about a company. The same could be said of many reported insider purchases. These often involve nothing more than the exercise of stock options nearing expiration. All insider purchases and sales must be noted on Form 4s filed with the SEC. These filings are the press's principal source of information for purchase and sale listings.

EQUITY AND EQUITY-LINKED FINANCINGS

Mature businesses rarely issue equity unless embarking on significant expansion or seeking to reestablish ties with public investors that had previously lost interest in a company. Mature companies generally finance growth with debt or internally generated cash flow. Both are less expensive alternatives. At times, they may also issue equity-linked instruments such as convertible securities. As previously discussed, convertibles may come in the form of debt or preferred stock. Debt versions typically carry a five- or seven-year maturity and are referred to as "notes" rather than "bonds" (instruments with maturities exceeding ten years are called bonds). Preferred stock versions may be structured to exist in perpetuity unless converted by the investor or redeemed by the issuer. Convertibles pay a lower coupon than straight debt and may be converted into shares of the issuer at a premium to the company's stock price at issuance. A convertible security can provide an attractive financing vehicle when a company's balance sheet is in need of capital that is subordinate to other debt, such as bank facilities. Convertible notes are a lower-cost form of capital than straight equity.

In essence, the issuer of a convertible security is selling two securities at once: (1) debt and (2) an option on its stock. As with straight debt, the buyer receives a security that pays a coupon (or dividend, in the case of a preferred stock instrument) and typically has a maturity period for the repayment of principal. The buyer also receives an embedded option to acquire the issuer's stock at a specific price using the face value of the convertible instrument. This option reduces the cost of the debt by driving down the coupon and allowing more lenient covenants, or issuer obligations, in the instrument. Given the bifurcated nature of convertible instruments, companies sometimes issue "synthetic converts" by issuing straight debt with warrants to accomplish the same objective. Converts provide investors with the upside opportunity of equity and the downside protection of debt.

The value of an option is influenced heavily by the volatility of the underlying stock—the higher the volatility (i.e., propensity for price swings), the higher the option value. For this reason, it is common for the market for convertible securities to become more active during periods of heavy volatility. Such periods allow companies to monetize the volatility in their stocks by issuing attractively priced convertible instruments—the greater the option value, the higher the conversion premium and the lower the coupon. The market's primary gauge for overall volatility is the Chicago Board Options Exchange Volatility Index, commonly known as the VIX. It measures the implied volatility of S&P 500 index options and therefore the market's expected near-term volatility. It is actively monitored by investment bankers, traders, and investors focused on options and convertible securities.

The market for convertible securities has advanced significantly over the past many years due to the influx of hedge funds and more sophisticated analytical tools and trading strategies. The terms and conditions of convertible securities can be tailored to meet the specific needs of an issuer. Subject to tradeoffs, the coupon, conversion premium, and maturity period all can be adjusted up or down. Aside from balancing these factors, pricing is driven by the state of the credit markets, the issuer's credit characteristics, and the volatility of the issuer's stock. The amount of "borrow" in a company's stock can also be important as convertible buyers often deploy hedging strategies when making purchases. These strategies involve shorting the issuer's stock. As noted previously, borrow refers to the number of shares across Wall Street that brokerage firms can lend to those looking to make short sales. A share can only be lent once at any particular time for such purposes.

The covenants contained within the indentures of convertible instruments typically place very few restrictions on the issuer. Unlike straight debt, they do not require the issuer to maintain financial coverage ratios or limit the assumption of additional debt. Buyers do require "no call" provisions that limit the right of the issuers to redeem convertible instruments before a certain period of time has elapsed after issuance, generally three or five years. Without this protection, an issuer would call for redemption once its stock traded above the conversion premium, thereby forcing the buyer to convert and forego interest payments.

Convertible securities may be sold pursuant to a registration statement or may be sold to institutional buyers without one. For sales in the United States, unregistered sales are made pursuant to Rule 144A. Sales to foreign investors are made pursuant to Regulation S. More than half of all convertible deals are 144A sales (including those with Reg S sales sprinkled in). Because the instruments appeal primarily to institutional buyers, there is virtually no pricing difference between registered and unregistered sales. Most 144A transactions, in fact, require the issuers to use their "best efforts" to register the convertible securities within a certain number of days after the initial sale, usually 90 days. A liquid aftermarket exists for unregistered and registered converts between institutional buyers, and most investment banks maintain dedicated and active trading operations in the instruments.

Whether registered or unregistered, convertible securities are sold through investment banks acting as either underwriters or agents. Investment banks are generally paid an underwriting or placement fee of 3 percent for their services. Issuers usually negotiate lower fees for larger transactions. Convertible issuances can range up to several billion dollars, though most involving growth companies fall below $300 million. Convertible issuances rarely exceed 30 percent of a company's market capitalization. Likewise, they are rarely under $75 million unless completed as PIPEs.

The bank selection process for a convertible security is similar to a follow-on equity offering. Bankers are chosen based on their past contributions to the issuer and expertise in underwriting and trading convertibles. Because convertibles have an equity angle that buyers look to understand, a bank's history with trading and researching the issuer's stock is also important. To avoid the risk of leaks, issuers do not typically conduct bake-offs for convertible deals. Convertible deals usually involve fewer investment banks than equity deals due to their smaller fees. Often, there is only one lead manager, and this party usually receives more than 70 percent of the economics. In most situations, co-managers receive 5 percent to 10 percent each.

The transaction process for convertible securities is also similar to equity offerings. After the banking group is selected, an organizational meeting is called with the issuer, the bankers, the lawyers, and the accountants. The meeting includes a review of the proposed transaction, due diligence, and drafting. Whether or not they are registered with the SEC, convertible offerings use marketing prospectuses that describe the company, the terms of the offering, and key provisions of the transaction's indenture (the contractual arrangement between the issuer and the investor describing the terms of the security, the obligations of the issuer, and the rights of the investors). The drafting process typically lasts under two weeks. The marketing process begins immediately after completion of the marketing document in the case of 144A transactions and those made pursuant to a shelf-registration statement.

Marketing involves presentations to the sales forces at the investment banks and a road show. The road show can range from one day to several days and typically includes conference calls, in addition to one-on-ones, with institutional investors. Institutional meetings and their follow-up are coordinated by convertible salespeople or equity salespeople who encourage their clients to invest or to refer the opportunity to an appropriate investment affiliate within their fund complex. A book of orders is generated from these meetings and then the transaction prices, assuming the terms are acceptable to the issuer's board. Leading up to this point, the commitment committees at the investment banks would need to approve the transaction.

Once priced, the transaction is allocated to interested buyers within the book of orders. This process is spearheaded by the ECM desk of the lead underwriter (the convertible effort typically falls within this department). Before the allocation process is complete and trading officially begins, convertible securities trade in the "grey market." Here, investors buy and sell securities that have yet to be issued. They fulfill their delivery and payment obligations when the securities become available. With the existence of the grey market, the issuer and its investment banks have an earlier view on a deal's success than in an IPO, where trading only begins after the official opening of the stock.

Because the underlying value of a convertible security relies heavily upon its opportunity to participate in the equity upside of the issuer, most convertibles are issued without credit ratings. Large convertible issues from more mature companies, as well as bonds, notes, and even syndicated credit lines, are rated by all or a subset of the main rating agencies: S&P, Moody's, and Fitch Ratings. Issuers pay these independent agencies to review their credit characteristics and the credit quality of specific debt instruments. Ratings are published for investors and are updated when warranted by new developments. Investors generally require ratings from at least two of the agencies before acquiring a debt security.

Each rating agency has a slightly different hierarchy of ratings. When a rating is warranted, the required coupon for a security and how it trades in the aftermarket are dictated by where it falls in this hierarchy. Unlike the equity market, where value is driven by the unique aspects of each company, bonds are treated as more homogeneous. Those with the same ratings trade within narrow interest-rate bands, the upper and lower ends of which are often created by speculation about improving or deteriorating credit quality. When a credit rating is upgraded, the security trades up and its effective yield decreases. The reverse holds true for credit downgrades. Coupon differences between the various ratings are referred to as "yield spreads." Spreads are described according to basis points. There are 100 basis points, or "bips," for each 1 percent.

When seeking a credit rating, the issuer prepares and presents a comprehensive review of its business and credit characteristics to the rating agencies. The review contains detailed historical and projected financial analyses and discusses the terms of the proposed financing. An issuer's lead manager is actively involved in this process, helping prepare and guide the contents of the rating-agency presentations. These are not released publicly and typically contain confidential information such as internal projections. Agencies are selected based upon their knowledge, history, and reputation within an industry. Rating opportunities are often steered to those considered to be more issuer friendly in a given sector. A lead reviewer from each agency is assigned to spearhead the rating effort. Reviewers and their teams typically have industry expertise and cover similar companies and instruments.

DEBT FINANCINGS

Debt financings can take several forms. Given the breadth and depth of the market, debt can be highly tailored to meet the objectives of the borrower. In broad strokes, the options are driven by length of maturity, balance-sheet priority, and collateral. Shorter maturity instruments are generally used to satisfy working capital requirements. These usually take the form of revolving lines of credit supplied by commercial banks. Companies may also sell their receivables to third parties to generate immediate cash, which is known as "factoring." A myriad of financial players make such purchases at discounts to the face value of the receivables. Much larger corporations may also fund short-term capital needs through the issuance of commercial paper—interest-bearing securities issued to institutions that carry maturities under 270 days. Commercial paper programs have credit ratings. Along with short-term instruments issued by governmental entities, commercial paper serves as a cornerstone of the money market for investors and financial institutions. Borrowings to fund longer-term projects, such as capital improvements and acquisitions, have longer maturities. They typically take the form of term loans, notes, or bonds.

Whether short-term or long-term, all debt is assigned a priority on the borrower's balance sheet. The priority is dictated by the contractual provisions in a company's lending agreements. In the event of a default or bankruptcy, priority dictates the rights of the lenders and the sequence through which they are to be repaid with available assets of the borrower. In this context, borrowings are typically defined as senior or subordinated. Senior, or higher, priority means less risk and lower interest rates. Subordinated instruments have lower priority and higher borrowing costs. Borrowings of equal rank are said to be "pari passu." All debt obligations rank higher in priority than common equity or preferred stock.

Closely linked to priority is collateral. This refers to assets of the borrower that have been identified to serve as security for a specific loan. The lender has recourse to these assets before other parties in cases of default. Secured borrowings may or may not permit recourse to other assets and the borrower itself. Collateral is required for many types of loans. Short-term borrowings are often secured by items such as inventory or customer receivables. Longer-term borrowings may be secured by assets such as real estate. When priority and collateral are considered together, the least risky debt is senior secured and the most risky is subordinated unsecured (note that the priority comes before security in an instrument's description).

The rights and obligations of investors and issuers for debt issued in the form of bonds and notes are dictated by the terms of a deed of trust, otherwise known as an indenture. For the most part, these are not negotiated by investors. Covenants in an indenture are negotiated by the underwriters and can be fairly standard or highly customized. Compliance with the indenture is supervised and enforced by a trustee, usually the trust department of a large bank. Debt taking the form of a more traditional loan is governed by specific contractual agreements between the borrowers and lenders.

Larger loans are often funded by lending syndicates comprising several commercial banks and, increasingly, other large financial institutions such as hedge funds. Term loans carry varying maturities and, unlike revolving credit facilities, are funded when made. Credit facilities are commitments to be used on an as-needed basis over a certain timeframe. Beyond interest payments, borrowers pay lenders up front (and possibly ongoing) commitment fees for most loans as well as drawdown fees in the case of credit facilities. On large syndicated loans, one or more lenders (typically large banks) serve as the lead lenders, or "arrangers." They negotiate terms, find other lenders, and pull together the syndicate. The arrangers receive an extra fee for this service. The arrangement fee may be shared with other members of the syndicate. Syndicated loans are marketed through a series of bank presentations coordinated by the arranger. All-in syndication fees can run 1 percent to 2 percent. Some large repeat lenders, like LBO firms, have started to self-syndicate loans to avoid these fees and lower their borrowing costs.

Many syndicated loans are part of broader financing packages developed to fund large acquisitions. Deals involving financial buyers almost always include them and may encompass several "tranches" of debt possessing distinct priorities and collateral—each bearing different maturities and interest rates. In these circumstances, there may be more than one arranging agent and an agent is often the investment bank that advised on the transaction in question. These agents may also be required to fund "bridge" loans to cover a portion of the acquisition until other equity or debt sources can be secured. In fact, investment banks are called upon to play three roles in some transactions—advisor, financier, and co-investor. Sophisticated borrowers, such as private equity funds, attempt to steer participation in their loans to certain lenders. They also attempt to place limits on a lender's ability to transfer a syndicate position to a new lender. In the event that the issuer runs into trouble and faces a default, the owners want the debt to be in "friendly" hands (lenders that are willing to negotiate adjustments rather than declare a default—albeit for a fee).

Bonds refer to debt raised through the sale of securities that mature in more than ten years; notes, in less than ten years. Most debt securities are issued with credit ratings and are not registered with the SEC. They are sold pursuant to Rule 144A and/or Regulation S.

How bonds and notes are sold depends largely upon the credit quality of the instrument. High-yield, or "junk" bonds, possess a lower credit quality and are typically sold pursuant to the same process as convertible notes. They involve underwriters, a marketing prospectus, and a short road show. Although they are purchasing debt, junk bond investors look for opportunities where the issuer's credit quality can improve, thereby increasing the value of its bonds. Like equity investors, they look to understand an issuer's prospects for the future. Those with promising "equity" stories can receive materially better terms than their more dubious counterparts. The underwriting fee on high yield offerings is generally 3 percent on an average-size deal but less on larger transactions.

Investment-grade bonds and notes have higher credit ratings and are more removed from the equity story of the issuer. The yield spreads on such instruments are generally tighter and, thus, improvements in credit quality produce only modest increases in value. Investment-grade instruments are more commodity-like and are purchased for current yield. As such, most are sold without the fanfare common to equity and equity-related securities. There is no detailed prospectus or road show. Instead, investment-grade debt securities are sold via the debt capital markets desks of investment banks. Typically, an issuer will shop a potential transaction to a few firms and award the business to the bank that offers the best terms. The transaction is then quickly documented by the issuer, the underwriter, and their respective attorneys using standard forms. The bank then purchases the securities and resells them to institutional investors. The entire process may be as short as one day. Unless sold pursuant to a shelf-registration statement, investment-grade deals are always sold without being registered with the SEC. They are sold to institutional accounts through Rule 144A or Regulation S.

The trading environment for bonds is notably different from that of stocks. Bonds and notes, irrespective of their investment grade, by-and-large trade with less frequency than equity issues and are traded by investors in an informal OTC market known as the "bond market." Registered bonds may be listed on the exchanges but unregistered bonds may only be sold to qualified buyers and cannot be listed on the exchanges (current securities laws forbid it). Trading is conducted between institutional investors directly and via large investment banks that serve as "dealers." The bond-trading desks of dealers buy, sell, and maintain positions in many debt securities and are the principal source of pricing information. Many argue that this approach results in pricing that is less transparent and efficient than securities traded on the exchanges or more formal OTC markets. In light of this perspective, there are currently initiatives underway to permit exchange listings for bonds (registered or unregistered) where the issuers have registered equity securities on the exchange.

Bond investors may protect their positions by acquiring credit protection for their positions. In essence, credit protection serves as insurance and protects the investor against losses resulting from a default. Investors purchase credit protection on the basis of the face value of the instruments they hold. As with other derivative investments and hedging tools, the market for credit protection has ballooned over the past decade.

SALE LEASEBACKS AND ASSET-BACKED FINANCINGS

Besides issuing debt, businesses may obtain capital by leveraging individual assets. This can take many forms. For instance, large manufacturing concerns may borrow against their equipment. One of the more common forms of this asset-backed financing is the sale–leaseback. Businesses with real-estate holdings that require the use of the holdings but want to free up capital held in them for other purposes, may chose to sell the holdings to another party and enter into a lease arrangement for use of the buildings or property. These sale–leaseback arrangements can be useful, particularly when a business has significant equity tied up in real estate due to its appreciation or otherwise. For most business concerns, holding real estate is not considered to be a core competency or the best method to generate returns on invested capital for shareholders.

SHELF-REGISTRATION STATEMENTS

Whether considering the sale of equity, debt, or other securities, mature businesses often put in place shelf-registration statements with the SEC to permit broad and fast distribution of such securities. Shelf-registration statements contain a description of the securities to be offered as well as other required information concerning the issuer. They are filed with the SEC. As with other corporate filings, sometimes they are reviewed and sometimes they are not (although, under recent rule reforms, some filings by large companies—"well-known seasoned issuers"—go effective immediately with no possibility of SEC review). Once finalized with the SEC, they are declared effective and permit the issuer to sell securities without further registration delays. Shelf-registration statements are public documents and are intended to describe securities that may be sold over the foreseeable future.

Shelf-registration statements may be prepared with the assistance of investment bankers. More often, they are drafted by just the issuer and its outside counsel. Upon filing, the document is typically tailored to satisfy only regulatory requirements rather than marketing objectives. The scope of the securities contemplated in a filing typically reflects the opinions of a company's investment bankers. When a "shelf" is used as the foundation for a marketed transaction, the document is amended by the underwriters before printing preliminary prospectuses to be shown to potential investors.

Shelf-registration statements are frequently used to enable "bought deals." Similar to the procedure outlined previously for secondary stock sales, bought deals involve an investment bank purchasing securities from the issuer at a set price. The investment bank then resells the securities to investors. The price is generally the outcome of negotiations with a small handful of banks. The mandate goes to the bank offering the best terms. Unlike marketed transactions, in which the issuer receives only what the investor is willing to pay less an underwriting fee, the investment bank assumes full price risk in bought deals. It pays for the securities and receives whatever price investors ultimately pay for them, whether for a gain or for a loss. Bought deals are standard for investment-grade debt transactions and are often used in equity deals with large issuers. They are less common, but not unheard of, for junk bonds and convertibles. Shelf-registration statements may also be used for PIPE transactions. Commonly referred to as "registered directs," securities "taken off" a shelf for a PIPE receive better terms than those that are not registered due to liquidity considerations.

DERIVATIVES

The topic of derivatives is long and complicated and cannot be addressed appropriately within the confines of this book, particularly given the ever-increasing range of derivatives available in the marketplace. As a general observation, derivatives are not a source of funding for companies. Rather, they enable companies and investors to better manage financial risks. Sometimes they also enable these players to profit in the process. In basic terms, derivatives are contracts between two or more parties that shift or transfer certain rights and obligations associated with other securities, assets, or financial arrangements—they derive from other dealings, hence the name derivatives. Derivatives may be negotiated directly between the parties involved (usually with the aid of a financial intermediary such as an investment bank). They also take the form of standardized contracts that can be purchased and sold, similar to stocks and other securities. Several exchanges specialize in these instruments. The largest is CME Group, which was formed in 2007 through the merger of the Chicago Mercantile Exchange and the Chicago Board of Trade. Unlike stocks that can be traded on or off their listed exchange, derivative contracts created by these exchanges are considered by the courts to be proprietary instruments that can only be traded on their exchange of origin.

Fueled by better technology, stronger analytical tools, and the expansion of interested capital sources (namely hedge funds), the market for derivatives has mushroomed the past several years. By some estimates, the total face value of derivatives globally now approaches $300 trillion, more than a three-fold increase since 2000. Companies use derivatives for everything from assuring stable pricing for commodity supplies, to managing currency fluctuations in global operations, to reducing interest-rate risks tied to outstanding loans and borrowings. Investors use them to reduce risks associated with existing investments, like interest-rate swings and borrower defaults. They also use them to make highly leveraged bets to generate returns.

From the very complicated to the very simple, derivatives generally possess the opportunity for greater gains or losses relative to the securities or financial arrangements from which they derive. Option contracts, for instance, one of the oldest and simplest derivatives, permit an investor to harness the price swings for a large number of shares of a company for a relatively modest sum. Option contracts trade in 100-share increments that can be purchased for a fraction of what the 100 shares would cost. Take a $50 stock for which an option to purchase at $52 can be had for $3 a share. The option would cost $300 for the 100 shares. If the stock ran to $56, this would provide a 33 percent return (a $400 gain that cost $300). When buying the underlying stock at $50, the $56 price would only produce a gain of 12 percent. Of course this works both ways. If the stock was below $55 but above $52, the option would lose money (the difference would be less than the $3 purchase price for the option). If the stock fell below $52, the option would result in a total loss (there would be no gain to offset a portion of the $3).

Figure 20.1. PEMCO's Financing Progression.

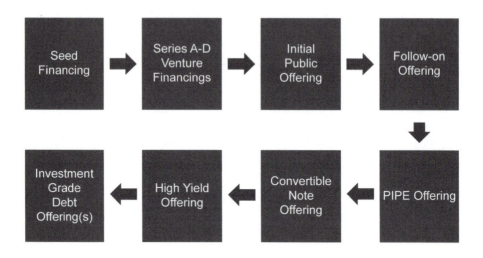

PEMCO's PATH

Having recovered from its defective product issues and shareholder suit, PEMCO pursued a financing path common to many successful, maturing businesses. It financed much of its expansion through bank lines and internal cash flow.

Technology improvements broadened the PEM's applications over time. PEMCO was able to produce much larger units with greater power-generation capabilities. These units provided an economical alternative energy source for homes. To fund the rollout of this initiative and to make some related acquisitions in the fuel-cell market, PEMCO raised capital through a convertible note offering and then a junk bond financing. When its efforts proved successful, the company experienced tremendous cash flow growth and unprecedented stability. The company ultimately achieved an investment-grade credit rating from the rating agencies. It then raised some investment-grade debt to retire its junk bonds and lower its interest payments. PEMCO also forced conversion of the convertible notes by calling the instruments after the "no call" provision expired. Instead of allowing the company to redeem the notes at par, the investors converted the notes to shares. With PEMCO's successes, the stock was trading well above the conversion premium. PEMCO would not need to raise additional equity capital.

Over this time frame, PEMCO was added to a few stock market indexes—most notably, it became part of the S&P 500. Indexes, particularly the broader ones such as the Russell 2000, routinely adjust their rosters to account for changes in the market. They add and drop companies based on their expanding or waning fortunes and influence. Being added to an index is a favorable event for a company. Beyond the prestige, it opens a stock to a long list of new buyers, namely index funds. The added demand from these can drive a stock price higher and lower a company's capital costs.

An Added Commentary on Technology and Its Impact on Wall Street

Throughout this book, there have been several discussions concerning the impact technology has had upon certain Wall Street professions and organizations. The theme is important and warrants summarization, if not further commentary.

Technology has fundamentally changed the way the Wall Street game is played. It has created tremendous opportunities for some players and challenges for others. At its core, improving technology has provided markets participants with: (1) stronger analytical tools, (2) better communication abilities, and (3) broader and more readily accessible information. These have had a profound impact on the buyside, the role of the sellside, and the competitive landscape within each group.

Consistent with the approach found elsewhere in this book, below are five observations on how the three elements just mentioned have impacted Wall Street. Please note that some of these have been touched upon previously.

1. *Technology has fueled the proliferation of new financial instruments available to issuers and investors.* Wall Street has experienced an explosion in the volume and range of exotic financial instruments. These include everything from complicated derivatives designed to manage previously unmanageable market risks to more pedestrian options targeted at retail investors such as those addressing price movements in the broader indexes. Better technologies have enabled the financial community to devise and deploy instruments that cost-effectively serve a much wider spectrum of specific objectives—both those to manage risks and those to capture speculative profits. This, in turn, has significantly expanded the amount of capital directed at such securities.

   It merits highlighting that these changes have had a big impact on more than just Wall Street. They have fueled changes in our overall economy, particularly with respect to the availability of capital and credit. For instance, better analytical and administrative tools have allowed loans of all sorts to be made, packaged together, sliced up, and then resold to investors such as hedge funds and other non-originating lenders. This has dramatically increased the amount of capital in the system and thus the amount of credit available to borrowers of all shapes and sizes. Of course, such changes have produced unforeseen complications and largely enabled the recent crisis in subprime loans.

2. *Technology has driven public investors to take a shorter-term perspective on their investments.* This is due to two closely linked factors. First, we have become an impatient society. When we want things, we want them now. We grow bored with solutions that do

not deliver immediate results. With the internet and other technologies, investors are able to constantly monitor prices, news, research, and message boards concerning their investments. So, like channel surfers buzzing through cable stations, we explore and rapidly shift between investments looking to capture near-term performance. Furthermore, this approach is enabled by today's low transaction costs and low commission rates. Second, whether they are predisposed to do so or not, many institutional investors must seek short-term performance given the attitudes of their investor base. They do not have the luxury of time and cannot rely upon company fundamentals and longer-term results for success. They must focus on short-term drivers and must act on the positive or negative sentiments in the market (real or perceived).

The beneficiaries of this short-term mentality are private equity firms and hedge funds. Both have strict limitations on investor withdrawals. This permits them to take a longer-term view on their investments and capture values produced by the shortsightedness of the public markets.

3. *Technology has radically reduced the value of traditional brokerage services.* Brokerage firms offer their clients two principal products: research and trading. Technology has blunted both.

   Historically, the buyside paid for sellside research with brokerage commissions. The buyside bought and sold stocks through a firm when its research analysts (directly or through institutional salespeople) provided good investment ideas, quality insights, and helpful updates on new developments concerning public companies. This type of information is now readily obtained via sources such as the internet and can be generated with much less effort than in the past. Thus, the buyside is no longer willing to pay as much for it. This is the case even with distinctive sellside research since it becomes commoditized almost from the moment it is released. In this day and age, word travels fast, so investors feel less obligation to pay for information and opinions.

   As for trading, the buyside paid brokerage firms with commissions for providing liquidity in the market. The buyside paid firms to unload unwanted securities and acquired desired securities at the best prices. In many cases, this role can now be accomplished with newly established electronic trading systems and networks that provide similar results with much lower commission rates.

4. *By impairing the value of brokerage services, technology has caused many investment banks to shift their attentions to buyside activities and higher-margin sellside offerings.* Every investment bank on Wall Street has adjusted its brokerage operations to confront the new realities of the business. They have reduced research, trading, and brokerage personnel and automated many of their functions.

Correspondingly, most banks have shifted resources to higher-margin activities, areas where they can generate larger revenues with smaller staffs. This has included initiatives that would otherwise be categorized as buyside activities, such as running proprietary trading desks and operating hedge funds and private equity funds. As for sellside offerings, new efforts have included expanding M&A practices and focusing more attention on large lead-managed financings since both activities involve small teams producing large fees. A byproduct of the shift away from brokerage services has been the rise of the M&A-focused boutiques. Historically, brokerage support for a company was critical to a banking relationship and almost a prerequisite to winning M&A mandates. With the commoditization of brokerage and reduced attention to it from the larger investment banks, it has become less important to many clients and, in fact, is sometimes even considered a potential issue or conflict in an M&A advisory relationship. As a result, several M&A-focused firms have emerged over the past few years that have been able to gain significant business traction without having to invest the time and resources to build credible brokerage operations.

5. *Technology has enabled new competitors to succeed in virtually every area of the market.* Whether it is competing against the New York Stock Exchange, Fidelity Investments, or Goldman Sachs, innovative thinkers deploying new technologies have created new business models and product offerings that have successfully challenged the services and products of the market's largest and most established players—upstart electronic communications networks have shifted trading volume away from incumbent intermediaries; upstart hedge funds have shifted investors away from incumbent investment managers; and upstart boutiques have shifted fees away from incumbent investment banks. In many areas, technology has proven to be the great equalizer. It has enabled the small to compete with the large and the young to compete with the old. In doing so, it has also offered tremendous leverage to the newer organizations. Unencumbered by all of the facilities, employees, and other baggage required to compete in the past, the successful upstarts capture massive financial rewards when they prevail. Being able to do more with less has also prompted the consolidation wave witnessed in certain corners of Wall Street, especially among exchanges and intermediaries, where tremendous cost synergies can be found. It bears mentioning that globalization of the capital markets has also played an important role in this trend.

Strangely, technology seems to have made some areas of the market more efficient and others less efficient. Not surprisingly perhaps, newer areas seem to fit in the former category and older areas seem to fit in the latter. The markets for derivatives and other financial instruments requiring strong quantitative tools and computing resources are now larger, more liquid, and more valuable to their constituents. On the other hand, stocks and markets historically influenced by mass psychology seem somewhat stunted by today's vast and unfiltered flow of both biased and unbiased information. Sure, technology has reduced transaction costs in these markets but it has also produced knee-jerk reactions, a short-term orientation, and a herd mentality that appear to unjustifiably reward some companies and securities and neglect others.

CHAPTER 21

When Things Slow Down: Creating Shareholder Value and Related Topics

➤ The primary financing methods used by mature companies to generate shareholder returns: dividends, stock repurchases, leveraged recapitalizations, divestitures, and more aggressive acquisitions.

➤ The general parameters and considerations of the bankruptcy process for troubled companies.

PEMCO's growth ultimately stalled. Insurmountable limits to the technology prevented continued expansion, and its stock price languished accordingly. PEMCO produced great cash flow from its existing markets but would need something more to renew investor interest. For the most part, the only attention PEMCO was drawing from the investment community involved activist shareholders and private equity funds. Both saw opportunities to create value in the company. With mounting pressure to act, PEMCO had several options to consider. Beyond seeking operational improvements, there were a number of financial strategies it could pursue:

1. **Dividends.** Many profitable public businesses issue dividends to their shareholders. These are generally quarterly or annual payments paid on each share of stock held by investors as of a set record date. Sometimes they are special one-time payments to return a company's excess cash balances to shareholders. Dividends and their record dates are announced either in quarterly earnings calls or separate press releases. Dividends serve several functions: They increase shareholder returns and open a company's stock to new shareholders, particularly certain mutual funds that are mandated to invest in dividend-paying stocks (e.g., certain growth and income funds). By reducing the shareholders' equity account on a company's balance sheet, they can also improve a business' financial

performance measurements, namely return on equity. Dividends are typically issued by slower-growth companies with fewer needs for internally
generated cash. Lending agreements generally place restrictions on the
dividend policies of a company. Many larger companies have dividend
reinvestment plans (DRIPs). A DRIP enables shareholders to reinvest
dividends directly into the company for newly issued stock or stock that
was previously repurchased by the company.

2. **Stock repurchases.** Rather than using cash for dividends or growth initiatives, companies also invest in their own stock via stock repurchases,
   especially when share prices are depressed. Historically, many companies preferred stock repurchases to dividends when it came to returning
   capital to shareholders. Stock repurchases lower the balance sheet's equity account and the number of shares outstanding, thereby benefiting
   ongoing shareholders. Perhaps more importantly, dividends were taxed
   to shareholders at higher rates than capital gains produced by stock sales,
   making repurchases more tax efficient. As of the date of this publication,
   this is no longer the case.

   Repurchases are conducted pursuant to stock repurchase plans adopted
   by a company's board of directors. These are publicly announced to
   shareholders. Once in place, a company generally works with several
   investment banks to effectuate the repurchases. Banks that are "in the
   rotation," as it is known, are selected on the basis of their trading history
   in the stock and relationship with the company. Each bank is given
   its turn to repurchase stock on the company's behalf, generally at the
   request of the company's CFO or treasurer. Progress in a repurchase plan
   is usually discussed in the quarterly earnings call. Companies are not
   obligated to complete repurchase plans and are often accused of using
   such announcements as public relations ploys to drive interest in their
   stocks. After all, if a company thinks its own stock is a good buy, it must
   be, right?

3. **Leveraged recapitalizations.** Besides using cash flow and existing cash
   balances to fund repurchases and dividends, a company may also borrow
   money to do so, assuming it has the requisite debt capacity. Known as
   a leveraged recapitalization (leveraged "recap" for short), this approach
   basically entails swapping out equity for debt on a company's balance
   sheet. Though it has been more common in privately held businesses
   than public companies, the onslaught of private-equity-funded buyouts
   and the success of this strategy for the new owners in many of those
   situations have prompted public boards and management teams to more
   carefully consider this option. That being said, public companies are
   likely to remain more conservative in this area than their private counterparts due to the nature and range of their stakeholders. When pursued,
   leveraged recaps usually result in a large one-time special dividend to
   shareholders.

4. **Divestitures.** Closely tied to operating strategy, a company may also sell or divest assets or subsidiaries to return capital to shareholders. Depending on the circumstances, divestitures can take the form of outright sales or spinoffs of separate publicly traded entities. Activist shareholders often focus on divestures when seeking improvements in stock price performance and campaigning management teams to take action. Divestitures can help operations and free up capital. Ironically, many of the same investment bankers who advise on poorly suited acquisitions are later paid as advisors to divest these businesses. Investment banking is a relationship business and the role of bankers is to put things together and, sometimes, to pull them apart.

5. **Broader acquisitions.** Rather than unleashing shareholder value by reducing the scope of a company's operations or unused cash balances, cash-rich companies may also take an opposite tack for producing shareholder returns. They sometimes seek to expand by broadening their acquisition strategy. They start to target businesses in less related areas. This approach allows executives to keep and possibly grow their empires. Without clear and defensible synergies, however, this approach is generally frowned upon by sophisticated investors. As a general rule, public investors prefer "pure plays" over conglomerates—Berkshire Hathaway and a few others being notable exceptions. Investors want to decide what industries and businesses to pursue instead of relying upon management teams and boards to make such decisions on their behalf. Similarly, diversified businesses create challenges for research analysts and portfolio managers, whose expertise frequently is limited to a particular sector. Many diversified businesses are valued in the public markets according to their core business. Other operations are often misunderstood, ignored, or steeply discounted.

Another, more drastic step PEMCO could take would be to sell the company. Many businesses choose this path when growth slows and there is no clear catalyst for renewed expansion. These businesses face stagnant share prices and a host of challenges, particularly when they are in dynamic industries and tight labor markets. Their issues include employee retention, higher-cost capital, and impatient shareholders—all of which lead executives and boards to seek graceful exits. Selling at a premium by capturing some of the value an acquirer (financial or strategic) hopes to create often fits this description. It can also accelerate large financial payouts found in executive contracts, thereby creating an added incentive for many to consider this option. As discussed in Chapter 17, most acquisition premiums are 20 percent to 30 percent.

When involving a financial buyer, these deals also give senior executives another bite at the apple to enrich themselves. Management teams are often retained and given equity participation to run operations even when a transaction is not a management-led buyout. While facing performance pressures from the new owners, private equity investors take a longer-term perspective than their public counterparts. This affords executives broader latitude to take the necessary steps to reposition a company to perform better. Of course, such investors can be unforgiving and have the power to quickly make management changes when goals are not achieved.

At times, companies with deteriorating businesses wait too long to find a buyer or choose financing strategies that later prove to be detrimental, if not disastrous. In many cases, these businesses end up in bankruptcy proceedings.

Although bankruptcies are not the focus of this book, they are related to Wall Street and therefore merit a few observations:

1. **Process.** Generally, companies elect bankruptcy when their financial obligations to outside creditors threaten their ability to fund ongoing operations. Assuming the company seeks to stay in business rather than liquidate, it files for a Chapter 11 bankruptcy or reorganization. Upon filing, the company's financial obligations are suspended and operations are permitted to continue. Companies contemplating Chapter 11 bankruptcies are always advised to hoard cash before filing to provide adequate resources to maintain operations during bankruptcy proceedings. After filing, creditors of equal standing form separate groups which, in turn, constitute the creditors' committee. For bonds, notes, and other debt securities, the indenture trustee represents the security holders in these proceedings. Through a long series of contentious (typically) and time-consuming negotiations, the company, the committee, and their respective advisors and legal representatives devise a reorganization plan. The plan outlines all aspects of the reorganization, including the future operating strategy and each constituent's stake in the post-bankruptcy business. The plan must be submitted to and approved by the bankruptcy court. The court must deem the plan to be fair and viable. Debt holders usually receive some combination of equity and new debt in the entity. Existing common shareholders usually see their positions wiped out. Despite their past failings, existing management teams often keep their jobs and are given equity incentives to stay.

2. **Legal representation and restructuring advisors.** The company and the creditors' committee are represented by legal counsel and restructuring advisors, commonly known as "work-out" groups. Along with some smaller, specialized firms, most large law firms have bankruptcy teams, and several large investment banks and boutiques have dedicated work-out groups. Unlike most investment banking services, which are paid according to a percentage of transaction value, these groups are paid on a retainer basis, generally monthly. Legal fees and the work-out retainer receive priority over other creditors in reorganization proceedings. The bankruptcy court, however, must approve fees and the terms of these arrangements.

3. **Vulture investors.** Often, the creditors in bankruptcy proceedings have self-selected the role. Frequently, the creditors are not the original lenders to the troubled company. They are hedge funds and other groups that purchase distressed debt, including bonds and syndicated loan positions, with the idea of generating returns through their post-bankruptcy ownership stakes. As part of these initiatives, creditors may force companies into bankruptcy by demanding accelerated payments on outstanding loans due to technical defaults (e.g., failure to maintain certain coverage ratios). Known as vulture investing, parties that successfully deploy these tactics are well versed in bankruptcy law and thoroughly understand their contractual rights under loan agreements and bond indentures.

4. **Debtor-in-possession (DIP) financings.** Many bankrupt companies require outside financial support to fund operations and reorganization expenditures during bankruptcy proceedings. Funds loaned for these purposes receive first priority in reorganizations. They must either be fully repaid under the plan or the lender is entitled to the business. Known as DIP financing, this tactic can enable a lender to gain control of a bankrupt business with little or no pre-bankruptcy financial commitments. The lender does, however, face some risks attendant with lengthy and unpredictable reorganization negotiations, such as continued erosion in the value of a business's operations and assets.

Fortunately, PEMCO was far from having to contemplate bankruptcy. It had the full spectrum of other options to consider given its balance sheet and operating characteristics. Of course, the company's founders, private investors, and earlier public investors had already profited handsomely from their involvement in the business. This had some influence on PEMCO's motivations and decision making. With this in mind, we end our story and leave it to your imagination to decide what path the board pursued to serve the company and its stakeholders.

Personal Observations on Public Companies

1. *Being public is expensive and fraught with headaches for senior executives.* All things being equal, a public company has significantly greater administrative burdens than a private counterpart. It requires more internal and external accounting and legal resources to adequately address its reporting and disclosure obligations. It must pay listing fees to its stock exchange, travel expenses for its executives to visit with investors, higher compensation to its directors, and insurance premiums for policies that protect directors and officers against personal liability to shareholders. Combined, all of these expenses often amount to several million dollars a year. Beyond

the cost, these factors consume management energies that would otherwise be spent growing and developing a business. In addition, the disclosure requirements for public companies can negatively influence management's actions by causing them to act or refrain from acting based on how they expect the market to react. Private companies operate without this consideration. They can focus on strategy and longer-term results without being swayed by short-term perceptions and stock price performance.

2. *Although burdensome in some respects, being public can be extremely advantageous for the right companies.* Assuming a company has the right mix of scale, opportunity, and leadership, being public provides ready access to capital, liquidity for shareholders, strong mechanisms for employee retention, and credibility with customers and business partners. These factors can have tremendous strategic value for a company. It is not surprising, then, that even some of the most vocal proponents of being and staying private ultimately choose to go public. Interestingly, in recent years, this has started to include several of the largest and most successful private equity firms whose core business is taking companies private.

3. *Even in this day and age, some CEOs run public companies like they are private fiefdoms or sole proprietorships.* Although they are careful to adequately disclose their actions and avoid formal accusations of self dealing, fraud, or abuse, these CEOs pursue agendas that serve their own interests first and the interests of their shareholders second. In doing so, they seem to adhere (consciously or unconsciously) to the theory outlined by the eighteenth-century economist and philosopher Adam Smith in his book *The Wealth of Nations*. Paraphrased as "in the pursuit of one's own self interests, society's interests are also served," this stance, for better or worse, has become an axiom of American business.

Nowhere are the self-serving agendas of some corporate executives more evident than in the area of sellside decisions. Negotiations concerning "corner office" considerations (i.e., who gets to run a business and maintain his or her authority) are often the stickiest to address and frequently derail otherwise meritorious acquisition discussions involving strategic buyers. When such discussions involve financial buyers, the opposite is often true. Senior executives often prompt these discussions. Some are anxious to see their companies sell to such players, knowing that they will get to keep their jobs and will benefit handsomely in financial terms (executives frequently receive equity packages that can be worth millions when a company is taken private and later sold or "re-IPOed"). Special board committees are designed to protect shareholder interests and guard against inappropriate executive actions in these situations but executives remain influential in the outcome of proposed transactions.

4. *Some boards of directors are very effective; some are not.* This is a corollary to the preceding point. Many boards vigorously guard and protect the interests of shareholders. They set high standards and hold executives accountable to them. Others blindly accept the questionable actions of senior executives. These boards are often handpicked by the CEO and are friends and former colleagues. Fortunately, this is beginning to change. Increased shareholder activism and liability concerns are driving more thoughtful board oversight where it did not exist previously.

5. *Leadership is the most important ingredient to a public company's success.* Give me a great management team with a mediocre platform any day over a great platform with a mediocre management team. Whether self-serving or not, great leaders produce great companies. They set the tone for their organizations. They develop strong strategies, products, cultures, and customer relationships. They communicate effectively with shareholders and earn their trust and confidence. These contributions may not be enough to justify the size of their paychecks but that is a debate for another day. Unfortunately, it is not easy to distinguish between good and bad leaders when they are hired. Most new hires have great resumes and pedigrees. Only time decides whether they can get the job done.

Schematics

Landscape of Capital Markets Players.

- **The Sellside**
  - Issuers
    - Corporations
      - Executives
      - Boards of Directors
      - Early Investors
    - Special Entities
      - REITs
      - SPACs
      - Partnerships
    - Governmental Organizations
      - Debt instruments only
  - Securities Issued
    - Equity (stocks)
    - Debt (notes/bonds)
    - Hybrids (convertibles)
  - Investment Banks
    - Banking Operations
      - Corporate Finance
      - M & A
      - Capital Markets
    - Brokerage Operations
      - Sales
        - ∞ Institutional
        - ∞ Retail Brokers
      - Trading
        - ∞ Position
        - ∞ Sales
      - Research
    - Types
      - Bulge Bracket
      - Universal Banks
      - Middle Markets Firms
      - Boutiques

- **The Buyside**
  - Private Investors
    - Friends and Family
    - Angel Investors
    - Venture Capitalists
      - Early Stage
      - Later Stage
    - Private Equity Funds
    - Hedge Funds
    - Crossover Funds
  - Public Investors
    - Institutional Types
      - Mutual Funds
      - Hedge Funds
      - Other Institutions
        - ∞ Pensions
        - ∞ Foundations
    - Institutional Personnel
      - Portfolio Managers
      - Analysts
      - Traders
      - Sales & Marketing
    - Retail Accounts
      - Traditional
      - Online
      - Managed
  - Related Entities
    - Independent Research Providers/Services
    - Debt Rating Agencies
    - Funds of Funds

- **Others**
  - Regulators
    - SEC
    - States
    - SROs
      - FINRA
      - NASD
      - Exchanges
  - Trading Enablers
    - Exchanges
    - OTC/Nasdaq
    - ECNs
  - Professionals
    - Lawyers
      - Securities
      - Class Action
    - Accountants
  - Related Services
    - Financial Printers
    - Stock Transfer Agents
    - Registrars

Typical Financing Progression of a Successful Venture-Backed Company.

(Use of Proceeds/Commentary in Parentheses and Primary Investors in Italics)

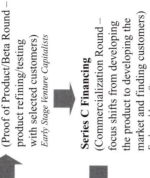

Company Formation
(Entrepreneur and an idea)

Seed Financing
(Startup Funding – hire team and begin development)
Personal Savings
Credit Cards
Friends and Family
Angel Investors

Series A Financing
(Proof of Concept/ Alpha Round – product development)
Early Stage Venture Capitalists

Series B Financing
(Proof of Product/Beta Round – product refining/testing with selected customers)
Early Stage Venture Capitalists

Series C Financing
(Commercialization Round – focus shifts from developing the product to developing the market and finding customers)
Early and Later Stage Venture Capitalists

Series D Financing
(Private Expansion Capital – often "agented" by an Investment Bank; Series E and later rounds may be warranted subsequently)
Later Stage Venture Capitalists
Private Equity Firms
Hedge Funds
Crossover Funds

Convertible Note Offering(s)
(Expansion Capital and Acquisition Financing)
Equity and Income Mutual Funds
Specialized Mutual Funds
Hedge Funds

High Yield Note Offering(s)
(Expansion Capital and Acquisition Financing)
Debt Mutual Funds
Specialized Mutual Funds
Hedge Funds

Initial Public Offering(s)
(Expansion Capital and Shareholder Liquidity – most companies are sold at or prior to this stage)
Equity Mutual Funds
Hedge Funds
Retail Investors

Follow-On Equity Offering(s)
(Expansion Capital, Acquisition Financing, and Shareholder Liquidity)
Equity Mutual Funds
Hedge Funds
Retail Investors

PIPE Financing(s)
("Private Investment in Public Entity" pursued when warranted by financial distress or special circumstances)
Equity Mutual Funds
Hedge Funds (many with this sole focus)

Investment Grade Debt Offering(s)
(Expansion Capital, Acquisition Financing, and Recapitalization Funding)
Debt Mutual Funds
Pensions, Foundations, and Other Institutional Investors

Note: Progression excludes working capital facilities, term loans, and other debt financings generally funded by commercial banks rather than institutional or retail investors.

Glossary of Selected Terms and Acronyms

Terms in *italic* type within an entry are cross-references to main entries.

2 and 20. The compensation structure for the managers of most venture capital funds, *hedge funds*, and *private equity funds*, referring to a 2 percent annual fee on the funds under management (known as the *management fee*) and a 20 percent participation in the profits generated by the fund (known as the *carried interest*).

Accredited investors. Organizations and wealthy individuals meeting particular guidelines that are permitted to invest in certain types of higher risk investments, such as *hedge funds*, under U.S. securities laws.

Activist shareholder. An investor in a public company who uses its stock position to put public pressure on the company's management to effectuate some form of change. This can be either financial change, such as divesting a business to improve share price performance, or non-financial change, such as adopting certain environmental protection practices.

ADR. The acronym for American Depository Receipt, a legal construct permitting shares of a company listed on a foreign exchange to trade domestically.

Aftermarket. The trading in a company's securities after a public offering.

Aggregate value. Sometimes also called *enterprise value*, the term refers to the total value of a business's outstanding debt and equity securities less its cash balances.

Alpha. A term referring to investment performance that exceeds a fund's competitive benchmark, such as the S&P 500 or some other relevant index.

Angel investor. An individual investor whose activities include committing funds to early stage financings. Angel investors are usually wealthy individuals with some expertise and interest in a particular industry.

Arranger. Sometimes also known as the lead lender or agent, the lead bank in a *syndicated loan* that bears responsibility for negotiating terms with the borrower, finding other lenders to complete the syndicate, and conducting administrative tasks, such as dispersing cash flows among the syndicate members after the loan has been funded.

Ask. A trading term referring to an offer to sell.

Bake-off. The formal competitive process used to select *investment banks* or other professionals to serve as a company's underwriters, agents, or advisors. Bake-offs generally entail a series of presentations made by competitors to a company's executives or directors.

Bear hug. A letter in a proposed M&A transaction provided by a potential acquirer to a reluctant target's board of directors outlining the merits of pursuing a dialogue or specific offer. Intended to catalyze a transaction, a bear hug contains a request for discussions and creates a formal record of the inquiry.

Best-efforts underwriting. As opposed to a *firm-commitment underwriting*, this arrangement provides that an *investment bank* will use its best efforts to find investors for the securities being offered without actually assuming any direct financial risk.

Bid. A trading term referring to an offer to buy.

Black-out period. Times during which executives and other corporate insiders are prevented from buying and selling stock pursuant to public company trading policies which generally prohibit stock transactions between the period beginning two weeks before the end of a fiscal quarter and ending shortly after the announcement of financial results.

Blank-check company. A publicly offered vehicle designed to raise a "blind" pool of capital to acquire a yet-to-be-identified business or businesses. Recently, the structure of choice for these vehicles has been the special-purpose acquisition company (SPAC).

Bond. A security representing indebtedness of a company or other issuer that has longer than a 10 year maturity period.

Bond market (The). The informal over-the-counter market in which debt securities, namely *bonds* and *notes*, are traded by investors and *dealers*.

Book. Within the context of Wall Street, "book" can have several meanings. For a securities offering, "the book" refers to the roster of interested investors gathered during the marketing phase of the transaction and subsequently allocated securities by the offering's lead managing underwriter. For a company sale, "the book" refers to the descriptive memorandum on the business that is provided to interested suitors. A "pitch book" refers to the materials prepared by investment bankers to present ideas and qualifications to prospective clients. And finally, a "board book" refers to materials presented by investment bankers to a board of directors regarding a particular transaction or *fairness opinion*.

Bookrunner. The lead *managing underwriter* of a securities offering designated with primary responsibility for the marketing phase of the transaction and, more specifically, the process of collecting and screening institutional orders for the *book*, setting the final terms of the offering, and, ultimately, allocating shares to interested investors.

Borrow. The number of shares of *common stock* held by *brokerage firms* across Wall Street that can be lent to investors looking to conduct *short sales*.

Bought deal. A transaction in which an *investment bank* purchases securities as a principal from an issuer or selling shareholder for subsequent resale to investors.

Boutique. An small *investment bank* focused on a narrower set of industries or services than those targeted by the *bulge bracket* or larger firms.

Break-up fee. A fee in a M&A transaction payable to the other side in the event that one party decides to terminate the deal prior to *closing*.

Broker. An individual or firm that trades securities for buyers and sellers in exchange for commissions. Brokerage is an operation typically conducted by *investment banks*.

Brokerage firm. *See broker.*

Bulge bracket firm. A large *investment bank* with global operations that underwrites stocks and bonds, provides M&A advisory services to corporate clients, trades an extensive range of securities, provides research on these securities, and may even provide office space and back office services to clients. A bulge bracket firm typically also conducts a range of *buyside* activities.

Buy-in. The act of closing an investor's *short sale* position through an open market purchase when the shares underlying the *short sale* are sold by their owner and thus are no longer available in the *borrow* at a particular *brokerage firm*.

Buyside (The). The term used to describe the broad group of institutions and professionals responsible for investing in securities.

Buyside advisor. An *investment bank* hired to represent a company when it seeks to buy another business in a M&A transaction.

Capitalization. The total value of a company's outstanding debt and equity securities. The term is also used to describe the capital structure of a company.

Carried interest. *See 2 and 20.*

CCM. The acronym for commitment committee meeting, the meeting of the committee within an *investment bank* that is tasked with approving or denying the bank's participation in a securities offering or other transaction. Such committees are composed of senior representatives from various departments within an *investment bank*. A transaction's deal team is responsible for preparing an extensive memorandum for the committee and presenting to the committee on the merits and issues of a deal.

CFA. The acronym for Chartered Financial Analyst. Held by many research analysts and other investment professionals, the CFA designation requires passing three exams offered by the CFA Institute, a global organization dedicated to advocating fair and transparent capital markets and setting high ethical standards and levels of professional excellence in the investment industry.

Charter documents. A corporation's basic formation documents, including the Articles of Incorporation and Bylaws.

Chinese wall. A term referring to internal policies and procedures at an *investment bank* designed to contain nonpublic information pertaining to transactions and companies to only personnel with necessary access, such as members of a deal team.

Closing. The term refers to when a transaction is finalized and the item being sold and the consideration being paid for it are exchanged.

Comparable. A transaction or company whose financial metrics are used to help value or assess another transaction or company. Comparables, or simply "comps," are the key components to many financial analyses prepared on Wall Street.

Co-manager. *See managing underwriter.*

Comfort letter. Prepared and signed by an issuer's outside accounting firm, this document helps shield an underwriting group from liability in a securities offering by noting that financial information contained in a registration statement corresponds to a company's audited and unaudited financial statements and other financial records.

Common stock. Securities representing the most basic form of equity ownership in a company.

Conversion premium. The term used in a *convertible offering* to describe the difference between the price of an issuer's *common stock* at the time of the offering and the price at which the convertible instrument being issued can be converted into such *common stock*. For example, a $50 million convertible security issued at a 25% conversion premium for a *common stock* that trades at $40 would convert at $50 per share, thereby resulting in the issuance of 1 million shares instead of 1.25 million.

Convertible offering. An offering of securities, typically *notes* or *preferred stock*, that bear a *coupon* and can be converted into *common stock* of the issuer at a subsequent date.

Corporate opportunity doctrine. A legal doctrine prohibiting corporate executives and certain other insiders from independently pursuing opportunities better suited to their companies.

Coupon. The interest rate or interest payment on a debt security.

Covenant. A restriction placed on a borrower pursuant to the terms of a loan or other debt financing.

Cram down round. A financing round for a private company that materially resets and reduces the rights and values ascribed to previously issued securities.

Credit rating. A rating provided by one of the main debt rating agencies—Standard & Poor's Ratings Services, Moody's Investors Service, and Fitch Ratings—opining on the credit characteristics and credit quality of a borrower or specific debt instrument. Those on the upper end of the grading continuum are deemed to be investment grade. Instruments on the lower end are known as high yield or *junk bonds*. The rating dictates how debt obligations are treated by investors and the terms and interest rates required of them when issued. Each rating agency has a slightly different hierarchy of ratings.

Dark pool. *See ECN.*

Data room. A location, now often provided online with special access and tracking software, organized and monitored by a *sellside advisor* in a M&A process that contains all material documentation on the seller (e.g., contracts, leases, and financial records) to assist potential buyers in their *due diligence* efforts.

DCF. The acronym for discounted cash flow, an approach to valuing an asset or business according to the present value of anticipated future cash flows generated from it.

Dealer. An entity, typically a *brokerage firm*, that maintains an inventory of securities and acts as a principal rather than just an agent when trading securities.

Definitive acquisition agreement. The final agreement between the parties involved in a *M&A* transaction setting forth every aspect of the transaction, including the respective parties' rights and obligations. Depending on a deal's structure, this agreement may also be called a purchase and sale agreement or a merger agreement.

Demand registration rights. *See registration rights.*

Desk. The desk generally refers to the trading desk of a *brokerage firm*, where position traders and sales traders conduct their affairs. It can also refer to the debt or equity capital markets departments of an *investment bank*.

Directed shares. Shares sold in an *IPO* that are directed to certain individuals at the request of the issuer.

Down round. A financing round for a private company conducted at a lower valuation than the prior round.

DRIP. The acronym for dividend reinvestment plan, a program enabling shareholders to reinvest dividends back into a company for newly issued stock or stock that was previously repurchased by the company.

DTC. The acronym for Depository Trust Company which, in essence, is an electronic storage and clearing house for securities that enables *brokerage firms* and other institutions to efficiently move securities and settle trades electronically.

Dual-track process. An *IPO* process undertaken by an issuer to generate interest from potential acquirers and possibly secure a sale of the company prior to completing the offering.

Due diligence. The process of ascertaining the accuracy and completeness of information obtained and required in *M&A* transactions or disclosed to investors in a registration statement or other materials used in a securities offering.

Dutch auction. A pricing structure used in certain securities transactions, such as online *IPOs* and selected *tender offers*, requiring interested investors or participants to submit offers or indications of interest denoting a price at which they would be willing to consummate a deal. After gathering such offers or indications, the deal is completed at the highest price containing the sufficient number of shares to close. Those parties indicating that price or better participate in the transaction at the final arrived upon price.

Earn-out. A provision contained in some *M&A* transactions setting aside a portion of the purchase price for payment at a later date upon the seller achieving certain performance goals.

EBITDA. The acronym for earnings before interest, taxes, depreciation, and amortization. Sometimes used synonymously with cash flow and often cited when describing the financial strength or value of a business.

ECM. The acronym for the equity capital markets department of an *investment bank*. ECM is integral to pitching and executing equity offerings. Typically,

ECM is divided into two functions—origination and execution. Those in origination work closely with bankers to identify and pursue financing candidates and structure transactions. ECM execution, a portion of which is called *syndicate*, works on engaged transactions and provides input leading up to a deal's announcement and then assumes the leading role during a deal's marketing phase. *Syndicate* maintains the *book*, sets the terms for the deal, and ultimately allocates the securities to investors.

ECN. The acronym for electronic communications network, a platform enabling buyers and sellers to trade securities outside of the exchanges and traditional OTC markets. These networks are sometimes also referred to as electronic trading networks (ETNs). When they permit major investors to trade large positions on a completely anonymous basis, they are called *dark pools*.

Enterprise value. *See aggregate value.*

EPS. Earnings per share, the net income of a company for a specified period of time, generally a fiscal year or quarter, divided by the total number of shares of *common stock* issued and outstanding during such time. EPS is the most cited metric on Wall Street for a public company's financial performance.

Equity. Refers to the ownership interest of common and preferred shareholders in a company.

Escrow (An). A provision contained in some *M&A* transactions setting aside a portion of the purchase price to fund liabilities or penalties associated with breaches in a seller's representations and warranties contained in the *definitive acquisition agreement*. These funds are placed in an escrow account for a finite time period. If unused, they are released to the seller's shareholders after the period expires.

Exchange ratio. In a stock-for-stock *M&A* transaction, the number of shares of the acquirer that each share of the target receives in the deal.

Fairness opinion. An opinion rendered by a financial advisor, typically an *investment bank*, to a company's board of directors concerning the merits, or "fairness," of a proposed material transaction, generally a merger or acquisition.

Financial printer. Commonly referred to simply as the printer in a transaction process, a printer that specializes in financial documents filed with the *SEC*, such as registration statements, annual reports, and proxy statements.

FINRA. *See SRO.*

Firm-commitment underwriting. As opposed to a *best-efforts underwriting,* this arrangement involves the underwriter purchasing securities from an issuer at a set price with a negotiated discount for the underwriting fee. The underwriter then resells the securities to public investors and bears the financial risk if it fails to do so. Almost all marketed offerings of *registered securities* are conducted pursuant to firm-commitment underwritings.

Flipping. The practice of buying a stock in an *IPO* and then quickly selling it at a profit when the stock begins its first day of trading.

Follow-on offering. An offering of *common stock* by a public company at any time following an *IPO*. Sometimes referred to as a *secondary offering* if it is composed of *secondary shares*, a follow-on offering can include *primary shares* or *secondary shares*.

Form 4. The form required to be filed with the *SEC* by certain corporate insiders of a public company to report changes in their ownership of the company's stock.

Form 8-K. The form required to be filed with the *SEC* upon the occurrence of certain material events concerning a public company such as a change of control or the announcement of financial results.

Form 10-K. A report required to be filed annually with the *SEC* containing extensive disclosure on the operations and status of a public company. The document must generally be filed within ninety days of the end of a company's fiscal year. The document serves as the foundation of the Annual Report subsequently provided to shareholders.

Form 10-Q. A less comprehensive version of a Form 10-K that must be filed quarterly within forty-five days of the end of a company's first three fiscal quarters.

Form S-1. The basic registration statement filed with the *SEC* to register securities for sale. Among other things, a Form S-1 is the most common document used in connection with *IPOs* and *follow-on offerings* that occur shortly after *IPOs*. The Form S-1 serves as the corpus of the *prospectus* delivered to investors in such transactions.

Form S-3. A more abbreviated form of registration statement filed with the *SEC* to register securities for sales. Form S-3s are available to public issuers that have been subject to the reporting requirements of the *Securities Exchange Act of 1934* for at least 12 months and have filed all of their required disclosure documents with the *SEC* in a timely fashion for the past 12 months.

Green shoe. The term refers to the *over-allotment option* typically granted to underwriters in securities offerings. Named after the legal case that legitimized the structure, a green shoe entitles the underwriters to purchase 15 percent more shares than noted in an offering in order to stabilize the share price, if necessary, after the offering begins trading. The option can be exercised by the underwriters within 30 days of an offering. Underwriters actually sell the shares covered by the green shoe at the time of the offering. This creates a large short position and provides the underwriters with proceeds from the sale that can then be used to buy shares in the open market if the aftermarket trading price dips below the offering price. When such purchases are made, this demand stabilizes and helps create a floor in the stock price. If stabilization is necessary, the open-market purchases cover the underwriters' short position. If it is not necessary, the underwriters cover the short position by exercising the option and the issuer receives the proceeds from the original sale. Green shoes can include both *primary shares* and *secondary shares*.

Gross proceeds. The total proceeds of a securities offering before underwriting discounts and fees are deducted.

Gross spread. The underwriting fee in a securities offering typically described as a percentage of the offering (e.g., 7 percent in a *IPO* or 3 percent in a *convertible offering*). The gross spread is divided into three components: the management fee, the underwriting fee, and the selling concession. Generally, these represent 20 percent, 20 percent, and 60 percent of the gross spread, respectively. The division of the gross spread and its components among an underwriting group is subject to negotiation and varies from transaction to transaction.

Hedge fund. A closely-held, loosely-regulated investment vehicle, typically structured as a limited partnership, created for wealthy individuals and institutions, such as endowments, foundations, and pension funds, that, subject to its formation documents, is able to deploy a much wider range of investment strategies than a mutual fund to generate returns for its investors.

Hostile takeover. A proposed acquisition that is strongly resisted by the target.

HSR. The acronym for the Hart-Scott-Rodino Act anti-trust filing. Required for many mergers and acquisitions exceeding certain threshold sizes, the HSR filing enables the Department of Justice and Federal Trade Commission to review the competitive impact of a transaction on the marketplace and challenge it if necessary to protect the interests of consumers.

In play. The term used to describe that status of a public target in a M&A process when the target has taken certain steps that legally obligate it to sell itself at what is deemed to be the best offer.

In the box. The trading term referring to when a *brokerage firm* has committed to being a *market maker* in an OTC stock and thus is required to post *bid* and *ask* prices that it must honor in the designated stock on lots of 100 shares or more.

Indenture. Otherwise known as the deed of trust, the contractual arrangement between the issuer and the investors in a *note* or *bond* offering describing the terms of the security including the obligations of the issuer and the rights of the investors.

In-house presentation. A presentation from the management team of an issuer to the institutional salespeople of the issuer's underwriters made at the beginning of the marketing phase of a securities offering. Typically 20 to 30 minutes in length and followed by a Q&A session, the in-house is intended to educate the salespeople about the company and the transaction.

Initiation of coverage. When a *sellside* research analyst begins offering a formal opinion on the investment merits of a particular public company and stock, typically involving the publishing of a report and ongoing analysis regarding a company's operations, strategy, performance, and prospects.

Inside market. The highest *bid* and lowest *ask* available in the market for a particular security.

Insider. A person with access to material information pertaining to a company before it is announced to the public who has a duty not to divulge or misuse the information. In a public company, the term includes officers, directors, and other key employees.

Institutional investor. An organization whose purpose is to invest its own assets or assets entrusted to it by other investors. The term includes mutual funds, *hedge funds*, endowments, foundations, pension funds, sovereign wealth funds, and the like. Those with responsibility for making the investment decisions within an institutional investor are called *portfolio managers*, or PMs. In some instances, they may also be called investment officers.

Investment bank. A *sellside* institution focused on serving issuers and the *buyside* through one or more business lines including, among others, brokerage, securities underwriting, private placements, and M&A advisory services. Unlike commercial banks, investment banks do not accept deposits from or provide traditional loans to consumers and businesses. *See also boutique and bulge bracket firm.*

IPO. The acronym for initial public offering, the process of offering shares and equity ownership in a company to the public for the first time.

Jump ball. A compensation structure for underwriters that divides a portion of the *gross spread* according to the wishes and opinions of the investors in an offering.

Junk Bond. Also referred to as high yield notes or bonds, junk bonds are debt securities issued with *credit ratings* below investment-grade status and thus carry higher interest rate obligations.

LBO. The acronym for leveraged buyout, a transaction involving the purchase of a business, often a public company, by one or more *private equity funds* using debt as a primary source of funding.

Lead manager. *See managing underwriter.*

Lock-up agreement. An agreement between the underwriters and an issuer or its principal shareholders restricting the ability of the parties to sell shares for a specified period of time following a securities offering.

LOI. The acronym for letter of intent, a document prepared prior to signing a more complete agreement expressing the intent of the signatories to enter into a specific transaction such as a merger or acquisition. Often referred to as a signed *term sheet*, an LOI may take this form when signed by both parties.

M&A. The common term for mergers and acquisitions often used in the singular to refer to a particular transaction (e.g., "the team is working on a M&A deal for XYZ")

MAC. The acronym for the material adverse change provision contained in most *definitive acquisition agreements*, which permits the acquirer to terminate the transaction prior to *closing* if there is a significant change in the seller's business.

Management fee. The meaning of this term depends on context. With respect to underwriters' compensation, see *gross spread*. With respect to the fee structure of certain investment funds such as *hedge funds*, *private equity funds*, and venture capital funds, see *2 and 20*.

Managing underwriter. The underwriter in a securities offering that individually or with other *co-managers* is responsible for preparing the registration statement, conducting due diligence, setting the terms of the offering, and marketing the offering. If a transaction involves more than one managing underwriter, one or more of them will be designated by the issuer as *lead manager* or co-lead managers. These parties take point on driving the underwriting process and coordinating the efforts of the *working group*.

Market capitalization. The value of a public company determined according to the combined market value of all of its outstanding *common stock*.

Market maker. A *brokerage firm* that uses its own capital, research, and trading resources to provide liquidity for a Nasdaq-listed stock. Market makers request this role and are obligated to buy or sell securities at prices quoted by them to the public.

MBO. The acronym for management buyout, a transaction involving the purchase of a business, often a public company, by the company's management team, usually with the financial support of one or more *private equity funds*.

Mezzanine debt. Used to finance buyouts and acquisitions, mezzanine debt has lower standing than other forms of debt issued in connection with a transaction and is generally issued with *warrants* or other equity participation mechanisms.

Mezzanine financing. Positioned between venture financing and public financing, the term frequently used to describe a late-stage private financing conducted just prior to when a company pursues an *IPO*. Also known as a "mezz" round.

MOE. The acronym for merger of equals, a M&A transaction structured to deem the two parties involved equals rather than one a buyer and the other a seller.

Money manager. A common term for an individual, such as an investment professional with an *institutional investor*, who is responsible for choosing and monitoring the investments of other individuals and organizations.

Naked on the shoe. The term referring to when a lead underwriter over-allocates a securities offering and creates a short position larger than the 15 percent contractually provided for in the *green shoe*. This occurs in rare instances, when an offering is almost certain to need stabilization due to weak demand or choppy market conditions,.

NASD. The acronym of the National Association of Securities Dealers, the former *SRO* operating under the oversight of the *SEC* that included nearly every broker-dealer engaged in the securities business in the U.S. public markets. In July 2007, the NASD was consolidated with the member regulation, enforcement, and arbitration functions of the New York Stock Exchange to form the Financial Industry Regulatory Authority (*FINRA*), which is now tasked with these oversight functions for the securities industry.

Net proceeds. The total proceeds of a securities offering after underwriting discounts and commissions are deducted.

NDA. The acronym for nondisclosure agreement, an agreement used in M&A discussions, *PIPEs*, and certain other nonpublic dealings requiring the special treatment of confidential information by a potential investor or counterparty.

No-shop provision. A provision contained in a *LOI* or signed *term sheet* for a M&A transaction that provides for an exclusivity period for a buyer and seller to agree upon a *definitive acquisition agreement*. This period of time also allows the buyer to complete its *due diligence* review of the seller. The exclusivity period is typically thirty days.

Note. A security representing indebtedness of a company or other issuer that matures in fewer than 10 years.

OEM. Acronym for original equipment manufacturer, a business responsible for designing and producing various equipment or electronics which are then marketed and sold under its own brands or the brands of other companies. An OEM strategy refers to selling a product to an OEM that, in turn, will use it as a component in one or more of its own products.

One-on-one meeting. A meeting held during the *road show* of a securities offering between the issuer and an institutional investor. Typically lasting 1 hour, a one-on-one provides the opportunity for the management team to make a short presentation on the company and the transaction and allows the potential investor to ask questions and engage directly with the executives (usually the CEO and CFO).

Option. An option is a financial instrument that provides its holder with acquisition or disposition rights, but not obligations, over another security, generally a specified *common stock*.

OPM. The acronym for other people's money, a term used by some members of the financial community to describe the source of funding used to make investments, take risks, and help achieve gains.

OTC. The stock market acronym for over-the-counter. The OTC market operates without a physical location. Its participants are connected electronically and conduct business in a virtual trading environment. The most notable OTC network and quotation system is operated by Nasdaq.

Over-allotment option. *See green shoe.*

Overhang. The shares of a company's stock held by pre-IPO investors that become freely tradable at a certain point following an *IPO*.

Oversubscribed. A term used to describe a securities offering, public or private, which has investor demand exceeding the amount of securities being offered.

Par. The face value of a debt security, generally $1000, which is the amount owed on the instrument by the issuer. For trading purposes, debt securities are quoted relative 100, a truncated version of par. For instance, a bond trading at 100 is valued at $1000 and a bond trading at 90 is valued at $900.

Pay-to-play round. A financing for a private company that requires investors from earlier rounds to participate in order for them to maintain their rights and preference on their earlier investments.

Participation rights. Rights often conferred to investors in a private financing that permit the investors to invest in subsequent financing rounds in order to maintain their ownership percentages in a company.

PCS. The acronym for private client services, the department within a *brokerage firm* responsible for providing brokerage services to wealthy clientele, including the executives of investment banking clients. PCS has different formal names across Wall Street, such as "wealth management" and "private client wealth services."

P/E or PE. The price-to-earnings ratio used within the context of a stock's valuation and calculated by dividing a company's stock price by its *EPS* for a particular 12-month period (generally the next calendar year). The P/E is quoted as a multiple (e.g., 15X or 20X). Note that PE is sometimes also used to refer to private equity.

P/E/G or PEG. The price-to-earnings-to-growth ratio used within the context of a stock's valuation. The ratio is calculated by dividing the *P/E* by the anticipated growth rate of a company's earnings for some period of time into the future, usually 5 or more years. As with the *P/E*, the P/E/G is quoted as a multiple.

Piggyback registration rights. *See registration rights.*

PIPE. The acronym for private investment in public equity or entity, a financing transaction involving a privately negotiated investment in a public company generally taking the form of cash for stock or stock with warrants.

Pitch book. *See book.*

Platform investment. An acquisition of a company by a *private equity fund* that can serve as platform for future acquisitions and investing activities.

Poison pill. A *takeover defense*, generally implemented with a shareholder rights plan, designed to delay the timing and raise the cost of an unsolicited acquisition attempt or *hostile takeover*, thereby encouraging potential suitors to negotiate with a company's board of directors.

Portfolio manager. *See institutional investor.*

Pot. Divided between the institutional pot and retail pot, the pool of securities in an offering that is ultimately distributed to institutional or retail investors. The list of those receiving such shares is referred to as the pot list.

PPM. The acronym for private placement memorandum, the document used to market private financings.

Preferred stock. Securities representing equity ownership in a company that carry unique rights and privileges distinct from *common stock.*

Pre-release. A public announcement made by a public company prior to its regularly scheduled annual or quarterly earnings release indicating that the company will materially exceed or fall short of performance expectations held for it in the market.

Pricing. The point at the conclusion of the marketing phase for a public securities offering when the final terms are set for the transaction by the underwriters with the approval of the issuer and/or selling shareholders.

Primary shares. Shares offered in a securities transaction by the issuer rather than pre-existing shareholders.

Private equity fund. A closely-held investment vehicle, typically structured as a limited partnership, created to generate investment returns by acquiring established businesses using a combination of equity and debt. Private equity funds may also invest in other opportunities including late-stage private companies. Subject to their specific strategies, private equity funds and the firms that manage them may be referred to by other monikers such as buyout funds, buyout shops, or LBO funds. Investors in private equity funds include wealthy individuals and institutions such as endowments, foundations, and pension funds.

Private placement agent. An *investment bank* that works with a company to identify and pursue investors in a private offering of securities.

Prospectus. The offering document used by the issuer and its underwriters to market a securities offering. The preliminary prospectus, also called the *red* *herring*, contains the bulk of material found in the *registration statement* and notes that certain information concerning the value of the securities to be offered may change. The final prospectus contains the final terms of the transaction and is delivered to the purchasers of the securities immediately following the offering.

Proxy statement. A document used to solicit shareholder votes. In a public context, proxy statements must follow certain procedures and contain certain information required by *SEC* regulations.

Public float. The number of shares of a company held by public shareholders rather than insiders and pre-IPO investors.

QIBs. The acronym for qualified institutional buyers, well-funded *institutional investors* meeting particular guidelines that are permitted to participate in certain higher risk securities transactions under U.S. securities laws, namely sales of unregistered securities pursuant to *Rule 144A*.

Red herring. *See prospectus.*

Registered securities. Securities registered with the *SEC* pursuant to a *registration statement*, which enables them to be sold to and freely traded among public investors.

Registration rights. Contractual rights of a shareholder to have all or a portion of its shares registered with the *SEC* pursuant to a *registration statement*. These may take the form of *demand registration rights*, which entitle the shareholder to demand that its shares be registered at a time of its own choosing, or *piggyback registration rights*, which entitle the shareholder to participate in a registered offering being conducted by the issuer.

Registration statement. *See Form S-1, Form S-3, and shelf registration statement.*

Regulation FD. Rules adopted by the *SEC* in 2000 to prevent the selective disclosure of material nonpublic information by issuers and to clarify certain issues pertaining to insider trading.

Regulation S. A regulation adopted by the *SEC* in 1990 to formally permit the sale of unregistered securities to investors in foreign jurisdictions.

Road show. A series of meetings and presentations made by an issuer to potential investors during the marketing phase of a securities offering. Typically lasting 1 to 2 weeks, road shows involve travel to multiple cities and the use of conference calls, group presentations, and *one-on-one meetings* geared to *institutional investors*.

Rule 144. An SEC rule that permits holders of unregistered securities to make certain sales in the *aftermarket* without registering the shares.

Rule 144A. A rule promulgated under U.S. securities laws that permits the issuance and resale of securities to certain *institutional investors* without the use of a *registration statement*.

Sarbanes-Oxley Act of 2002. Federal legislation enacted following the collapse of the technology bubble that made a number of significant changes to the regulation of public company reporting requirements and corporate governance.

SEC. The acronym for the Securities and Exchange Commission, the federal agency created to administer the *Securities Act of 1933* and the *Securities Exchange Act of 1934*.

Secondary offering. *See follow-on offering.*

Secondary shares. Shares offered in a securities transaction by pre-existing shareholders rather than the issuer. Those offering secondary shares are called selling stockholders or shareholders.

Securities Act of 1933. The federal statute regulating the offer and sale of securities. The statute also contains antifraud provisions prohibiting false representations and disclosures made in connection with securities transactions.

Securities Exchange Act of 1934. The federal statute regulating, among other things, certain trading practices, insider trading, tender offers, and the reporting obligations of public companies. It also established the self-regulatory system of market oversight conducted by the *NASD* and the exchanges (now *FINRA*).

Seed capital. The financing round to start a company composed primarily of funding from founders and their friends and family.

Sellside (The). The term used to describe the broad group of institutions and professionals responsible for selling, supporting, and trading securities for issuers and the *buyside* in exchange for fees and commissions.

Sellside advisor. An *investment bank* hired to represent a company when it seeks to sell itself in a M&A transaction.

Settlement date. The date on which a public securities offering or other securities trade closes whereby the securities are delivered to the purchaser(s) and the proceeds are delivered to the seller(s). The amount of time between the transaction/trade date and the settlement date varies by offering or trade type. The settlement date generally ranges from same day to trade date plus three days (T+3).

Shelf registration statement. A *registration statement* filed by a more mature public company that permits the company to sell the securities described in it at any time following the date that it is deemed effective by the *SEC*. The securities described in a shelf registration statement are supposed to be those that the company intends to offer over the foreseeable future. A shelf registration statement may also be used to register *secondary shares* for selling shareholders.

Shell corporation. A publicly traded company with limited or no operations that may be acquired by a private company as a means of becoming a public company without conducting a traditional *IPO*. When a shell corporation is purchased, the buyer merges into the public entity, thus becoming its operations and identity.

Short sale. A securities transaction involving the sale of a particular security, typically a *common stock*, borrowed from a *brokerage firm* that can then be replaced at a later date by the purchase of the same security in the open market. Short sales are conducted with the belief that the security involved will decline in value between the sale and subsequent purchase thus generating a profit for the investor.

Specialist. A stock exchange member responsible for monitoring trading activity in a specific stock and, when necessary to maintain an orderly market, for buying and selling the stock for its own account if no natural counterparty exists for a trade. There are several firms dedicated to being exchange specialists. When a company decides to list with an exchange, it interviews several specialists and presents a short list to the exchange which in turn selects one for the company.

SRO. The acronym for self-regulatory organization, an organization sanctioned by the government to oversee and police certain activities of its members. On Wall Street, the Financial Industry Regulatory Authority (*FINRA*) serves this function. *See also NASD.*

Standstill agreement. A document frequently signed during discussions in a proposed M&A transaction involving a public company, which limits the ability of a potential acquirer to take certain actions, such as making purchases of the target's stock.

Stock purchase agreement. The agreement between the issuer and investors in a private stock offering, also called a private placement, setting forth the terms of the investment and the rights and obligations of the parties involved.

Stock registrar and transfer agent. An agent appointed by an issuer, typically a commercial bank, responsible for maintaining the records of security ownership. The agent is also responsible for issuing and canceling stock certificates and resolving issues associated with lost, destroyed, and stolen certificates.

Strike price. The price at which an *option* or *warrant* may be exercised.

Syndicate. A group of underwriters selected by the *managing underwriters* to be included in marketing and supporting a securities offering. The term also applies to certain functions of an investment bank's ECM department—see *ECM*—and the lending group in a *syndicated loan*—see *syndicated loan.*

Syndicated loan. A large loan funded by a group of lenders known as a syndicate, which is typically arranged by a lead bank called an *arranger.*

Synergies. A term used in M&A transactions to describe the potential financial benefits of an acquisition or merger produced by revenue enhancement or cost containment opportunities generated by the combination of the two entities involved.

Takeover defenses. Structural protections contained in the *charter documents* of a public company to guard against unwelcome advances and to encourage potential suitors to negotiate with the company's board of directors. Such defenses include, among others, a staggered board, a *poison pill*, and special limitations on shareholder voting.

Teach-in. The presentation regarding an issuer made by an underwriter's research analyst to the underwriter's institutional salespeople prior to the marketing phase and *road show* of a securities offering.

Teaser. A brief document describing a company to potential suitors in a M&A transaction or potential investors in a *PIPE* transaction, which is designed to generate and gage interest in the opportunity prior to divulging more specifics. Often, teasers do not refer to the company described by name.

Tender offer. An approach used in certain M&A transactions involving public companies in which shareholders are solicited to submit, or tender, their shares in exchange for the consideration being offered in the transaction.

Term sheet. A document containing the primary terms of a proposed securities or M&A transaction submitted by an interested investor or suitor.

Ticker symbol. A three or four letter symbol assigned by an exchange or OTC market to identify a particular security. Note that many older, more established securities possess ticker symbols with fewer letters.

Tombstone. An announcement, often placed in *The Wall Street Journal*, commemorating a recently completed securities offering or other important transaction.

Tranches. The term referring to the different layers of debt issued in connection with a *LBO* or *MBO*. Each tranche of debt possesses different maturities, priorities, and/or collateral and thereby interest rates commensurate with its level of risk.

Underwriter. An *investment bank* that offers and sells securities to investors in a public offering.

Underwriting agreement. The principal agreement between the underwriters and the issuer and/or selling shareholders in a public offering of *registered securities* outlining the terms of the relationship and the transaction.

VC. The acronym for venture capital or venture capitalist, the investment funds or those who manage them, which are used primarily to finance private growth companies early in their development. Venture capital funds are closely-held investment vehicles, typically structured as limited partnerships, targeted to wealthy individuals and institutions such as endowments, foundations, and pension funds.

Venture debt. A financing alternative to traditional venture capital for private growth companies which is provided in the form of a loan secured by a blanket lien over all of the assets of the business, including intangibles like patents and other intellectual property. Venture debt lenders receive interest payments and typically participate in the equity upside of their borrowers through *warrants* that they are issued in connection with their loans.

VIX. The Chicago Board Options Exchange Volatility Index, which measures the implied volatility of S&P 500 index options and therefore the market's expected near-term volatility.

Vulture investor. An investor, such as a *hedge fund*, that purchases distressed debt, including bonds and syndicated loan positions, with the intent of generating favorable returns through the outcome of bankruptcy proceedings. Successful vulture investors are well versed in bankruptcy law and thoroughly understand their contractual rights under loan agreements and bond *indentures*. The term vulture investing is sometimes applied more broadly to any situation in which an investor seeks to profit by acquiring securities impacted by distressed circumstances.

VWAP. The acronym for volume-weighted average price, a term used in the trading of securities that is calculated by dividing the gross dollar amount of all trades in a security during a given period of time by the total number of securities traded during the same period of time.

Warrant. A security issued by a company entitling its holder to purchase shares of *common stock* at a pre-defined price in the future.

White knight. In the context of a M&A transaction, a potential suitor, also known as a friendly bidder, that is viewed as offering a more favorable transaction to a target than that being proposed by a hostile party, also known as a unfriendly bidder or black knight.

Window dressing. The practice conducted by some mutual funds of selling poorly performing stocks and buying strongly performing stocks just prior to the end of a fund's public reporting period in order to show a more impressive set of holdings to investors.

Working group. The group of individuals from a company and its advisors responsible for executing a transaction. For a securities offering, the working group is composed of key company executives and representatives from the *managing underwriters*, underwriters' counsel, the company's outside counsel, and the company's outside accountants.

Yield spread. The difference in *coupons*, or interest rates, between debt instruments possessing different *credit ratings* or maturities. Yield spreads are described according to basis points, or "bips." There are 100 basis points for each 1 percent.

Index

About the Author

JASON A. PEDERSEN has been a Wall Street professional for over fifteen years. He was an attorney in the corporate and securities group for Pillsbury Madison & Sutro, a managing director in the equity capital markets and investment banking departments at Montgomery Securities (Banc of America Securities), and a founding partner in the investment banking firm Thomas Weisel Partners. He has worked on an extensive range of public and private financings and M&A transactions. Pedersen holds a J.D. from Georgetown University and a B.A. from the University of Utah.